THE
GULF
BREEZE
SIGHTINGS

Introduction by
Budd Hopkins

Photo Analysis by
Dr. Bruce S. Maccabee

WILLIAM MORROW AND COMPANY, INC.
NEW YORK

THE
GULF
BREEZE

SIGHTINGS

THE MOST ASTOUNDING MULTIPLE SIGHTINGS of UFOs IN U.S. HISTORY

Ed Walters
Frances Walters

Library of Congress Cataloging-in-Publication Data

Walters, Ed.
    The Gulf Breeze sightings : the most astounding multiple sightings
of UFOs in U.S. history / by Ed Walters and Frances Walters;
introduction by Budd Hopkins; photo analysis by Bruce S. Maccabee.
        p.   cm.
    ISBN 0-688-09087-7
    1. Unidentified flying objects—Sightings and encounters—Florida—
Gulf Breeze.   I. Walters, Frances.   II. Title.
TL789.3.W33   1990   89-13255
001.9′42—dc20   CIP

Printed in the United States of America

First Edition

1 2 3 4 5 6 7 8 9 10

BOOK DEISGN BY PATRICE FODERO

FOREWORD

I have a Ph.D. in physics. For the last sixteen years I have been employed by the United States government as a research physicist. I have worked in the area of optics and on other subjects including the Strategic Defense Initiative.

Over the last twenty years I have studied the UFO phenomenon. I have done both historical research and sighting investigations; I have published numerous papers on the subject, specializing in UFO photo cases. My investigation of this case has included personal interviews with the witnesses, on-site inspections, and photographic analysis (including computer-aided techniques).

I have concluded that there is no evidence of a hoax and that the photos in this book are authentic. They show unconventional aerial craft that have appeared over Gulf Breeze, Florida, and surrounding areas.

—DR. BRUCE S. MACCABEE

ACKNOWLEDGMENTS

Duane Cook and Dari Holston were the first to recognize the significance of the Gulf Breeze sightings. The investigation started at the *Gulf
Breeze Sentinel,* supported by the numerous Gulf Breeze witnesses who
had the courage to come forward and describe their sightings in spite of
possible ridicule. A special thanks goes to the open-minded people of
Gulf Breeze, a "class act."

Both Walter Andrus, international director of MUFON, and Budd
Hopkins, author of *Intruders* and *Missing Time,* supported the investigation and gave my family much-needed personal advice. The on-location
research team of Don Ware, Charles Flannigan, and Gary Watson carried
on a detailed investigation while the sightings were occurring. Along with
Bob Reid, a special researcher in charge of surveillance, the local team
has my sincere appreciation.

Many people have supported the photographic analysis, including
Robert Oechsler, Robert Nathan, Vincent DiPeitro, Joe Greco, Dr. Mark
Carlatto, Dr. Brian O'Leary, and Dr. Bruce Maccabee, who I personally
thank for his hundreds of hours of research.

Authentication of the photographic evidence required the expertise of
those professionals and others like Harro Limbo, a technical expert with
Polaroid Corporation, and Richard A. Vandenberg, a photographic expert. Professionals from many fields of study, such as electronics engineer Edward Weibe and acoustical physicist John Gardner, have reviewed
the evidence.

The decision to come forward was difficult and was based on the
combined support of these people. Many others, such as Jerry Clark,
Richard Hall, Dr. James Deardorff, Dan Wright, and Jim Moseley, offered convincing advice to write these events for the record.

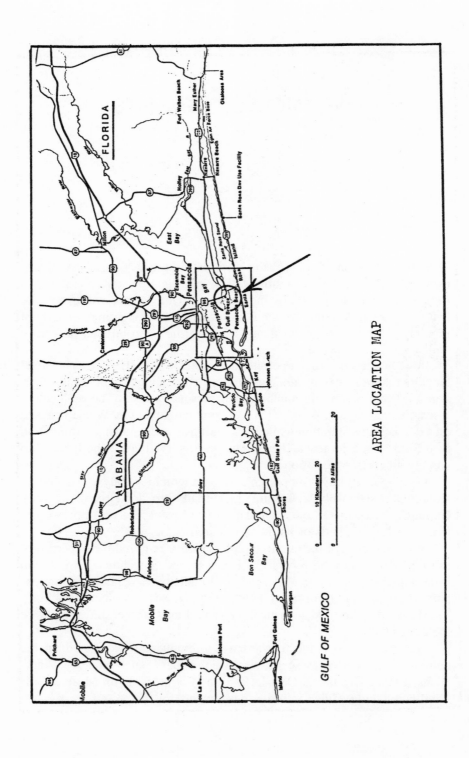

AREA LOCATION MAP

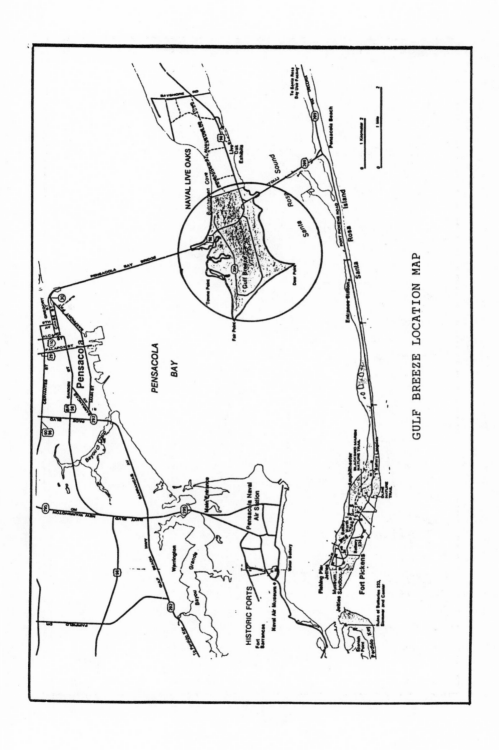

GULF BREEZE LOCATION MAP

CONTENTS

INTRODUCTION

by Budd Hopkins

Whatever your current view of the UFO phenomenon, that opinion will be forever changed by the book you hold in your hands. Until now, whether we were casually curious or skeptical or intrigued or downright scornful of the UFO reports that have been amassed over the past four decades, we've at least had the luxury of regarding the phenomenon as something extremely distant from our lives. If UFOs existed at all, they were "out there somewhere," to be thought about every now and then perhaps, with little flashes of hope or dread. Now, it is an all-too-human habit to think of many other disturbing phenomena in much the same way—reports of holes in the ozone layer, for example, or the warming greenhouse effect on our planet's surface. We may see these issues as puzzling, odd, distressing—or possibly even nonexistent; nothing, surely, to interfere with our normal, day-to-day living. It's true that Chernobyl and Three Mile Island caused ripples of genuine concern, but memories are short and life goes on. We want it that way. I want it that way. It is difficult enough to handle the daily emergencies of children and money and health and family without having to consider—vividly—possibilities of nuclear destruction or unexpected encounters with extraterrestrials.

The public's acquaintance with UFOs has largely been through sci-fi films or an occasional newspaper article or TV talk-show discussion. Photographs of UFOs usually depicted blurry, remote objects, and though an optical physicist can glean a great deal of valid information from such photos, the rest of us, after an uninformed glance or two, are not so impressed. But after acquainting oneself with the spectacular Gulf Breeze sightings and photographs presented in these pages, UFOs will never again be regarded so casually—nor as so safely, reassuringly distant. In the spring of 1988 I sat in the living room of a Gulf Breeze resident, listening to her account of a UFO that hovered at treetop level about thirty feet from the back of her house. The witness's daughter then told me her version of this incident, describing how she and her mother huddled together in bed, too terrified to move, silently praying for the thing to leave. She told me how the shifting, pulsating lights on the craft shone through the closed curtains for what seemed like hours. I watched this lovely, vibrant, but still frightened young woman as she recalled what had been for her a virtually traumatic event. Her hands worked nervously. She continuously interlaced and then unclasped her fingers, speaking all the while in a low, fearful voice, as if she felt she was running a risk even by talking to me about her encounter. She confided to another investigator—a woman—that she was afraid to go to sleep at night in the house and that the experience was beginning to affect her health. The object that had appeared behind her home was no vague, distant blur. It was very like the UFOs that her neighbor Ed Walters and several other people had photographed clearly and up close. This thing was real, and the fear it engendered could not be rationalized away as the result of a frivolous mistake—the photographs demolished that possibility once and for all.

My involvement in these matters began in December 1987 when I received a phone call from a Florida radio station asking my opinion of the Gulf Breeze UFO sightings. I confessed that I knew nothing whatsoever about them, but the rather vague description the caller provided sounded intriguing, and my curiosity was piqued. A month later I received a full account of these startling and still-unfolding events from Donald Ware, a friend and colleague who was one of the central investigators in the case.

After outlining the salient facts and chronology of the Gulf Breeze sightings, Don told me he had called for two reasons. First, he wanted to know if I would speak to Ed Walters, the key witness, and offer him some advice having to do with publishing issues. Ever since his dramatic UFO photos first appeared in the local newspaper, and other witnesses had provided corroboration, various publishers and writers had called offering contracts of one sort or another, talking books, magazine and newspaper articles, exclusive rights, and so on. Ed was a businessman whose expertise lay elsewhere; he had no idea what to make of any of this. Don Ware had decided to contact me because I had written two books on the UFO abduction phenomenon; both had been issued by major publishers and both had been well received. He hoped that because of my experience I might have some ideas as to the best way for Ed and the other investigators to handle these matters. He explained that so far Ed's credibility—and that of the other Gulf Breeze witnesses—was intact, and the amazingly clear, close-up photos appeared to be genuine. He felt that if, after thorough investigation and analysis, the case remained valid and the photographs authentic, then the events at Gulf Breeze should be presented in all their complexity to the full scientific community and to the general public as well. I felt that the only way I could properly evaluate the situation would be if I looked into it firsthand.

No matter what I might learn from a trip to Gulf Breeze, the information was sure to have value for future UFO investigations. We might discover something new and useful about the nature and ingenuity of hoaxes and the psychology of their perpetrators—or we might find ourselves with invaluable new photographic evidence.

Don Ware's second purpose in calling me was to say that he had reason to believe at least one of the local witnesses may have been physically—and temporarily—abducted by the UFO's occupants. Since my experience with this sort of case was extensive, Don hoped I might be able to visit the area and begin my own investigation into this possibility. I listened, as always, with curiosity and skepticism; my fingers were crossed and there was the usual doubt in my mind. But shortly after our conversation I spoke to Ed by telephone and heard his side of the story; I knew, then, what had to be done. The next day I bought my airline tickets and in early February was on my way to Gulf Breeze.

My first encounter with the UFO phenomenon had occurred years before, in the summer of 1964. While driving with my wife and a friend near the tip of Cape Cod, we watched a round, apparently metallic craft hover and then zoom away in broad daylight. Since then I had investigated hundreds of similar sightings as well as the more graphically detailed abduction accounts I dealt with in my books *Missing Time* and *Intruders*. In carrying out such investigations one actually becomes a detective, searching for clues and attempting to learn whether the witness is lying, is somehow psychologically deluded or confused, or is recalling, to the best of his or her ability, the unvarnished truth. One learns, for example, to listen for certain small, highly significant details that suggest a real, observed experience rather than an abstract, concocted tale. One of the Gulf Breeze cases I eventually looked into involved a woman who described with a great deal of fear an encounter that began one night when she found herself virtually paralyzed and staring at a small figure standing in the doorway to her kitchen. We were seated comfortably in her living room as she told her story, and when I asked her how tall the figure was, she replied, "His head came up to the bottom of the microwave." I had to go into the kitchen a little later to find out that that meant about four feet tall.

During my three visits to Gulf Breeze I was to hear over and over, from Ed Walters, his family, and other local witnesses, the same kinds of "trivial" but inherently credible details. Ed told me that the night of December 2, when he suddenly confronted a small UFO occupant at his bedroom door, the shock caused him to stumble backward and fall. But he recalled that the figure's black, staring eyes "seemed shiny, almost like they were wet, the way a person's eyes look just before they begin to cry . . . the eyes get kind of misted over. That's the way they looked." It was a realistic description of the aliens' eyes, generically similar to dozens I had heard before, but flavored by Ed's particular, personal choice of imagery. He was either a remarkably subtle liar with hidden literary skills or a good observer who had, indeed, stared into a pair of shiny, wet-looking alien eyes.

It was quite clear to me at the outset that the Gulf Breeze events had to be either a massive, orchestrated hoax or an extraordinarily important new development in the slowly unfolding UFO mystery. Despite my cautious skepticism, everything I learned from the very beginning supported the latter hypothesis. When I first drove up to the Walterses' prosperous residential neighborhood, I saw neatly tended grounds, a basketball hoop on the garage door, a clean, efficient-looking truck, and several cars—all signs of a stable, conservative, middle-class businessman's family. From years of experience in UFO research I knew of two infamous UFO contact hoaxes that included as supporting evidence photographs of purported craft. The George Adamski case of the 1950s involved a man who gave his address as Mount Palomar and allowed his followers to assume he was an astronomer. It turned out that he worked in a small roadside souvenir and hot-dog stand on that mountain and that despite his adoption of the title "Professor," his education had been less than imposing. Billy Meier, the Swiss contactee, enthralled his followers with tales of visits backward in time with personages such as Jesus Christ. He presented believers with hundreds of pages of arcane lore that he said the Space Brothers had asked him to pass on to a needy world. Meier was a poor, one-armed handyman in his village, a person who some UFO investigators decided was entirely *too* handy when small models of UFOs were found in Meier's garage, models that looked exactly like the "beam ships" in his photographs. (Meier ingenuously explained that he saw the UFOs first, photographed them, and *then* constructed the scale models.)

Both Meier and Adamski presented themselves as seers or gurus—privileged men who had been selected by cosmic beings to bring eternal truths to the rest of us mere earthlings. For a period of time each made money from his role as a kind of New Age priest—more money, surely, than either man made previously from odd-job carpentry or hot-dog sales. I thought of these archetypical hoax cases when I parked in front of Ed Walters's house for the first time that day in early February 1988. Though I am not in the least dissatisfied with my style and standard of living, I still found myself envying Ed's swimming pool, his video camera and equipment, his huge "industrial-strength" television screen, and especially his pool table, a memorable treasure in my own childhood. But above all I wondered what Billy Meier or George Adamski would have thought had they seen this kind of middle-class prosperity. I knew one thing at the outset: Ed Walters did not have to manufacture a UFO account and fake some pictures because he needed the money.

Just as significant a departure from the standard hoax scenario was the absence, in Ed's case, of the would-be guru's special claims. Unlike Adamski and Meier he did not insist that he and the Space Brothers had a special relationship and that they had specifically selected him as the ideal one to pass on cosmic wisdom. Those earlier "contactees" would have been appalled to hear that instead of feeling honored, Ed was frightened, confused, and apprehensive and that he had begun carrying a gun in his truck for protection. The hoaxer insists, "I am the Chosen One with the eternal truth," whereas Ed, like hundreds of other honest witnesses in this situation, simply asked, "Why me? What is this all about?"

Ed Walters, when I met him, turned out to be a warm, outgoing man with a ready smile and an obviously generous spirit. He has curly, longish hair and a respectable beard, and there is something about the angularities of his face and his prominent forehead (the product of good bones and a receding hairline) that put me in mind of Clint Eastwood—but Eastwood in his more engaging role as a small-town California politician. Ed welcomed me into his home and introduced me to Frances, his wife, and Laura, his thirteen-year-old daughter. Everything seemed typical and stable—the family, their house, and Ed's business. He is a builder whose office at home resembles that of one of my closest friends, another independent designer and home builder. It was all familiar. Elevations and floor plans were neatly tacked up on the walls, rolled blueprints were stacked away, carefully labeled, and a well-used Xerox machine sat on a worktable near the door. I realized that if Ed were perpetrating a hoax, he had put all of this at risk—his wife, his teenage children, his business, his reputation in the community. Everything that hard work and eighteen years of marriage had gained would be swept away . . . for what possible reason?

The day before I returned to New York, Ed told me that after his anonymously submitted UFO pictures appeared in the local paper, a book publisher dispatched a scout to Gulf Breeze to inquire into the authenticity of these sightings. As a result Ed had received a dazzling offer from this publisher, an offer that included a six-figure advance, if he would allow his story to be written and his photographs reproduced in book form. The offer included a cutoff date, and Ed was being pressured to sign a contract. He wanted to know what to do, since he was not at all sure he was willing to make his identity known and thereby risk ridicule and even damage to his business. He loved the small, conservative community of Gulf Breeze and felt very much at home there. Involving himself in such a controversial subject as UFOs might bring short-term rewards *and* long-term disaster.

I replied that before a book was undertaken, three things should occur. First, the case must be thoroughly investigated; second, the original photos must be handed over to a first-rate photoanalyst for careful, scientific examination of their authenticity; and third, Ed must submit to a polygraph test. Then, I went on, if the case passed all those hurdles, a book could be negotiated with this or another prestigious publisher. I laid out these conditions as a kind of test. I knew of course what a hoaxer would have done at that point—the six-figure standing offer would have been signed that afternoon. But my sense of this man told me what he would do. Ed nodded and said that all of this—the long-term investigation, the polygraph test, and the extensive photoanalysis—made sense to him. He would reject the standing offer and proceed with the intensive investigation as I had outlined it. It was a course that only a truthful man—a man with nothing to hide—could accept.

While I visited with Ed, I tried to learn everything I could that might shed light on the truth or falsity of his story. I wandered through the house in search of indications that Ed, his wife, or his children were skilled model makers or photographic hobbyists. There were no models anywhere, even though a builder-designer might conceivably find them useful. Photography, likewise, seemed absent from their interests. Several times I made deliberate attempts to test the consistency of Ed's account. Sitting in his office one afternoon he told me where he had fallen on the street when the blue beam first released him. A day after that conversation, standing now in his front yard, I pointed to a place about five feet *away from* the point he had originally described. "So you were dropped here?" I asked, and he instantly corrected me, with no sense whatever of having to recall a complex, invented story. "No, it was over there," he said, pointing to the spot he had described the day before. A tiny detail, of course, but it illustrates a wonderful remark of Mark Twain's: "Always telling the truth means never having to remember anything." Ed *knew* where the UFO had released him; it was something he would never forget.

With something as dramatic and as potentially important as the Gulf Breeze photographs, the pessimistic skeptic in me gives up slowly. The whole thing was almost too compelling to be true. I had always predicted that when we would finally get good closeup UFO photos, they would inevitably appear to be fake, and this is what seemed to be happening. Nevertheless, when I was interviewed during that first visit by a Pensacola TV station, I pointed out that my present inclination was to accept both the witnesses' accounts and the photographs as authentic, for one very cogent and powerful reason: I had not yet found a shred of evidence of a hoax. I went on to state, however, that the idea of a hoax should not be rejected out of hand. The nonideological pragmatist must carry on a careful investigation, keeping all the doors of possibility open—because the true believers of one persuasion or another can always be expected to rush around busily slamming them shut.

This, unfortunately, began to happen at Gulf Breeze when a few individuals decided that the photographs and sighting reports constituted a vast and carefully orchestrated hoax, involving perhaps dozens of perpetrators. That this counterattack occurred is hardly surprising. We know from historical precedent that the UFO phenomenon had always engendered unease or even fear in many otherwise orderly minds. Most of us, including supposedly inquisitive scientists, have convenient mental carpets under which we habitually sweep such disturbing information. Our need for boundaries—a desire for the known and the predictable—is simply too strong, too basic a human trait. The Gulf Breeze photographs were too disturbing to deal with, so they had to be explained away at all costs. The "chain of evidence" typically went this way: Ed Walters, as a prominent businessman, knows a few law enforcement officers in his community. Two sheriff's deputies in a nearby town have reported UFO sightings. *Therefore* we should suspect a plot! This and many other similarly mindless "connections" appeared over and over again in official-looking "newsletters" and press releases issued by the same few individuals. Reading them, one doubts that even Senator Joseph McCarthy would have ventured so far out on such thin ice. In the pages of this book Ed and Frances Walters give a personal, deliberately subdued account of the pain they suffered as a result of these widely circulated attacks. (One broadside even suggested that Ed Walters, the family man and pillar of support for the local PTA and his children's high school marching band, might be a sociopath, on the grounds that since he passed two lie detector tests and *cannot possibly* be telling the truth, he might well be a pathological personality!) The triumph of the Walters's ultimate vindication, though sweet, cannot erase all memory of the insults and ridicule that were heaped upon them and their innocent children—just because they *did* tell the truth.

The most unprecedented aspect of the events in Gulf Breeze is the presence of so many excellent UFO photographs. Though we have never before had such a series, many other details in this case are familiar from the historical record. In a famous 1975 abduction a man named Travis Walton, in full view of six co-workers, was hit—like Ed—by a blue beam of light from a hovering UFO. The beam lifted him up and then dropped him back onto the ground, causing his terrified friends to drive off in panic. After a later, fruitless search they went to the police and reported Walton's disappearance. He was found five days later, dazed and severely dehydrated, with partial memories of having been inside a UFO lying upon an examining table. Again, like Ed, Walton's co-workers passed polygraph tests about the incident, as did Walton himself, three months after his abduction.

The telepathic communication Ed Walters describes so vividly in this book is also frequently reported by those involved in close encounters and apparently functions as a kind of controlling device. Typically an individual may be awakened from a sound sleep by hearing his or her name being called. The person is then "told" to go into the kitchen, or outside into the yard, or even to get into the car and to drive out into the country, where inevitably a UFO awaits. Sometimes these commands are sensed rather than heard in so many words, but the effect is the same. Ed's "humming sound," a signal that led him to most of his UFO encounters, is a variant, then, on an old theme.

The circle of dead grass and peculiarly altered soil discovered near Ed's home is still another clue familiar to UFO investigators the world over. This phenomenon, usually reported in conjunction with UFO landings, constitutes an area of reliable, testable physical evidence. Hundreds of these "landing trace" cases have been studied over the years; the results of the various soil analyses performed so far conform closely to the analysis of the Gulf Breeze soil. But on a more disturbingly human level my study of the UFO abduction phenomenon led me to discover a pattern of "family connection." I learned that when a man or woman becomes the target of UFO curiosity, it is highly likely that other family members are also being studied or observed. Ed and his older brother both seem to have been such objects of curiosity, as the reader will learn. My trips to the Gulf area have uncovered five other families apparently in the same distressing situation. Three of these family reports predate any publicity about the Gulf Breeze incident, but seem, in their own way, related to aspects of Ed's case. In one of them, a harrowing 1974 close encounter with a low-flying UFO, the description of the craft seemed remarkably close to the objects seen in Ed's photographs. The Walters's UFO encounters can be viewed, then, both as conforming to historically observed and reported patterns of UFO behavior and, because of the photographs, as diverging from these patterns. It would seem that a very familiar phenomenon is beginning to change its behavior, in and around Gulf Breeze, Florida.

The account that Ed and Frances Walters present in these pages is different from anything yet published on this bizarre, unnerving subject. One will not find here the professional journalist's artful construction or the UFO investigator's dry objectivity or the mystical writer's cloudy peregrinations. Instead, what Ed and Frances have given us is a clear and touching family saga, the story of a man and his wife and children learning to deal with the unimaginable. Perhaps no moment in this very human account is more typical and more revealing than the night shortly after Christmas when the Walters family together stared in amazement at a UFO hovering and gliding only a few feet from their home. Ed quietly slipped outside with his video camera to record the spectacle while Frances comforted her frightened daughter and tried to prevent her son from bravely joining his father on the back deck. Thirteen-year-old Laura and her brother, Dan, were seeing a UFO for the first time. Each was aware that this unearthly object—or one very much like it—had once lifted their father off the ground in an apparent abduction attempt. Frances's own incipient panic at that moment was tempered by an instinctive need to protect her children and to reassure them that their father was safe, that he would not be taken away from them. Her account is not so much the story of a UFO encounter as it is a moment of family crisis, told with the kind of emotion we have all unfortunately experienced at one time or another.

My own daughter, Grace, is only a year older than Laura Walters. The first time I interviewed Laura, I could not help but think of my daughter's very similar innocence and vulnerability. I realized I was selfishly thankful that Grace had not undergone the traumas that Ed's and Frances's children had had to endure. It is virtually impossible for anyone to hear Laura's account and not be aware of the anguish and fear that lay barely concealed beneath her words.

And this is the final, tragic side of the Gulf Breeze story. However benign or ''scientific'' its ultimate purposes may be, the UFO phenomenon has inevitably brought pain and terror to innocent people, to a decent man, his loving wife and children, and to countless others in small towns and large cities, in states like Florida and Indiana and California, and in countries on every continent throughout the world. Ed and Frances Walters deserve our profound gratitude for sharing with us their family's harrowing story—and for presenting the photographic evidence that grounds it in hard, unavoidable fact.

—BUDD HOPKINS
Wellfleet, Massachusetts

The Photographic Evidence

A philosopher once said, "One picture is worth a thousand words"! In today's high-technology society, where science fiction becomes science fact and fantasy becomes reality, we use higher standards of scrutiny before a stamp of authenticity can be justified. The Gulf Breeze photographs have clearly earned such a stamp of approval.

Authentication of the photographic evidence required the expertise of many noted professional analysts, including Dr. Bruce Maccabee, a civilian optical physicist with the U.S. Navy, and top technical experts with the Polaroid Corporation. Dr. Maccabee performed the initial analysis using standard acceptable field-measurement practices and evaluated each photograph using optical and/or digital enhancement equipment.

Since the bulk of the photographic evidence was in the form of Polaroid original prints, relatively uncommon in UFO archives, my job became the task of defining the unique chemical process of Polaroid prints and negative peel-off strips and developing a basis for analysis. The greatest difficulty in the analysis process centered around the facts that the original pictures are extremely dark and the anomalous UFO images are generally quite small. In order to overcome this problem, an independent project was initiated to rephotograph the originals using techniques to increase the overall brightness of the photographs and to enlarge the subject images for close-up analysis.

My analysis criteria included the evaluation of the effects of expired film dating (involved in the first nine photos), a thorough examination and identification of various film defects, and a detailed study of the cameras used to determine (a) the causes associated with the discovered print emulsion defects and (b) the capability and viability of double-exposure techniques that might have been employed should that be alleged. The study included an evaluation of how the film type was processed and packaged and involved a series of experiments that took over seven months to complete. Many of the experiments involved the photographer of the originals, and several took place at the exact site that the original photographs were taken.

In addition to the Polaroid photographic analysis, conducted with the assistance of professional photographer Richard A. Vandenberg, I used my former background credentials as mission specialist to gain access to the television production studios at NASA's Goddard Space Flight Center in Greenbelt, Maryland. Electronics Engineer Edward Weibe and I conducted a five-month analysis of the videotape taken of a flying UFO over the field behind the Gulf Breeze Senior High School. Omega Studios in Rockville, Maryland, and the Noise Cancellation Technology Center in Columbia, Maryland, were used to perform an audio analysis of the sound track to the videotape with the assistance of acoustical physicist John Gardner.

The inescapable conclusion: The photographs shown in the pages that follow represent genuine physical objects of unknown origin. The analyses have determined approximate size and distance relationships with the surrounding terrain. The variety of equipment used to photograph the objects leaves a very narrow window of low probability for an exotic deception. My year-long character evaluation of the primary photographer removes all doubt for me relating to his ability to perpetrate any such deception. The evidence, in my estimation, can support itself through time.

—BOB OECHSLER
Annapolis, Maryland

These photographs were taken in early evening, early morning, or late at night; most of them are very dark and many of the details are obscured.

The corresponding copies and enlargements have been enhanced by photographic experts. Through a technique of intense light blasting, the originals have been brightened, exposing details to aid in the analysis. This technique makes the UFO appear to be much brighter than it really was, but in no other way does it alter the image.

By presenting the originals along with the enhancements, it can be better understood that the UFO was actually quite dull as compared to the pronounced glowing of the enhancements.

There are a great many emulsion streaks and defects (white spots) created by the rollers of the seventeen-year-old Polaroid camera. These defects, exaggerated by the darkness of the originals, have been identified by Polaroid chemistry experts and should not be considered part of the pictures.

NOVEMBER 11, 1987—FIRST SIGHTING— FAILED ABDUCTION

Veterans Day—About 5:00 P.M.

Gulf Breeze is a small city in the west Florida panhandle, surrounded by water on three sides and closed off by a national park on the fourth. Our community is made for family life—parks, water sports, public ball fields, tennis courts—and only six thousand of us enjoy it all.

I've lived here with my wife and two children for five years, and we all love it. It's the ideal place to raise children, although many retirees, a number of them ex-military, also call it home. Though not as conservative as some of the people in surrounding areas, the citizens of Gulf Breeze are far from liberal. They are, by and large, religious, family oriented, and hardworking. They are the people I've been glad to call my friends and neighbors.

The local residents surely would have preferred the UFO to show itself across the three-mile-long Bay Bridge in Pensacola. After all, Pensacola is where the Naval Air Station and numerous air training fields are located. Or it could have gone thirty miles to the east to Hurlburt Air Field, or a little farther on to Eglin Air Force Base, the largest military reservation in the Southeast.

But Gulf Breeze it was, and on that day there was nothing unusual happening—at least not that I had seen or heard of. As the evening hours approached, the weather was beautiful. A slight patch of cloud cover hung in the west, and the sun gave up its last rays to glow off the bottom of the clouds. The air was cool, but at this time of year short-sleeved shirts were still a common sight.

As a builder-developer I have always dealt with the practical details of any problem. Every book in my office concerns, in one way or another,

26

my business, which totally involves me. I had never speculated about otherworldly phenomena, nor given any thought to UFOs. In fact, I had always laughed at people who said they believed in little green men. My attitude was, I'll believe it when *I* see it.

My office is in the front section of our house. Its location allows me to bring clients straight in from the foyer without disturbing my family. Sitting at my desk on that November evening, I had no reason to think I would ever have to worry about a UFO. It was about dinnertime. My wife, Frances, stepped into the office long enough to tell me she needed something from the store. She'd go get it and be right back.

My daughter, twelve, was still out, I assumed with one of her neighborhood girlfriends. I wasn't worried. Residents of all ages wander our streets well after dark. Gulf Breeze is that kind of place. My son, a high school senior, was in the rec room blasting the new big-screen TV to its audio limits. In all, it was a typical evening.

I heard Frances start up her van, back out, and leave for the store. I didn't look up. On our quiet, little-traveled street I had no need to worry about her. Had I bothered, I would have expected to see the quite normal view I look out on every day.

The window faces west, overlooking our front yard and its large circular drive. My pickup truck was parked to the left. On the opposite side of the street sits a neighbor's brick house. A thirty-foot, short-needled pine claims the middle of our yard. Its fairly full branches occupy only the topmost ten feet of the tree.

Some minutes later I did happen to look out. My eyes caught a slight movement of light between the pine's limbs. I sat up and leaned over my desk to get a better look. It was still behind the tree, but I could now see that the glow was unusual—quite different from any of the commonplace planes and helicopters that populate the sky with their comings and goings from the Naval Air Station right across the bay.

I still couldn't see clearly enough through the pine boughs to satisfy my curiosity. I went to the front door and opened it. Whatever it was I had seen was still behind the tree. But I could tell now that this glowing, bluish-gray craft was like none I had ever seen before.

This was right out of a Spielberg movie that had somehow escaped from the film studio. It was impossible, but there it was, glowing and gliding along like a cloud. There was a quiet in the air. As I stared at the craft, the hairs on my arms bristled. This was no movie prop gone astray.

My first thought was to call the police but then I realized no one would believe me without proof. I rushed back into my office and grabbed the old Polaroid camera I use so frequently on my job sites. Quickly I stepped back out onto the small porch area. I took my first picture (photo 1) as the craft came from behind the pine.

The craft was still partially concealed by a branch. I moved the camera from my eye to get a better look. My mind told me there was some perfectly logical explanation for it all. My eyes told me something I absolutely didn't want to believe. This was a UFO, something that just could not be.

My brain was numb. I was out-and-out stupefied. *This was a UFO.* The camera in my hand almost slipped from my grip. All my attention focused on the bright glow of the power source radiating energy unlike any earthly craft.

But for a UFO to slowly descend over a peaceful, residential neighborhood made no sense. Why was it so low to the ground? Someone was sure to see it. Surely if its occupants were observing or photographing, their equipment could do that from a much higher altitude. Were they having some kind of mechanical trouble? Was this an experimental U.S. military craft?

What I was looking at is probably not what you would expect if you closed your eyes and imagined a UFO. It was unlike science fiction and Hollywood depictions of a "flying saucer." The pictures I took are clear, but it's not like seeing it firsthand. In person it was an awesome sight and an unforgettable experience.

It seemed to be nearly as big as the houses below it and three times as high. It glided along without a whisper of sound. There was no hum, no wind, not a single disturbance to the air, trees, or houses as it passed over them. While rocking back and forth, it did not seem to spin, so I never saw all sides, only what is in the photographs.

I estimated it at two hundred feet above the ground, sixty feet in diameter, and thirty-five feet from the top dome to the bottom of the "power light." (Later it became very obvious that the UFO wasn't nearly this large. But having nothing to compare it with and not knowing just how far away it was made it impossible to be sure of the size. Being excited didn't help either.)

A lot of small details don't show up in the pictures. Central between the large black squares that look like windows were small openings that I believe were portholes. Some of the portholes were lit, some were not. There were also some diamond shapes between some of the large black squares and, unseen on the photos, there were definitely horizontal lines going around the main body. (See drawing following page 64.)

As I lowered the camera I could see the power light clearly, and I ran out into the street to shoot a picture. My knees threatened to buckle. In one burst of speed it had moved almost directly overhead.

What a sight. The inside ring of the power source was throbbing and pulsing with energy. No sound came from what should have been blasting like a 747 jet. The outer ring glowed bright white. I was overwhelmed with awe. How can I explain it? It was like when a crowd sees an extraordinary fireworks display and all breathe, aaahhh. Well, my whole body was screaming, aaahhh!

Bang! Something hit me. All over my body. I tried to lift my arms to point the camera. I couldn't move them. They were blue. I was blue. Everything was blue. I was in a blue light beam. The blue beam had hit me like compression. It was pressing me firmly, just enough to stop me from moving.

I screamed, with my mouth frozen half open, but the sound was hollow. Dead, like a vacuum. I couldn't even move my eyes or eyelids. I thought that I was dying. I was trying to breathe, there was air, but my chest wouldn't expand. I had to pant to get enough air, each breath shallow.

This was it . . . I was dying. My brain was being squeezed and felt like it was going to crack open. The right side of my forehead felt like it had a knife piercing through to the back of my eye socket. No air . . . I needed more air. Panicky, I tried to suck in air.

The best I can tell, this all took less than twenty seconds. Then my feet lifted off the ground. I screamed. A voice groaned in my head. "We will not harm you."

I screamed again.

The deep, computerlike voice said, "Calm down."

But it was in my head, not my ears.

I screamed, as well as I could, "Put me down!"

A few seconds passed as I slowly rose away from the pavement. A dream? Hell no! This was real. The feeling of helplessness was the worst. No control—just a piercing smell, a little scent of ammonia mixed with heavy cinnamon that scorched, then stuck to, the back of my throat.

My heart was pumping so hard I could feel its throb as it thumped against my unmoving chest. I could feel the thumping vibration pass down my legs.

The voice groaned, "S-t-o-p i-t."

I screamed, "Screw you!"

All this happened fast. Now I was about two feet above the street. I panted for air, but the smell stung my lungs. My brain started to black out, so I screamed, "Aagghh!"

The scream was black and dull, just outside my mouth. Almost the way you feel if you dive deep to the bottom of a swimming pool with the pressure holding everything, even your own voice, close to you.

The voice came back, but now it seemed to be female. An easy hum filled my head. Suddenly, from within my head, came the sharp vision of a dog. Then another and another. I was confused. What are these dogs? Rapid visions, one after another, on and on. It seemed that I could almost see words beneath the dog visions. Something was flashing dog pictures in my head just as if they were turning the pages of a book. The hum continued. I had the sensation I was four feet above the ground.

Wham! I hit the pavement hard and fell forward onto my knees. The blue light was gone. The hum was still in my head, but it quickly decreased and was gone, like the hum of a speeding car that races by. I collapsed onto my chest in the middle of the road, filling my lungs with real air. My stomach turned and I choked, trying not to throw up.

The sound of an airplane passed overhead. I rolled over onto my back. There was no sign of the UFO. I didn't see where it went, but it was nowhere in the sky. There was just the single airplane to the north, headed west toward the Naval Air Station.

Perhaps that airplane had saved me from being picked up by the UFO. It stayed on course. It had just happened to be passing by at the right time. I wondered if the pilot had seen anything.

My neighbors must be deaf. How could they not see and hear what had happened? I stood up and called out, "Hey, can anybody hear me?"

Again . . . nothing.

I called for my son, but he didn't answer. Later I found out that, despite the television's high volume, he had fallen asleep on the rec room sofa. He, like my neighbors, had neither heard nor seen a thing.

I shot an anxious look at the sky, but saw nothing odd. Doubt flashed through my mind. Was I crazy? Was it a hallucination? No, damn it! I'd seen it. I'd photographed it.

The pictures were scattered on the ground, each where I had taken it and let it fall. I had begun to gather them up with shaky hands when Frances rounded the curve. She drove on into the garage, then came out to see what I was doing. Before I could say anything, she asked, "What's that awful smell?"

That stinking ammonia-and-cinnamon scent was still on me. I looked up at her and I guess she could tell something had happened by the expression on my face.

"Ed, what's the matter with you?"

"Not here, let's go inside." I'm not sure whether I wanted to go inside to get away from the craft in case it came back or so that no one would hear what I had to say. It was probably a little of both.

My heart was still racing as we went into the house. I sat down at the breakfast bar in the kitchen. Frances brought me a glass of tea, then watched over my shoulder as I peeled the backing off the pictures.

There it was, on the film. It hadn't been my imagination, or some sort of hallucination. What I had seen was real. That wasn't a comforting thought.

The pictures brought it all back to me again, the excitement and the fear. It took a few minutes before I could begin the story. The more I recalled the details, the angrier I got. How could I ever make anybody believe me? Show the pictures? Maybe. They did look good. But my own wife was looking at me as if I were crazy, and she had already seen them.

I couldn't really blame her. If anyone had told me such a tale, I'd probably have laughed. But damn it, this was real. I knew it was. It had happened to me.

It wasn't that Frances didn't believe me. She just didn't want it to be true. The idea that extraterrestrials not only existed but went around picking up people was something neither of us wanted to admit. But the evidence was right there with us. The photographs, and the smell that still clung to my clothes, couldn't be explained away.

If only somebody else had seen the craft too. But how could I find that out? I wasn't going to ask anybody, and I wasn't going to go to the police either. I didn't want my name linked to a UFO in their public records. Besides, what could they do?

I was mostly concerned about other people's view of my credibility if I reported what had happened. I might be known as the crazy builder who saw UFOs. That wouldn't be great for business. Would people involved with me in various community projects decide they didn't need my help anymore? What about our friends—mine, my wife's, the kids'? How would they react?

Frances and I talked over what to do. At first we thought we'd keep it to ourselves, not tell anyone. But what if this UFO continued to fly around our community? Didn't we have an obligation to our friends and neighbors? What if that had been our daughter, or some other child outside? Would they have been taken? We finally decided we couldn't just keep quiet about it.

My first thought was to send the photos to the *Sentinel,* our local weekly newspaper, with an anonymous letter explaining what had happened. But I was afraid no one would take it seriously. I decided I'd have to take them in myself.

Frances was against it. What if the *Sentinel* refused to keep my identity a secret? She and I could handle anything people might say about the "nut." It was our children she was concerned about, especially our daughter. Our son would be off at college next year, but our youngest had five more years of school ahead of her, and children can be cruel. So can adults. We decided to give it more thought before we did anything.

November 11, 1987—Frances's Account

As was frequently the case around our house, dinnertime meant a mad dash to the store for some forgotten item. I don't recall what it was on this particular evening. I simply told Ed I was going and took off.

A round trip to the store took about seven minutes of driving time. But I could never go and pick up just the one thing I went for. By the time I reached the checkout counter I had at least six or seven items from various aisles around the store.

It was almost dark as I headed back. I don't like driving at that time of day. I can't see as well and because of that I kept a close watch on the road ahead, alert for kids on bikes or one of the multitude of cats that live on our street.

If I hadn't been so concerned about watching the road, maybe I would have looked up at the sky and seen the UFO. Instead I rounded the last curve before our house and only saw Ed picking up what I thought were small pieces of paper.

Pushing the automatic opener for the garage door, I drove in. I parked, got out with my bag of groceries, and went to ask Ed what he was doing.

The first thing I noticed was that the pieces of paper were Polaroid pictures. Why Ed would have snapshots scattered all over the yard I couldn't guess. Then I noticed the smell. A strange, awful, pungent smell. It was sweetish, yet it wasn't. It was acrid, but not exactly. And it wasn't in the air. It was on Ed.

I asked him what the smell was, and he looked up at me. I knew something was wrong. He was breathing hard, as if he'd been running. But it was the wide-eyed look of fear on his face that scared me. Ed had always been my rock, the one I knew would always keep me safe, no matter what. To see him so shaken stunned me.

My questions, what was wrong, what had happened, were answered by a quick "Not here, inside." I picked up the last photo and we went through the garage into the kitchen. I put my bag on the counter. Ed sat down at the breakfast bar.

"Would you pour me a glass of tea, baby?"

At last! Something normal. Maybe now he'd explain what was going on. I set the tea in front of him and asked him what had happened.

"In a minute. I want to peel these pictures first."

I stood behind him, looking over his shoulder, as he separated the films, one at a time. What emerged, shot after shot, was unbelievable. Ed spread the five photos out on the breakfast bar and just stared at them for a few minutes before he started to describe what had happened.

Somewhere along the way I sat down on one of the other chairs, dumbstruck. It was hard to believe, but the photos were right there in front of me. And Ed was obviously upset. The further he got into his story, the more agitated he became, especially when he told me about the blue beam.

I realized I was shaking my head, as if to deny all he was telling me. It wasn't that I thought he was lying, but things like this just didn't happen. Not in Gulf Breeze. Not to my family. But although I didn't want to believe it, I couldn't deny it. The evidence was right there. I could see it. And I could smell it.

Ed and I had a long "discussion" about what we should do. I agreed that someone should be told. The newspaper? The TV station? The police? That was the problem. Who? And how?

Under no circumstances did I want Ed to say he had taken the photos. And telling about the blue beam was totally out of the question. He agreed wholeheartedly. We could both imagine what would happen then—what people might say, things their children would repeat to ours. "Nut case," "crazy," and "weirdo" were just a few of the words that came to mind.

Gulf Breeze is a beautiful community full of warm, caring people. People with one of the highest education levels in the state of Florida. But I wasn't sure what they would think of a guy who saw flying saucers and I didn't want to find out.

We finally decided the first thing to do was tell our own children. Before dinner we showed them the photos, and their dad told them his story. They were flabbergasted, excited, and a little afraid—especially Laura.

Dan was sorry he hadn't heard Ed yelling so that he might have helped him. I told him he would probably have been caught in the blue beam too. Laura said she didn't think she'd run around so late anymore. That kept me from having to tell her I'd already made that decision for her.

We explained to the kids that somehow we had to let people know about the UFO, but we didn't want anyone to know who had taken the photos. They both agreed not to say anything about it to anyone. Neither of them wanted all the facts spread around town either.

Ed went to take a shower. I finished preparing dinner, then put his clothes in to wash while we ate. Later I wished I hadn't done that. There might have been some important evidence on them. But at that moment all I wanted was to try to make things as normal as possible. All of us were feeling the aftereffects of Ed's shocking encounter.

The children's rooms are completely on the other side of the house from ours. That fact had never bothered Laura before. But when I told her it was bedtime, she asked me if Dan would be in his bedroom studying. I assured her he would be and that I'd turn the intercom on monitor so I could hear if anything unusual happened. Finally she settled down.

It wasn't much easier for the rest of us. Dan at least had his schoolwork to keep him busy. The midterm grades he'd be sending off to colleges were foremost in his mind. Ed and I had nothing pressing to do, so we talked, and worried, and tried to find answers. Why Gulf Breeze? Why now? And most of all—why Ed?

We'd both read news accounts of UFO sightings, but neither of us had any real interest. Sure, we'd both said, if they exist, it would be fascinating to see one.

I wasn't so sure it was fascinating anymore. Not if it meant having someone you love abducted. And I had no doubt that was just what they had tried to do. How dare they? What gave them that right? Were they so far advanced that we were like animals to them? It was a frightening thought.

Over the next few days things gradually returned to normal, more so for the kids than for Ed and me. Since nothing else had happened, Laura went back to running around the neighborhood with her friends as she always had. Dan was preoccupied with school and college applications.

I didn't tell them how little sleep their father and I had been getting. There was no point in saying anything that might worry them unnecessarily. The truth was, every little sound at night woke us. Ed had always slept like the dead. Now he was the one asking *me,* "What was that?"

I liked to think that our dog, Crystal, would warn us if she could. After all, she looked up at birds flying overhead in the daytime. But she didn't bark at them, or at airplanes. Would the UFO be something she felt deserved a bark?

Maybe those dog "photos" Ed had seen meant something. Maybe they could control dogs; or maybe the dogs just didn't sense the UFO was there. I didn't know. That was the hard part—the not knowing.

Was this a one-time thing? Would they be back? Maybe, but not to us. At least I hoped not. I had always said I wouldn't believe it until I saw a UFO with my own eyes. No more. The photos and Ed's word were good enough for me.

I had always assumed the aliens, while maybe more intelligent than we, would be friendly. These weren't. I didn't want any more close encounters for myself, or my family. If this was the way the aliens behaved, I didn't want it for anyone.

Ed and I were still debating how to get the news out. I wasn't enthusiastic about any of his ideas, even the solution to which I reluctantly agreed. But it had to be done somehow, and I had learned years ago that once Ed made up his mind that he'd found the right way, nothing I could say would change his mind. Usually he *was* right. I hoped he was this time.

NOVEMBER 17, 1987—PHOTOS GIVEN TO PRESS

Early Morning

I came up with an idea I hoped would work. With my wife's help I wrote a letter, pretending to be somebody else—Mr. X, a fictitious friend who had taken the pictures. We deliberately omitted any mention of the telepathy and blue beam. Just telling about the sighting was threatening enough. Above all, I wanted to protect my identity, so we also changed some of the minor details, hoping nobody would suspect that I was Mr. X.

After I'd finished some business calls, I carried the letter and photos to the newspaper office. The editor, Duane Cook, wasn't there. His secretary wasn't sure when he'd be back, and I couldn't stay; I had a job site to get to.

Although I didn't want to turn what I had over to anyone but Duane, I did show the photos to his secretary. She was interested and thought Duane would be too. I told her I'd come back later, but I wasn't very happy. It had been hard enough to carry out my plan once. Now I'd have to do it all over again.

When I returned, Duane was there. He told me he'd heard from his secretary that I had something strange to show him. I laid the letter and photos out on his desk. When he saw that the photos were Polaroid shots, he was more interested, telling me Polaroids were hard to tamper with.

I could have told him I knew they hadn't been tampered with, but that would have blown my cover story. Instead I just waited while he and his photographer looked them over, anxious and more than a little nervous. I wasn't worried about the photos; I knew they were real. It was what Duane might ask me about the photographer that had my heart pumping too fast.

Sure enough, he asked me who Mr. X was. I told him the letter had the only answer I could give him. When Duane realized I wasn't going to say anything more, he told me he wanted to make some halftone blowups to see if he could get something decent in black-and-white for the paper.

I waited until the photographer brought in the print. The clarity and quality impressed me. The original shot was fairly dark, and I was amazed they had been able to brighten it so much.

Duane was happy with the result too. He told me he needed to make halftones of all the shots, which gave me the impression he intended to run the story. That's what I had hoped for. I told him he could keep the photos, that I'd pick them up later.

I knew a lot of the newspaper staff who were there. I worried that they might talk. Before I left, I stressed again that I was just acting as a messenger and wanted my name kept out of it. Duane agreed. I felt better, knowing I'd done something to get the story out while still protecting my family from any publicity.

When I got home for lunch, I told Frances everything that had happened. She had only one thing to say.

"I hope we don't regret this later."

So did I.

NOVEMBER 19, 1987—PUBLICATION OF PHOTOS

couldn't wait for the late-afternoon mail delivery of our *Sentinel;* soon after breakfast I went out and bought a copy. The photos and letter were front-page news. I was delighted. Surely someone else had seen the UFO. Now that I had come forward, even if it was anonymously, maybe others would too.

In the letter I made no mention of the failed abduction attempt. I wasn't prepared to come forward with that, even as somebody else. It was just too traumatic.

There were other changes, all ploys to try to lessen the chance that anyone might figure out who Mr. X really was. But the basic facts were there. What I really wanted was to see the photos published, to find out if anyone else had seen anything, to alert people.

Along with the letter, the *Sentinel* ran two of the five photos I submitted, numbers 1 and 5, and a blowup of photo 5. Following is my letter just as it appeared in the paper.

To Whom It May Concern:

On the night of November 11th I took the pictures you now see before you. I was reluctant at first to show them to anyone but my family, but my wife convinced me to show them to Ed. Ed in turn said that the photos should be shown to the press. That is why he is presenting them to you.

I had just sat down to dinner when I saw the object from my window. I rushed to my bedroom to get my Polaroid. I rushed outside and started taking pictures. I got off four good pictures (1, 2, 3, 4) and

38

then had to change film. I got one more good picture (5) before it shot straight up and disappeared.

There may be some reasonable explanation for what I saw but I don't think so. The ''ship'' looked about the size of a small house. It was, however, quite some distance away and hard to tell. It hovered in the sky for several minutes and then left. It did not spin or rotate but it did seem to bob up and down while weaving slightly. It glowed from the bottom as if that may be the power source. The markings (windows?) on the upper and lower section were aligned and spaced equally. On the top there appeared to be a dome or bump that was quite bright. There was nothing colorful about it—no flashing lights, no beams coming from it. None of that *Star Wars* stuff; it was just a dull gray-blue ''thing.'' I don't think that it was military but you may want to check. It was quite big and I don't think I was alone in seeing it. I wish to remain anonymous but if these photos and story spark any interest from your readership I may identify myself. I am a prominent citizen of the community and need anonymity at this time. I know what I saw and would feel much better if I knew I was not alone.

Let me reassure you that this is not a hoax. I saw what I saw, took pictures of it, and have given these pictures to you. I wish I could come forward but cannot; for while I have nothing to gain, I have everything to lose. Thank you for your time and understanding.

The only editorial comment appeared under one of the photos. It read:

These Polaroid photos were taken from the front yard of a Gulf Breeze residence Wednesday evening, November 11th. If anybody saw it or knows any information regarding this, please contact the *Sentinel*.

I went home with the paper so that Frances could see that Duane had kept his word, leaving my name out of it. Even so, she was upset that we had written that Ed had taken the photos to the paper. She felt like we should have left that out completely. I did my best to reassure her that we had nothing to worry about. But seeing even just half my name in print shook me up a bit. I just didn't tell her so.

NOVEMBER 20, 1987—SECOND SIGHTING—THE HUM

I finished my work at the last job site early, anxious to start home. Friday nights were always rushed at our house during high school football season, especially for home games. Frances worked at the stadium concession stand and was always one of the first to arrive to start the food cooking. I had to be at the band room early to chaperon the band and accompany them to the football field.

This Friday was more pressured than usual. It was Homecoming at the high school. There had been a parade in the afternoon, and I knew that everything would start on an earlier schedule.

As I drove home at about four o'clock, the newspaper still lay in the front seat of my truck. I had carried it around all day from job site to job site. Some of the craftsmen had already seen the front-page headlines. But most of them lived in Pensacola and didn't receive the *Sentinel*.

At one job I calmly asked if anybody had seen the UFO report in the paper. The job came to a standstill as everybody crowded around my truck with comments like, "Holy shit," "Ah, come on," and "That damn thing looks real." Most of all they wanted to get a copy of the paper to show their families and friends. Some of them asked, "Who took the pictures?" Of course I said I didn't know.

A small glow of satisfaction grew in my chest as the workers continued to talk about other people they knew who had seen strange lights in the sky. Maybe my idea had worked. Taking the pictures to the press was the best way of getting people to watch and report on what they saw.

Most people seemed to be fascinated by the idea that the pictures were real. Even those who didn't believe still wondered what it could be. They were thinking, asking questions. And that was what I had hoped for.

My construction crews range from hard-core "honky-tonkers," who insist on trying to sneak a beer onto a job site, to the other extreme, who would never take a drink or utter a curse word. How I managed to get them all to work together amazed even me. Now they had something in common to argue about and discuss.

Some of the men kidded about the aliens and sex. They even told a few jokes. One of my carpenters guaranteed me that the UFO meant that the end was near and I must prepare to meet my maker. Surely, he said, the UFO was the work of the devil.

I was frightened of the UFO, but only because of the apparent advanced technology. The blue beam had such power, and the craft could move without noticeable effort. In addition, it had tried to take me against my will. Had someone said, "Hey, Ed. Want to take a ride?" I might have agreed to go. But force me to obey? Lift me off the road? Freeze my body solid? Treat me like an ant or a dog? No way. Not in this country. It's un-American.

Nine days had passed and I was finally feeling pretty good about it all. Already the town was buzzing with UFO talk. While driving from job site to job site, or just sitting quietly working, it would hit me. I'd begin to smile.

I had seen it. I knew the truth. I had always said I would have to see one to believe. Well, I had. And I was still here. I had a light-headed feeling at having had the experience.

In the evenings I tried to share the "I know" feeling with my family. As we ate dinner, I couldn't help bringing up the subject of the UFO. I must have talked the subject to death, but I couldn't help it. They were very understanding, but nobody can really know without seeing for themselves. That was an experience I wanted them to have only from a safe distance. Even so, what had happened to me had opened all of our minds to new ways of thinking about what was possible and what wasn't.

An open mind was what was needed in order to deal with seeing the UFO. Just imagine what would have happened to that fellow who insisted that the UFO was Satan had he actually seen it. Or worse yet, had he been lifted up into the UFO. It might have pushed him past his breaking point. Yes, an open mind was best. And that kept the questions churning in my head.

Was it an accident that the UFO had shown itself to me through my office window? Did it specifically want *me* to come out, or could it have been anybody? Though I had sometimes thought of UFOs in passing and had always figured there might be life on other planets, I wasn't a believer. I had no reason to be.

I didn't even try to prepare myself for a return visit. There was no way to. Besides, the chances of seeing the UFO even once must have been millions to one.

So, without suspecting anything more than my family doing normal football-game-night activities, I parked in the driveway on November 20th, walked in the front door, and called out that I was home. At that moment I noticed a slight ring in my right ear—that strange, high-pitched ringing one hears sometimes for no apparent reason. That little sound that, if you ignore it, goes away.

On my way into the kitchen I asked if everybody was getting ready for Homecoming and what time Dan had to be over at the band room. Frances told me he had already gone and I was to be there at six. Laura was in her room dressing.

The ringing in my ear got louder, and I tried shaking my head to stop it. By now I was in the kitchen and the sound was so piercing that I felt as if Frances should be able to hear it coming out of my head. Moving my head wildly, I tried to make it stop. It grew louder. Maybe outside . . .

I hurried into the backyard, next to the swimming pool, and frantically shook my head and rubbed my ear. Frances followed me, asking what was wrong. Was I ill? Our arms around each other's waists, we walked to the far end of the pool. The sound moved deeper into my head and softened to a vibrating hum.

"Damn, humming. My head is humming. What the hell is going on?"

The right front of my brain was humming. I was scared, and Frances looked as if she was going to cry. She held me close, and we both sank to the concrete deck. Frances put her hand over my right ear and pulled my head to her shoulder. She must have thought that I was losing my mind, that I had snapped under the pressure of seeing the UFO and almost being taken by it.

I knew what was doing this to me. This was the same hum I had heard while trapped in the blue beam. How could this happen? Maybe I *was* losing it. Maybe I had some kind of UFO madness. Maybe a disease.

As the hum shook my head, I took a deep breath and said that I was okay now. Frances held me tight, and tears ran down her cheeks as I eased my head from her shoulder. She tried to insist that I go to a doctor, while I kept telling her I was fine. I smiled and pulled her up with me, using the edge of the diving board to steady myself.

"I'm fine . . . I'm okay . . . Really," I insisted as we walked back toward the house.

Laura was standing at the back-door window and said nothing as we walked in. Her eyes were big, and I knew the question "What's wrong?" was about to pop out of her. I touched her shoulder as her mother and I walked by and said that everything was okay, nothing to worry about.

Frances and I went to my office at the front of the house, and I told her that the hum was the same as the one I'd heard in the blue beam. She didn't know I was still hearing it. She was pale and upset, and there was no way I could stand to see her cry anymore.

She asked if I thought the UFO was back. I said maybe, but chances were that the hum was just kind of left over and everything would be all right. We walked out onto the front porch and looked around.

It was 4:30 P.M., daylight—clear sky. We looked over every inch of open space, across every edge of forest, and past each telephone pole. Nothing to be seen. No UFO. Frances must have thought I was losing my mind. Thank goodness for the pictures. At least I had them, and they could be seen on the front page at any newsstand.

The tension eased, and we went back into the house. I still didn't tell her that the hum was even then roaring in my head—but not as loudly as it had been in the blue beam. It was more like the sound of a hand vibrator held against my head. I told her to finish getting ready and went back into my office.

I sat in my office staring out the front window. Maybe that blue light *had* screwed my brain up. I tried to shake it off and do some work. My building schedules still had to be met.

The hum stayed. Then I suddenly heard a blast of air, just as if I were standing next to a bus just releasing its air brakes. This part is hard to describe. I heard the UFO voice again. It started softly. I couldn't understand anything, not a single word. I have no idea of how to write any of it—not one syllable. My best guess is that it was an earthly foreign language. Maybe an African dialect.

I knew this telepathy would be unbelievable when I tried to describe it, but it happened. I didn't see a vision of the being doing the speaking or see anything surrounding a being. Only a voice.

There I was, sitting alone in my office with that voice grinding out sounds. I felt dizzy. My heart pounded as I sat there bent over staring at the floor. I held my hands to my ears, supporting my head, and tried not to freak out. I thought that people in insane asylums who heard voices could be like me, or I like them.

The hum had stopped when the voice began, and the voice was better than the maddening hum, even though the "words" made no sense. It was the voice from the blue beam, deep and heavy, with an almost mechanical tone. I recognized it.

How could this be? How could I hear that voice? Why did my brain hear the sound and not my ears? Later I would have time to speculate as to why I could hear the UFO, but then I just sat there and shook, with cold sweat beading on my forehead.

The voice would pause, then continue again, as if I were hearing only one side of a conversation. Then it dawned on me—they were near. Somewhere out there in the sky, the UFO must be there.

I didn't call my wife again, just sat and listened. A little while later Frances came into my office and told me it was time for her to leave for the stadium. She asked if I was okay. I told her I was fine and that I'd see her at the game. For once Frances planned just to get the food started, let someone else serve it, and watch the game with me.

A few minutes later I heard her drive off with Laura to pick up one of her girlfriends, who was spending the night at our house. I hadn't told Frances about the voices. I wasn't sure I could explain what was going on inside my head. And I didn't want to frighten her.

Now it was close to five o'clock, with the sun all but gone. The house was empty, and I was thankful not to have my family see me like this. I listened to the one-sided conversation as I picked up my camera and slipped out the front door. I stood between the house and a bushy tree, looking over the horizon—still nothing.

The neighborhood was quiet. I was alone, but instinct told me something was there, and after me. My breathing echoed in front of my face as branches from the tree pressed against my cheek. Droplets of sweat ran down to my waist, wetting my neck and back. The evening air seemed to be thick around me. Everything was so quiet. I wanted to scream.

"I hear you, you bastard," I shouted.

The voice stopped.

"I know you're there," I said, this time quieter.

A rush of air blasted into my head. Maybe "it" had been talking to an African who was being held in a room with an airtight door. If so, not anymore. Everything was still and silent. Then a small speck of light appeared very, very high in the sky. It was falling at an incredible speed.

The voice sounded again. I flinched back against the brick wall with a jolt that made me bite my tongue and curse.

"Damn."

"Be calm. Step forward," came the forceful voice.

I raised the camera again, following the downward path of the UFO.

The UFO voice: "Don't do that."

Another voice, definitely a female voice that sounded distorted: "Please, don't do that."

Another voice, in Spanish: "*Los fotos son prohibido.*"

The female voice: "You can't expose them. They won't hurt you. Just a few tests. That's all."

"Right. If I want to be examined, I'll let you know." I shot picture number 6 as the UFO suddenly stopped its fall and hung there frozen, just beyond the power pole at the front of my yard.

Somehow I could hear them talking to me, just as if we were all on the telephone. All the voices were deep, garbled, and somewhat computerlike. Whether they were actually hearing me or just reading my mind, I didn't know.

The UFO shot over to my right, almost like a humming bird, and hovered there. It seemed to be spinning from right to left, but very slowly. Ever so slightly it would tilt toward me and then away, which I noticed because the big power light at the bottom grew larger and smaller. This craft lit itself up and was bright. It was so bright, in fact, that I still can't believe someone else didn't see it hovering there. I took picture number 7.

The UFO voice: "Step forward. We will bring you aboard."

"No way. What gives you the right to suck people up into your ship against their will?"

The UFO voice: "We have the right."

I remember thinking that the being was talking to me as if I were an animal: "Here, Rover. Sit, Rover. What a good Rover."

Click. I took shot number 8, next to the tree.

The female voice: "You must do what they say. They haven't hurt us, and we are going back home now."

Remember the dog visions? Dog after dog. Well, now visions blasted into my brain of naked women. These were not drawings of naked women, but actual naked women. Flash after flash, each lasting about five seconds. Big women, little women; fat, black, white women from every race and every age. There were even pregnant women.

If this was meant to encourage me to come aboard, it didn't work. I stayed right where I was.

The UFO voice: "We will come for you."

I snapped picture number 9. The craft moved forward and then shot straight up, disappearing into the dark so fast I couldn't see it leave.

This second sighting, with photos 6, 7, 8, and 9, was scary. They had threatened me, and I didn't know when they might try again to take me. If the voices from the UFO were real, then so were the people. At least I assumed they were, and some of them seemed to be human. But maybe it was all a trick. Well, I didn't know and I didn't want to go find out.

If they came back, as the voice had said, what then? I didn't want to start carrying a gun. But I thought, *What if it comes to that?* The reality that this UFO could be flying around Gulf Breeze, just out of sight, and suddenly drop from the sky to snatch somebody up with that blue beam sent chills down my back.

I was late for my date at the high school band room. It was the last game of the season and also the last chance I'd have to see my son march and play. The band had prepared a special exit from the field for halftime, which Dan swore would hold the crowd spellbound. I wasn't going to miss it, UFO or no UFO.

In the band room a lot of the kids were quick to ask if I was the Ed in the paper. I laughed it off with, "Well, I'll believe in UFOs when one lands in my backyard."

Soon Frances came in, but there was no chance to tell her the latest news. As we marched over to the stadium with the band, she did manage to get in a quick "Are you all right?" which I answered with a simple yes.

At the football game Dan played his quads (four drums connected together), but I knew he had more on his mind than playing drums. We would look at one another in silent disbelief as his friends laughed and talked about the UFO pictures they had seen.

Bundled against the cold, Frances and I huddled together under a blanket and listened to the conversations around us. Everything was UFO this and UFO that. Some of the vendors were selling "UFO burgers." The cheerleaders were even in on it. Someone told me that they had hastily worked out a UFO cheer.

I tried to join in the spirit of the evening, but I couldn't, not really, so I faked it. Laughing in all the right places and cheering each touchdown, I was determined that no one would suspect that anything was wrong.

Later, back at home, Frances rushed to get the girls settled, then joined me in my office. I told her about the sighting and showed her the pictures. She couldn't believe it had come back. When I told her I had been hearing the voices before she left, she was upset.

I don't remember all we said. I do recall her asking me why I had risked going to the game. "What if they had zapped you right there in the stadium? It wasn't that crowded, and I have a feeling those guys would be pretty accurate with their blue beam.''

She agreed with my answer that ''they'' probably wouldn't do anything with so many people around. But she didn't appreciate my black humor that if they had, at least everyone would have seen it and known the truth.

We went to bed, but the night of the 20th was a sleepless one for me. The voices hung in my thoughts. ''We will come for you.'' Every noise, every creak of the house, the wind in the trees, each sound quickened my pulse.

Sometime that night I loaded my shotgun. I loaded the .32-caliber pistol. I loaded the .22 rifle. If I'd had a machine gun, I'd have loaded that too. I didn't know if it would do any damage if I shot the UFO, but I felt less defenseless, even though I hadn't fired any of the guns in years.

I was counting on hearing the hum to let me know they were near. I worried that they had figured that out. Maybe they could stop the hum. The idea of a visit with no warning scared me. I would be an easy target for the blue beam.

What about the blue beam; how did it work? Might it just come through the ceiling and nab me? I didn't really think so. The voices had wanted me to ''step forward.'' Apparently, even with all the UFO's power, it couldn't just swoop down and grab me. It seemed they needed me out in the open.

I began to carry the shotgun in my pickup truck, behind the seat. The seat would have to be tilted forward to reach it, but at least it was there. Each night was agony and each morning a relief. My work began to suffer. I was thankful for my years of work with the same subcontractors. They knew how I wanted things done, so the work continued at each house site uninterrupted.

I decided not to tell anyone else about the pictures. I didn't want to press my luck in maintaining secrecy. If I showed up again with more pictures from Mr. X, people might begin to suspect that I was Mr. X.

NOVEMBER 25, 1987—WITNESSES COME FORWARD

The front page of the *Sentinel* was covered with stories of witnesses who had called in to report seeing the UFO. What a gratifying way to start the day. I was not alone. My fellow residents had responded with a flood of sightings, some of which were very reliable.

Jeff Thompson, a local resident, called in and reported a daylight sighting at 8:15 A.M., when he spotted the UFO near the Oriole Beach Elementary School. The UFO shot up and hovered for thirty seconds before speeding away. Thompson said that moments later he saw two jets, which appeared to be chasing the object. (The complete account of this sighting appears in Appendix 2.)

When the air force was questioned about Thompson's report, an unofficial spokesman replied that there were no air force "flying saucers," and if a UFO *were* intercepted, the information would no doubt be classified. Perhaps the air force doesn't know what is happening, in which case, those of us who have been witnesses would be glad to tell them— and many have tried.

It was months later that I discovered the official government position on UFOs. They don't exist, the government says publicly. But in 1977 and 1978 the Citizens Against UFO Secrecy (CAUS) discovered through lawsuits that the CIA is withholding somewhere between 57 and 200 files on UFOs, and the NSA has another 135. Although some files were released, CAUS failed to gain access to most of them under the Freedom of Information Act after the two government agencies involved argued in the federal courts that release of that information would seriously jeopardize the work of both agencies and the security of the United States.

I'm no expert, but even I know that if something doesn't exist, then there is nothing to keep secret. You can't have it both ways. And just saying something doesn't exist doesn't make it so. I know what I saw, and so did the others who told their stories to the newspaper.

At about 6:00 P.M., only an hour after I took the first five pictures, Linda Lubé was outside barbecuing and saw a strange light moving southeast across the sky toward Gulf Breeze.

"I had a feeling it was from another place," said Lubé. "I didn't have my glasses on, so I couldn't see the form, but I could tell I've never seen anything like it."

One week later Mrs. Lubé saw the UFO photograph in the *Sentinel* and knew she had seen the same craft.

There was also a report from Diana Hansen, with a sighting at 7:30 P.M. And another sighting at 9:30 P.M. of an object "in an apparent landing mode" that lit up the woods behind the house of an executive who wished to remain anonymous.

On November 11th, at about 2:00 A.M., fifteen hours before my first sighting, Mrs. Joseph Zamitt says she was awakened by her dog growling. She got up and, holding on to the dog, was led to the door. The dog began to bark when she opened the door. Mrs. Zamitt says that she looked up into the sky and saw the same craft that was later depicted in the *Sentinel*. "And there was a stream of light which came down into our canal." Not mentioned in the paper was the fact that the stream of light Mrs. Zamitt saw was blue and that she had been afraid the blue light would take her dog.

(All these sightings happened on the same date as my first sighting, November 11, 1987.)

Four days later "Cathy" and three friends saw an object hanging over Bayou Texar. I mention this report because of the way she described the object's departure. My account had not yet been published, but Cathy said that after a few minutes, the object dipped toward the right and disappeared. (She's correct. That's what it does. Just blink and it's gone.)

These reports were being forwarded to the Mutual UFO Network (MUFON) by the editor of the *Sentinel*. MUFON describes itself as a nonprofit organization composed of people seriously interested in studying UFO phenomena. The members are generally professionals, with certain expertise, who contribute to the quest for a final answer to the UFO question.

These MUFON representatives have guidelines to follow and forms to use when recording interviews with witnesses. Ultimately this international organization compiles the data at their headquarters in Seguin, Texas. There international director Walter Andrus keeps tabs on the latest sightings and enters appropriate sightings in the MUFON *Journal*, distributed worldwide once a month.

As of November 25, 1987, I hadn't spoken with anyone from MUFON. My only contact had been with Duane Cook, *Sentinel* editor, and then only as a spokesman for Mr. X. In time that changed. State MUFON representative Don Ware, along with Charles Flannigan and Gary Watson, were the investigators who would later become involved with my sightings.

With all these sightings, how was it that all the military bases around the area knew nothing? The FAA Air Traffic representative at Eglin Air Force Base, George Hobgood, was asked if he knew of an experimental aircraft that might look like a "flying saucer." Hobgood said that Eglin designs and tests weaponry but would not say if any top-secret craft were flying that evening. The Eglin Public Affairs Office said that nothing unusual had happened and that likewise nothing had been spotted on radar. The Naval Air Station, which is only three miles across the bay from Gulf Breeze, also reported no unusual radar sightings.

"But," said Earl Pitts of the Pensacola Air Traffic tower station, "that does not imply that what was photographed and observed by witnesses was not there."

Pitts explained that any aircraft not in communication with the tower is considered an unidentified object. He went on to say that it's well within reason to have stealth capability that would render a craft invisible to radar. Also, there are so many unidentified targets that one more wouldn't raise any questions, "unless it did something extremely unusual."

I don't want to get off the subject of the Gulf Breeze sightings that night, but to make another point about radar, let me digress for a moment to report a sighting recorded on February 5, 1976, by Deputy Sheriff Sonny Privett.

Privett saw several motorists pulled over on the shoulder of Highway 98 in Navarre (ten miles east of Gulf Breeze) at about 2:00 A.M. The motorists were watching a strange light hovering in the sky. Privett called Florida Highway Patrol Officer Bevis by radio.

When Officer Bevis arrived, the object was over the Gulf of Mexico directly out from the radar installation east of Navarre Beach. Officer Bevis called the dispatcher to have Hurlburt AFB and Eglin AFB check this on radar. The reports came back negative. Officer Bevis used a 200mm lens and tripod and took pictures of the light that were published in a local newspaper. Surely something was there, even though the radar was negative (or the "reports" were negative).

There was yet another important sighting on November 11, 1987. Here is the firsthand account written by Charles Somerby:

It was a few minutes after sunset on Veterans Day and wife Dari and I were just finishing up our evening walk along Hickory Shores Boulevard in the Midway area.

We looked out over East Bay to admire the cloud formations when our attention was drawn to a round object moving in a southwest direction toward downtown Gulf Breeze.

There were bright lights around the bottom, another at the top. None of the lights were colored or flashing.

Our thought—it's not an airplane, not a helicopter, not a bird. What is it!

Movement of the unidentified flying object was steady. No hesitation and no apparent change of course.

Watched the local news on television that evening and looked through the morning paper to see if anyone had reported the apparition.

When it appeared no one else had been looking up at the sky at the moment, we forgot about the incident until the pictures appeared in last week's *Sentinel*.

Unfortunately didn't have a loaded camera or binoculars with us at the time of sighting.

When the Somerbys last saw the UFO it was moving in the general direction of my house. It appears they spotted the UFO only minutes before I saw it. Later Charlie Somerby wrote this follow-up article:

Except for a tornado and a few hurricanes, few happenings in Gulf Breeze in recent years have stirred up so much interest as the unidentified flying object spotted by several area residents soon after sundown on Veterans Day.

For the Gulf Breeze *Sentinel*, it was one of a very few "scoops" in the past 27 years, with television and radio personnel plus representatives from an international scientific organization descending upon the newspaper office in unprecedented numbers.

There were a lot more indicating great interest in the unidentified flying objects.

None doubted the actual sighting of the apparition.

Wife and I still can't figure out what it could have been.

In two wars spent four years in combat areas and saw dozens of "bogeys" but nothing like this one. Things that stick most in memory is the complete lack of any sound from the object and the straight course which it glided.

One person who talked to us asserted "this must be the biggest local story of the year without question."

No one would get any argument from me on that score. For me personally it was more than the biggest local story of the year. The Iran-Contra scandal, Gorbachev's visit, the latest arms treaty—all paled by comparison. They were all interesting and important, but they were national and world news. This was not only local, it was happening to me.

Why me? That's what I couldn't figure out. If anyone had asked me to describe myself, I'd have said, "Lucky and blessed." I have a happy marriage, great relationships with my two children, good health, and financial security.

I couldn't understand what these beings wanted with a forty-one-year old contractor who'd been connected with the building industry in some way most of his adult life. If it was just because I'd been available, then why hadn't they gone after any of the dozens of other people in our town when they failed with me? Maybe they had; it was possible the UFO had intruded into the lives of others in Gulf Breeze who might also be afraid of going public. And why come back? None of it made sense.

NOVEMBER 30, 1987—FRANCES'S ACCOUNT

The long Thanksgiving weekend just over, Laura came home from school bursting with news of all the talk about the UFO. This had been her first chance to see many of her friends since the *Sentinel* had published the accounts from the new witnesses, and I had hoped that knowing that other people were seeing the UFO would make her feel better about what had been happening to us. It hadn't. Nor had the continued speculation at school about who had taken the photos and why the UFO had chosen Gulf Breeze.

We discussed the things she had heard at school and what she really thought about the UFO. How could I reassure her? I couldn't understand or explain it. It scared the hell out of me and made me afraid and angry.

Ours had always been a tranquil, happy household. Not anymore. These encounters with the UFO had disrupted our lives, upsetting each of us. And there didn't seem to be anything we could do about it. It wasn't right or fair.

At night in the privacy of our bedroom or during the day while the children were at school, Ed and I seemed to talk about nothing but the UFO. But for all the hours we spent asking and reasking the same questions, we could come up with no answers.

My hope that this was a one-time episode had already been shattered. They had come back and said they would come again. When? Where? How were we supposed to go on with our everyday lives with that threat in our minds?

Our neighborhood being what it is, we had all had a casual attitude about our safety. If Laura was late coming home from school or play, I didn't worry. I knew she just hadn't noticed the time. Now I found myself calling to check on her.

The rest of my family had their concerns. My daughter was afraid when her father went out at night. My son was ready to join forces with Ed and do battle against the UFO if necessary. Ed now carried a 20-gauge shotgun with him whenever he left home.

Things certainly had changed in our house.

DECEMBER 2, 1987—THIRD SIGHTING—FRANCES SEES UFO

A week after the second *Sentinel* article ran, two of the local television stations aired reports on the sightings. At this time my identity was still known only to certain members of the *Sentinel* staff, and even they didn't know that I was Mr. X. I hadn't talked to anyone at the TV stations; all their information had come from the *Sentinel* and other witnesses.

I was pleased with the television coverage. They weren't treating it like a joke, although there was some nervous laughter and banter among the anchors. I didn't mind that. I'd already learned that laughing, when I could, helped relieve the tension and kept me sane. Twelve days had passed since the second sighting, and my life was almost back to normal.

As I did most nights after dinner, I went into my office to work until bedtime. Every now and then I went to the window for a quick glance at the sky, and I remember thinking how black the night was. As I worked, drawing on the floor plan taped to my drafting table, memories would disrupt my concentration. In my mind's eye I could still see the blue haze glow all over my body and smell the strange cinnamon and ammonia that I'd never forget. Finally I decided to call it a night.

After checking all the door locks and leaving the front porch light on, I went to bed. I relied on our dog to warn me of any problems in the backyard. Crystal is a pure-white spitz and absolutely hates anybody coming close to her fenced-in yard. I'm told it's the nature of a spitz to be very protective of the family it belongs to. Crystal lives up to the reputation of the breed.

She has certain barks for certain problems. A squirrel or another dog receives some yapping attention, but a person drives her crazy. Rapid-fire barking, jumping at the fence, and scratching the ground like a bull are what greet even the oldest friend over for a visit. On that night Crystal was on guard in the backyard, as always. I felt better knowing that. If she barked at a squirrel in distrust, she should go nuts over a UFO.

I don't know how long I'd been asleep when something, not the dog, woke me. The clock's red numbers glowed in the dark. It was late, three o'clock in the morning, and very dark outside. As I rolled over, I noticed that the pool pump was running. We'd forgotten to cut it off again. I knew I should get up and turn it off, but I was in that half-asleep, half-awake zone and so relaxed. Then I heard a baby cry.

Baby cry? Strange. We don't have a baby. Our neighbors don't either, and if they did, how could I hear it from so far away? I listened closer but without rising from bed. In a few minutes I heard distinct voices. I shook myself awake and realized the voices were in my head.

They were back! No mistaking that voice—like a computer-type machine sound—very deep and almost as if it were coming through a blown-out speaker. If you ever talked through a comb with a piece of paper over it when you were a kid, you know what I mean. The voice is like that, deep and distorted. Even though I couldn't really "hear" the words, my brain somehow understood the sounds.

They were out there. I knew that. Were they waiting for me? I wasn't sure. I was afraid they intended to fulfill the parting promise to come for me. But why? The questions were shooting through my head.

Why come for me? Why show up and then disappear so quickly? Why hover long enough for me to take some pictures? Why not land? Why not just get it over with and let everybody see? Just go ahead and land in the middle of the Orange Bowl with seventy thousand football fans watching. That would do it. But that didn't seem to be the way they did things.

I lay there, afraid to move. I just listened. I felt stiff, and my neck muscles started to twitch. I slid my hand over to Frances and touched her on the side. She shifted in her sleep but didn't wake up. Again I poked her with my fingers. This time she turned on her side to face me and laid her left arm across my chest. She started to snuggle a little closer and must have noticed something wasn't right.

Quietly she asked, "What's wrong?"

I didn't say anything. The last time I had said something out loud, they had heard me. I lay there staring at the ceiling in the dark. Should I get up? The pistol was just to my right on the nightstand. I listened. They spoke in Spanish and were tending to the crying baby. I've translated as well as I can.

Female voice: "She wants some milk."

Male voice: "If they don't give us something other than bananas, I'll—"

Female voice: "Hush, they'll hear you."

Male voice: "But why do they just eat bananas?"

I know this sounds bizarre, and I was tempted not to tell it, but bananas are what they were talking about. I lived in Central America for about five years and speak Spanish to a modest degree, although I can understand it even better.

Male voice: "*Y jue puta.*" (I'm not sure about the spelling, but it translates to a slang version of "son of a bitch." I mention this because I remember hearing it in parts of Nicaragua and Costa Rica, maybe the voices' home.)

Male voice: "Son of a bitch. Look at all those . . . Maybe twenty . . . *Y jue.* . . . What is this action? [rough translation] What's happening?"

Female voice: "I saw them like that last night. The chief [her word was *jefe*, apparently referring to the one who talks to them] said they were taking on power fuel."

The baby was still crying. By now, of course, I was wide awake. Sweat soaked my back and rolled down my underarms. I was afraid to move and afraid not to. I knew the UFO was there, but did they know I could hear them?

I had to do something. Should I call the police? My relationship with the officers on our local force had always been good. We'd worked together on different projects. If the UFO was here for the police to see—great—but what if it was gone and all I could tell them was about the voices in my head? Sure, sure. There goes my reputation. But what if I needed help? They had said, "We will come for you."

There was almost no time to think clearly. I moved the sheet off my legs and slid my feet to the floor without sitting up. I slipped off the bed still on my back until I lay on the floor with shoes under my shoulders. I whispered for Frances to stay put, that everything would be fine.

The baby still cried in the background as the voices began talking about food again. The female must have begun to nurse the baby, because it was suddenly quiet. The male said something about wanting his clothes and not having leather for skin. Was this an indication that the UFO beings had leather for skin?

There was no time to think about that because as I lay on the floor next to my bed, I raised my hand to take hold of the .32-caliber pistol on the nightstand. I planned to creep around looking for them alone. Frances wouldn't have any of that. She got down beside me. Instantly there was a rush of air, the voices stopped, and a slight hum began.

Moving along the floor on our knees, we crawled to the front door in the dark—I had no intention of turning on the lights. I peeked through the leaded glass in the door. Nothing looked out of place in the front yard. I eased the door open and crouched on the porch, looking at the sky. It was black. There may have been clouds in the sky to hide the UFO craft, but it was so dark—no way to tell.

I crept back inside and closed and locked the door behind me. Kneeling on the floor, I listened to every sound of the house. Crystal, the dog, was quiet. Maybe asleep. Maybe I should check. I made my way through the living room to the kitchen, bent over to try to stay below the level of the windows. Frances followed me. I could hear her breathing heavily in the darkness.

From my position I could see little more than black sky through the half glass in the kitchen door. I raised myself up until the pool and the wooden monoliths that serve as windscreens around it were in full view. There was no sign of Crystal. Don't go outside, I told myself. I'd just crack the back door and call to the dog.

"Crystal," I whispered. "Crystal, Crystal." A little louder.

Nothing—so I eased out onto the pool deck. Crystal lay sleeping on the bench next to the house—no problem there. But I could still hear the hum. From out of the darkness came a soft glow. Directly overhead it was coming down—fast. I mean fast: From the size of a dime to half the size of my pool in about two seconds.

Panic and shock hit me and I shot back into the house. I slammed the door and locked it. The craft stopped about one hundred feet above the pool. It hovered there a few seconds, then sort of drifted to the east, away from the house.

I still had the gun in my hand. I tried to be rational, to think. No shooting. Not yet. Maybe we can talk. Maybe not. They have a super craft, they have telepathy and all that, but advanced culture—I doubted it. Advanced cultures should be civilized—maybe try some manners. Perhaps, "Please, may I suck you up into our craft?" "No, you may not." "Okay, thank you anyway." And they'd leave you alone.

Not these guys. They didn't bother to ask. They just did what they pleased. I cracked the door again. The UFO stopped.

The UFO voice ordered, "Step forward now."

"Not in this life," I muttered as I took the Polaroid camera from the breakfast bar.

I pointed the camera with my right hand and aimed the gun with my left. The craft moved a little farther away from the house. Then they just hovered there, out over the field, waiting. I wasn't exactly sure for what.

Knowing it was crazy, I slipped out the door and dashed to the first windscreen. I made my way to the far end of the pool, from windscreen to windscreen. Hiding behind the fourth one, I leaned my left shoulder against the right wooden edge, peeked around it, and watched.

The UFO changed color and almost disappeared into the darkness. The bottom power light turned from white to orange. The dome also turned orange, but the portholes that I could see were still white. I raised the camera and took photo 10.

Flash! The flashcube was in the camera. In the dark I hadn't noticed. It lit up my position like a spotlight. I might as well have just stood up and yelled, "Here I am!" Instead I screamed, "Damn, damn," and started running for cover, back to the kitchen door.

When I reached the door, Frances was yelling in a whisper, "What was that flash?"

I quickly explained it, then tried to convince her it hadn't been completely stupid for me to go outside. She continued to scold me as we watched the UFO through the window.

Seconds later, as quickly as it had dropped from the sky, the UFO shot straight up. No sound, no wind, just a flash as the bottom turned white and it was gone. How could anything move like that? When I say that it shot straight up, that is more of a sensation I had than actually seeing it move out of sight. It was so fast that it just disappeared, and I had the feeling that it had gone up.

The hum in my head faded, then stopped. I told Frances that, strangely enough, I was grateful for the hum. The hum would alert me. If they could stop it, I felt sure they would. She shivered beside me, and I told her to go on back to bed, I'd be there in a minute.

Earlier I had mistaken the UFO hum for the pool pump. That wouldn't happen again. From room to room I checked for anything that hummed. The refrigerator—unplugged it. The aquarium pump—turned it off. The central heater—off. By the time I was through, the house was quiet. Satisfied, I returned to my bedroom.

Frances was sitting up in bed waiting for me. We lay in bed and talked about it all. Maybe it was over. Maybe not. Three times it had been here. Three times, and for what reason?

The chances of seeing a UFO are slim, but the chances of seeing a UFO three times are incredible. And more outrageous than that—this one was making house calls. I was afraid of it, but also fascinated by it. If they would just stop all this cat-and-mouse stuff.

I was going to need some help to figure this out. Had this ever happened to anybody else? Was it life-threatening? Should I call the military?

The UFO hadn't really hurt me physically, yet. Would it? Why was it here? Why me? Again the "why" questions, for which I had no answers. But I was ready to look for some.

As Frances and I talked, there was a scary feeling in my stomach, but there was also a strong sense of satisfaction. We knew a truth, much like knowing something important that almost nobody else in the world knows. But perhaps many people knew and were too afraid to report it.

The other witnesses who had come forward in the newspaper were comforting. They knew, just like I did. Even though we hadn't talked, I felt a kinship. I just hoped that all the television and news interest would spread the word. Maybe more people would keep watch and report their sightings of this visitor to our city. Maybe someday we could all get together, share our experiences, and look at the photographs.

I picked the latest photograph up from the nightstand. Frances and I studied the shades of color that created two dark bands across the UFO. One band was at the middle of the main body. The other was between the power source and the main body.

The UFO was much more detailed to the naked eye, and I was disappointed with the photograph. It clearly showed the bottom oval, which was really a circle when the craft was overhead. But other things were impossible to see the way they really were. The outside edges seemed to fade. In reality the UFO was wider in diameter than the photo showed. Also, the small points of light in the dark band were not just light; they were portholes. I distinctly remember trying to stay hidden so that "they" couldn't see me through those portholes.

Well, at least I had another photograph. As dark as it was, the UFO was there. Now there were ten pictures in all. Some were better than others, with blue sky, background and foreground, clearer details. The UFO was real, and I knew it. The photos were real, and I welcomed the photo experts the reporters intended to have study them. When it was all over, nobody would be able to deny the existence of other beings in the universe.

Finally, when we both calmed down, I suggested we get some sleep. I knew Frances had to get up early the next morning, and neither one of us had slept through the night for some time.

Dropping the photo on the nightstand, I turned out the light. Sleep came quickly. I was exhausted.

December 2, 1987—Frances's Account

Life had pretty much fallen back into its normal pattern: kids fighting, Ed in his office working, and me typing Dan's college applications after dinner. By ten o'clock Laura was in bed, Dan was in his room studying, and my eyes and back couldn't face another page of blanks to be filled in. I went in and said goodnight to Ed and got ready for bed.

It had been almost two weeks since Ed's second sighting, and I had nearly convinced myself that despite the last thing he had heard, the UFO wasn't coming back. But a few hours after I fell asleep the night of December 2, 1987, I was roused by the insistent prodding of Ed's fingers in my side.

I rolled over to snuggle up to him and knew something was wrong. His entire body was rigid and his heart pounded under my hand. I was wide awake in an instant, asking in a whisper what was wrong. He didn't say anything; instead he placed his fingers lightly on my lips to warn me to be quiet. I lay there beside him, straining to hear whatever it was that had awakened him.

The fact that he had heard something that I hadn't would have once been odd. Normally, once Ed fell asleep, he stayed asleep until morning. I was the one who responded to our children's calls in the night, and Ed never even knew I had been up. But that was before the UFO entered our lives. Then it hit me. What he was hearing I would never hear. It was in his head. They were back.

After what seemed an eternity Ed slid out of bed and onto the floor. "Stay put, everything will be fine," he whispered.

I moved over to the edge of the bed and looked down at him. I could just make him out, lying flat on his back beside the bed. He reached up to get the pistol, and I quietly asked him, "What are you going to do?"

"I'm going to see if they're out there somewhere."

"Not without me you're not."

I slid down onto the floor beside him, scared of what we might find. Ed started off on all fours. I crawled along behind him, hampered by my granny gown. Finally I pulled the skirt up above my knees and tied it into a loose knot. The last thing I wanted if Ed yelled, "Run," was to find myself tangled in yards of flannel.

We crawled to the front door, and the chill of the foyer tile on my bare skin added to the goose bumps I already had. While Ed peeked out the door, I tried to rationalize it all, but couldn't. He reported that he couldn't see anything out of the ordinary, locked the door, and we headed for the kitchen. By now my teeth were chattering with cold and fear.

Ed opened the back door just a bit and softly called to Crystal. When she didn't come, he called louder. Still no wiggling, white body came bounding over to be petted. Before I knew what he intended to do, Ed had slipped out the back door and onto the deck. I grabbed for him and missed.

"Ed, get back in here!" I put as much authority into that whisper as I could.

He was looking up at the sky and didn't seem to hear a word I said. Before I could repeat my demand a little louder, he nearly knocked me down running back into the house. I saw why. I had my first live view of the UFO.

Panic doesn't descibe the way I felt. My entire body tingled as adrenaline flashed through me. I wanted to run, but couldn't. No force from the craft held me, unless you count being overcome with awe at what I was seeing as some mental tie.

The photos had amazed me. The real thing was almost beyond belief. It moved with an effortless grace, almost the way a sailboat floats with the breeze.

Neither Ed nor I said anything, or if we did, I don't remember. All I could think of was how frightening, yet beautiful, the craft was. After maybe thirty seconds Ed pointed the camera and the gun at it. It edged away, not quickly, then stopped out over the back field. Without giving me any warning, Ed dashed back outside.

I was afraid to yell at him. It might draw their attention to him hiding near the end of the pool watching them.

I debated if I should go after him, but I wasn't sure I had the nerve. Before I could decide, I saw a flash. Then Ed headed back for the door at a dead run. This time I got out of his way.

While we watched the UFO, I let him know exactly what I thought about what he'd done. I was angry because I felt he had taken a stupid risk, and he'd scared me half to death doing it. I didn't want to lose him to some alien creatures.

"The way that thing can move, how did you know it wouldn't zip over here and hit you with that beam before you could get away? Don't ever do that again."

Then, as if to prove my point about how fast it could move, the UFO just seemed to disappear straight up. One second it was there, then it was gone.

Ed told me to go back to bed, that he wanted to check all the doors before he came to bed. I made him promise he wouldn't go back out if the UFO returned, and then I went to our bedroom to get warm and try to steady my nerves.

When Ed came in, we lay in the bed, looked at the picture, and talked. Seeing the UFO wasn't a novelty to him anymore. But it was for me. The question each of us kept coming back to was one we couldn't answer. Why?

DECEMBER 2—FOURTH SIGHTING— THE CREATURE

The Same Night—About 3:30 A.M.

Crystal barked—once. My eyes popped open. Crystal never, never barks once. Were they back? I listened. No hum. *Were* they back? Come on! Don't they have to sleep? As I threw the covers off and jumped out of bed, Frances whispered, "Oh no, please, not again."

This time I wanted them to hear me, so I grabbed the pistol and said aloud, "If they're back, this time I'll use this thing."

Since I'd last seen the UFO out back, I assumed that was where it would be again. The pistol in one hand, the camera in the other, I walked over to the French doors that lead from the master bedroom out to a screened-in porch overlooking the pool.

Cloth miniblinds covered the glass. I could tell it was still dark out. Only the faint glow from the school's security lights, across the field behind us, showed around the edges of the blinds.

I felt for the draw cord and pulled it down quickly, leaning forward as the blinds came up. On the other side of the glass was a small creature. Big black eyes stared into mine. Just inches separated us. I screamed and fell backward onto the floor as my feet got crossed. My head and shoulders hit the closet door.

The creature just stood there, staring in at me. It was maybe four feet tall. A dark, grayish-black, box-like thing hid most of its body. The "helmet" over its head had a clear insert that revealed its eyes, really big eyes that covered the top half of its head. It grasped a glowing silver rod in its right hand.

Lying on the floor, I was about fourteen feet away from the door. The creature hadn't reacted to my scream, or the way I recoiled from the door.

63

It simply stood there for a few long seconds, calm and just looking in. Straight in, not turning its head or leaning closer to the glass.

I stole a quick look at Frances. She was on her knees, crawling across the bed toward me. At that moment she was closer to the creature than I was. What if it came after her?

I still had the pistol in my hand, so I quickly raised it and pointed it at the creature. I wasn't going to shoot unless it tried to get through the door.

The creature stared at me with eyes that showed no fear. Eyes that were calm. Eyes that were almost sad. Eyes that somehow seemed curious.

It felt like time was standing still. Frances was looking at me, then at the creature. What was going to happen? Would I shoot. No. Would the creature try to come in? No. It simply turned to the left with a deliberate movement and walked out of my view.

Anger swept through me. That little bastard had just scared me out of my mind, and now it was just going to walk away! The hell with that. I wanted him.

I scrambled from the floor and got back to the door in a few steps. The dead bolt and passage lock were impossible to operate without putting the camera and gun on the floor first. I unlocked the door, and without picking back up either of them, ran onto the porch.

The creature was steadily moving across the deck and toward the stairs. I was about twenty feet behind, intent on capturing it. Moving as slowly as it was, I could catch it in no time. I'd throw a body block and drag the little critter back into the house.

I pushed the screen door open and took two steps onto the wooden deck . . . bang! The blue beam angled down from the sky. My right leg, from the knee down, was hit. Frozen. Like it was nailed to the floor. Being squeezed. I fell. My forward momentum made me pull and twist my knee as I fell. My right leg was stuck in place.

"Shit!" I screamed. Frances ran onto the porch to help me, and I yelled at her to get back.

The blue beam began to lift my leg and pull me out from under the roofed porch. I leaned back and grabbed the screen-door jamb. As I leaned back, I was looking straight up into the bottom of the UFO.

It was maybe fifty feet up, with the beam just clearing the eave. The sight was enough to make me shudder, and I almost lost my grip on the doorjamb. No wonder the creature was in no big hurry to get away. Its buddies were there, and maybe this was all a trick to get me outside. If it was, it had worked.

My left foot tipped into the blue beam as I tried to pull myself away.

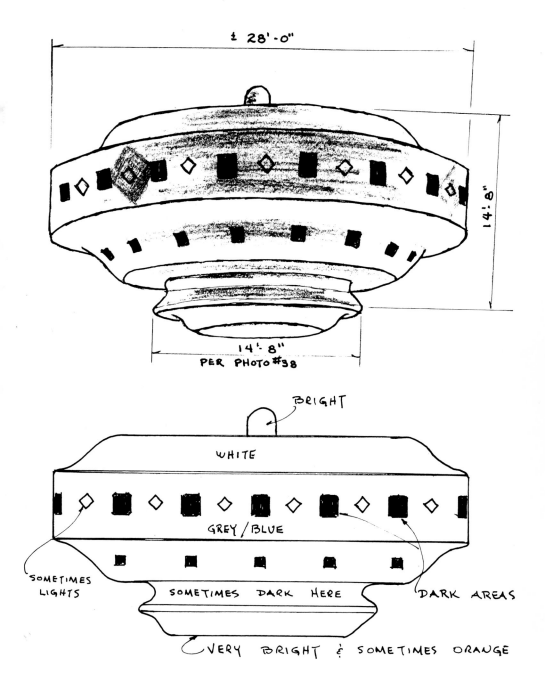

± 28'-0"

14'-8"

14'-8"
PER PHOTO #38

BRIGHT

WHITE

GREY/BLUE

SOMETIMES
LIGHTS

SOMETIMES DARK HERE

DARK AREAS

VERY BRIGHT & SOMETIMES ORANGE

Above are my two drawings of the UFOs that I photographed so often. The color varied from gray-blue to a rich orange-brown. The ''power ring'' was usually bright white with a darker orange core. The UFOs appeared larger during a few sightings than at other times. This proved to be the case. The stereo photos determined that there were crafts of several types and sizes in the sky over Gulf Breeze.

Photo 1

Just before dark on November 11, 1987, I noticed a strange glow beyond
the pine trees in my front yard. A UFO came from behind the trees as I took this
photo. Because the UFO was partly blocked by a tree, a computer analysis could be
made to study the overlap of the UFO by the tree, offering conclusive evidence for
authentication.

Photo 1, light-blasted and enhanced for detail

Photo 2, reduced original

Photo 3, reduced original

Photo 4, reduced original

Photo 5, reduced original

About 130 feet away and only 50 feet off the ground, the UFO glided slowly over the house across the street. It was later calculated to be 13 feet in diameter. Its flight was soundless and the "power light" at the bottom throbbed with energy. I took photos 1, 2, and 3 before the UFO changed direction and began moving straight toward me. I shot photos 4 and 5 and hurried into the street so I could photograph the UFO as it passed directly overhead. Once in the open road, I was suddenly struck by a blue beam that immobilized me.

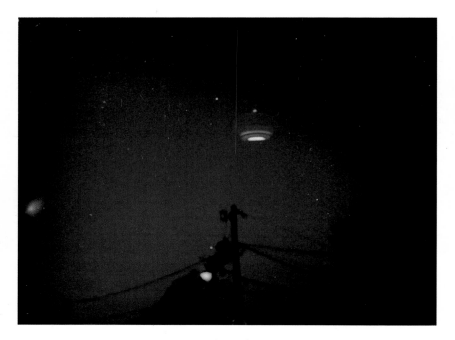

Photo 6

Photo 6, light-blasted and enhanced for detail
I was astounded when the UFO returned nine days later, on November 20, again just before dark. Far overhead, a light that looked like a star swiftly dropped from the sky. I aimed the camera, followed the UFO, and took this photo as the craft moved up and then off to my right.

Photo 7, reduced original

Photo 8, reduced original

Photo 9, reduced original

Daytime photograph at the location of the November 11 and 20 sightings

The UFO hovered toward my right and was partly blocked by the nearby cedar tree. A great deal of study was done on photo 7 and it showed that the cedar tree overlapped the edge of the UFO image; digital photo processing authenticated the photo. In photo 9, the UFO had moved closer to me. I followed it with my camera, not wanting to move or take my eye off the object.

Photo 10

On December 2, 1987, my wife and I experienced an early-morning sighting. We watched as the UFO pulsated from near invisibility to a rich orange color. After a few minutes it flashed away, straight up and out of sight.

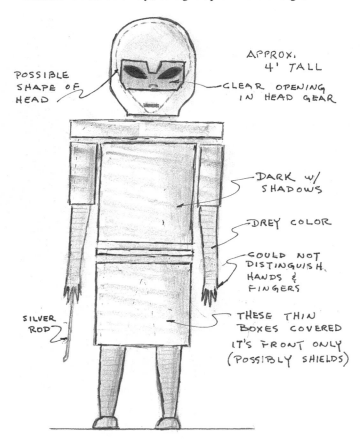

POSSIBLE SHAPE OF HEAD

APPROX. 4' TALL

CLEAR OPENING IN HEAD GEAR

DARK w/ SHADOWS

DREY COLOR

COULD NOT DISTINGUISH HANDS & FINGERS

SILVER ROD

THESE THIN BOXES COVERED IT'S FRONT ONLY (POSSIBLY SHIELDS)

The UFO returned in less than half an hour. I pulled up the bedroom window shade to see this small, shielded being standing just on the other side of the glass, looking into my eyes.

Photo 11

I gave chase. As my feet left the shelter of the back porch eave, I was hit by the blue beam and held immobile while the creature fled into the vacant field behind my house. As soon as I could move, I retrieved my camera from the porch and took this photo of the UFO shooting the blue beam into the field. I believe that it was picking up the creature I had seen.

Photo 11, light-blasted and enhanced for detail, enlargement

Photo 12

Photo 12, light-blasted and enhanced for detail

Just before sunrise on December 5, 1987, this UFO hovered above the treeline near the high school, about a block behind my house. It seemed different, somehow larger than the other UFOs I had seen, although it had the same basic shape. (A combination of camera shutter speed and UFO movement may be responsible for the double ring at its bottom.) The UFO moved toward me. As I fled back toward the house, I heard a voice grind into my head: "Do not resist . . . Zehaas."

I felt the pressure on my toes and wrenched it away. I jerked wildly, but my right leg stayed fast in the beam. Frances held me from behind. I pulled harder. Slowly and steadily my leg came out. I was free.

The blue beam disappeared, and the craft hovered toward the field. The creature had gone across the back field. I had heard it go through the chainlink gate in our fence. I scrambled to get my camera.

By the time I got back with the Polaroid, the craft was near the trees. Suddenly the blue beam shot down to the ground. No way to see the creature, but I figured they were picking up the back-porch visitor. I shot photo ll.

Frances called me. She was afraid the creature hadn't been alone, that there were others in the house. I ran back to help her check.

December 2, 1987—Frances's Account

I hadn't even gotten to sleep again, when Crystal barked. Ed stiffened beside me. I knew he was as wide awake and alert as I. Not again. I couldn't believe it, not again.

Ed flipped off the covers and jumped out of bed. He grabbed the camera and the pistol, threatening to shoot.

"How do you know that won't just make them mad?" I sat up and tried to focus on him in the dark.

"I don't care. I've had it." Ed started across to the outside bedroom door.

"Wait." I rapidly crawled toward the cedar chest at the foot of the bed. "Don't just go charging out there."

"Don't worry, I'm going to check first."

My heart pounding, I knelt on the smooth wood and waited. Ed took hold of the cord on the mini-blinds. With one quick downward stroke the blinds zipped up.

Ed's scream startled me. For a moment I didn't know what had frightened him. Then I saw that what I had mistaken for Ed's reflection in the glass was actually a creature. My scream echoed his.

I tried to scramble backward. My toes caught in the covers, and I tumbled into the center of the bed. "Oh, my god, what is that?" I yelled.

"Jesus, I don't know." Ed sprawled on the floor staring at the door.

I wanted to be closer to Ed. But was that a good idea? Thoughts flashed through my head. It would be easier for the creature to get us with that rod if we were together. Apart we might have a chance to outmaneuver it. Was that even a weapon? I decided it didn't matter.

Back on my hands and knees, I edged toward the corner of the bed nearest Ed, keeping my eyes on the creature. It didn't seem to notice I was there. It never even looked at me. It just stared at Ed.

All I could think of was that "they" had sent this creature to get my husband. Could it come through the locked door? Was it alone?

By now Ed had the pistol pointed at it. The creature's expression—if it had one—didn't change. I looked from it to Ed and back again in a near panic. It wasn't that it was ugly. Or that it made any threatening moves. It just didn't belong there.

Then it turned and left. It didn't run. It didn't seem afraid. It simply walked away, calm as you please. The creature was hardly out of my sight when Ed jumped up and ran to the door.

"Ed, what are you doing?"

He fumbled with the locks. "I'm going to catch it."

"Are you crazy?" I screamed. I tried to get to him before he could follow the creature outside.

The camera and pistol discarded, he unlocked the door and threw it open. I grabbed the shotgun and ran after him. I had never shot at any living thing in my life, but if that creature was waiting out there with its glowing rod, I would. Even shaky as I was, I knew I couldn't miss. I reached the door just in time to see the blue beam flash down.

Caught by one leg, Ed toppled to the side. I ran over, dropping the gun on the chaise lounge. Maybe I could drag him out of the beam.

"Get back! They could get you too."

Ed's warning made me look up. Above us the bottom of the UFO glowed a golden orange. The center writhed like an energy storm. Shadings from dark to blindingly bright undulated within it. I had the feeling I was looking up into awesome power.

Ed ordered me away again. I ignored him. Instead I grabbed him under his arms, braced myself as well as I could, and pulled with all my strength. He didn't budge.

His foot was off the ground, lifted by the beam. He continued to struggle. I hoped that, if nothing else, I could keep him from being pulled any farther. I was afraid that at any moment he would be snatched away from me up into the craft.

Suddenly he was free, and we tumbled backward. The blue beam was gone. We crawled back under the better shelter of the porch. The UFO moved slowly off to the east.

Ed stood up, pulling me with him. He assured me he was all right, then ran back for his camera. With Ed out of danger, I thought of the children. I snatched up the shotgun and ran back into the house. Ed was already out the screen door and onto the deck.

I hurried through the darkened dining room. Halfway across the living room I stopped. Something shadowy had moved in the unlit rec room. I strained to see, but could make out nothing.

Terrified of facing one of the creatures alone, I ran back to the kitchen door to call Ed. Through the glass I saw the blue beam connecting the craft and the field. Ed lowered the camera as I opened the door.

"Ed, I think there's something in the house!"

He ran back to me and I explained my fears. We hurried toward the children's side of the house, planning as we went. Shadowy figures again seemed to dart about as we entered the rec room. Ed flicked the light switch.

The mirror on the opposite wall threw our reflections back at me. Maybe that was what I had seen. There was nowhere in the thirty-foot room for anything to hide.

Quickly, quietly we crossed to the short hallway that connected the children's bedrooms. Light from the window in Dan's bath softened the shadows cast in the narrow hall by the rec room light.

Ed turned right to Dan's open door. I went left. With an unsteady hand, I turned Laura's doorknob. The door swung inward, bumped against something, and stopped. It's just some of her junk on the floor, I told myself.

I flipped on the light and stepped inside. I was greeted by the usual chaos of her room and a grumble about the light as she turned in her sleep. Steeled for anything, I peeked behind the door.

Wedged between the door and wall was the chair from Laura's bath. I let out the breath I hadn't realized I was holding. There was no other place to hide but the closet.

I crossed the clothes-strewn floor to the open closet door. A quick check revealed nothing. Two feet away a connecting door led to Laura's bathroom. I took a deep breath and pushed open the door.

The motion-sensitive light came on, reassuring me. If anything had entered the room, the light should have already been on. Unless it was in the shower. The light automatically went out if movement stopped. There was nothing to do but check.

The blood pounded in my ears so loudly I could hear nothing else. Terrified, I stepped around the corner. The shower was empty. Relief washed through me. I turned around and came face to face with Ed. I clamped my hand over my mouth to stifle my scream, then scolded him for sneaking up on me.

"Don't do that." Nervous laughter softened my words.

"Sorry." He squeezed my arm. "Nothing in Dan's room or the spare room."

We recrossed the bedroom to turn off the light. There was only one other place on this side of the house: the laundry room. It took little time to be sure it was unoccupied.

Just to be certain nothing had escaped us, Ed entered his office from the rec room, while I cut back through the still-dark living room, turning on lights as I went. We met in the foyer. Still nothing.

Though I felt better, there was a chance something had doubled back behind us. A flick of the switch lit up the dining room. There was nothing out of the ordinary. We backtracked through the living room, turning off lights, and went to relock the kitchen door.

Looking through the glass, we could see no sign of the craft or the creature. Something clunked behind us. We whirled around. I yelled, and Ed thumped against the wall. Startled, Laura's parakeet woke up and fluttered around her cage, sending seed hulls and feathers flying, scaring us even more. A long, breathy hiss filled the room.

For a moment sheer panic held me. Then I laughed. Ed looked at me as if he thought I was crazy, or hysterical. I was only relieved.

We had been terrorized by the icemaker dumping a load, then re-filling. I explained it all to Ed as we walked back to our bedroom, our arms around each other.

This had been my first experience with the blue beam, and it terrified me. If the UFO had waited to fire, Ed's entire body would have been caught again. Would they have taken him? Or had they just wanted to keep him from following the creature?

We talked about that and what they wanted with Ed until it was time for me to wake the children for school. Ed turned on the television. The morning local news lead story was "UFO sighted over Gulf Breeze."

ED'S ACCOUNT

I did not tell anyone about the December 2, 1987, sighting. Later I learned about another sighting early that same morning, which was recorded by investigator Robert E. Reid. Here is his report, as forwarded to MUFON headquarters:

Midnight Flyover

Just after midnight [early in the morning of] 2 December 1987, Pat and Elsie McClellan of Navarre Beach [about ten miles east of Gulf Breeze] were watching a late movie on television. Thru the west-facing picture window Pat saw a bright light apparently hovering over the water [Santa Rosa Sound] some distance away. He assumed it was a helicopter or aircraft landing light until it started making anomalous movements [e.g., bobbing up and down].

The couple went out onto the balcony to get a better look. The lighted object now appeared to have a searchlight that was shining down on the water. As they watched, the light seemed to pulsate and move slowly toward them, then, at an estimated distance of about seven miles, it suddenly winked out. Straining his eyes to the west, Pat asked his wife, "Where'd it go?" No more than five seconds had elapsed when Elsie replied, "Look up!"

There, approaching slowly from the west and already at an elevation of about sixty degrees, was the dimly lighted silhouette of a circular object, an object so close that its outline appeared 20 or more inches in diameter at extended arm's length. Accompanied by a low humming sound, the object continued its steady course and passed directly overhead. The couple were incredulous that this could be the same craft they had seen so far away only a few seconds before, however this seemed the only explanation. Both Pat and Elsie had seen news reports of the Gulf Breeze UFO, and these thoughts immediately came to mind. This was obviously not a type of aircraft the McClellans were familiar with. Elsie, fearful for the safety of their young daughter, rushed inside. Any concern Pat might have felt was quickly overridden by curiosity, and he hurried around to the other side of the house to watch the object as it proceeded toward the southeast. After continuing on this same course for several seconds, the craft veered right and took up a southerly heading. As it moved out over the Gulf of Mexico, its bright lights came back on again, and it rapidly accelerated out of sight.

The McClellans were mystified; neither could figure out what they had seen. About five to ten minutes later Pat, who had re-sumed watching TV, saw two more lights coming up the sound. He immediately went out on the deck to investigate. This time it was obviously two aircraft [apparently jet fighters] following the same path as the object had traveled. These jets even made the same right-hand turn and proceeded out over the gulf on the iden-tical trajectory the UFO had taken. The McClellans had lived at this address since September, and never before had any aircraft flown over their house in this way.

About a month later, when investigators asked me to draw what I remembered of the creature, chills ran down my back. As I worked on the drawing, I tried to reenact the event.

When I had pulled down the cord to raise the blind on the door, I had bent forward and down, lowering my head. There it had been, only inches from me. For a few seconds we were eyeball-to-eyeball, with just the glass separating us. The creature hadn't flinched, but I tumbled back-ward.

I was yelling as I fell, and now that I think about it, I'm surprised I didn't shoot myself. The panic and shock of seeing anybody standing there would send you reeling, let alone a four-foot creature in a shield with huge eyes.

Just writing these words, with the vision of that four-foot dark-gray being coming to mind, made me shudder. On the drawing you see the strange eyes. They resembled the contour of the eyes on a grasshopper. They were definitely angled, and very black.

It was the eyes that got to me. I couldn't tell what was going on inside the creature's head. Was it just curious about us humans and figured it would take a closer look? Or was it me it was interested in?

The creature just stood there, even when I pointed the pistol at it—nothing. There were square boxes covering most of its body. The boxes kind of hinged at the middle and at the shoulders. I've speculated that these boxes were some kind of shield and therefore it was unafraid of my pistol.

As it turned to leave, it didn't run from me, but merely turned and started walking away. The profile showed that the boxes did not enclose its sides or back. The creature opened the screen door to exit the screened porch. I know it used the door, even though I didn't see it, because that door has a piston closer and it was still swinging the door shut as I rounded the corner.

I called the rod a silver rod because it glowed silver. It was more like an energy glow than a solid color. The rod was perhaps the diameter of a pencil, but the glow made it look about the size of a broom stick.

The dashed lines in my drawing show what I think it looked like behind the shield. I've described the creature as well as I can, but it was dark and I was scared.

DECEMBER 3, 1987—WITNESS PRESENTS TWO MORE PHOTOS

L ooking for more news of reported sightings, I was impatient again for the newspaper delivery, and on the way to a job site I stopped off at a newsstand to buy a *Sentinel*. There it was, front page:

UFO—FOLLOW-UP—MORE SIGHTINGS REPORTED

I tried calmly to pick up the newspaper without giving much notice to the headline, but my eyes were glued to a new photograph. Without a doubt, it was of the same object as the one I had seen. The caption said the photograph had been taken more than a year before. It had been mailed to the *Sentinel* with the following letter:

Dear Editor:
I am very relieved to see the UFO photos. They look just like the photos (enclosed) I took last June '86. I never showed mine to anybody for fear of ridicule.
They were taken with a 35mm after dusk, facing west in Shoreline Park South. It came from behind the north trees very fast, and then stopped perfectly still (photo 39).
It stayed there for five or six seconds before flashing off to the north and out of my sight.
It happened so fast that I doubted what I had seen. The film came back from the developer with no prints of the object—but then I checked the negatives and there it was. The developer had not printed them—thinking they were too dark.

Like the other person, I too don't need the headaches that this can bring, so I withhold my name.

Photo 39 is one of the two photos taken in June 1986. These two photos were taken in Shoreline Park eighteen months before my first experience. Only photo 39 ran in the newspaper. Photo 5, of mine, was also reprinted for comparison purposes.

This new photo was a revelation. I sat in the parking lot and stared at the new picture. Frances was going to love to see this, so I went straight home to share the news.

At the time I was too excited to realize that this new photo would have been much more important if the photographer had given his name. Later, when I did think about it, how could I blame him when I had also withheld mine? Who better could understand the decision to withhold identity?

Another witness had written a letter that was in the newspaper and directed to me. The letter described another sighting on November 11, 1987, the day of my first sighting.

Dear UFO Sighter:
My husband and I feel you are not alone. However, I'm not sure if we saw the same thing. It was about 5:30–6:00 that evening. We were in our car. The object was overhead. At first we thought it might be a plane or helicopter; however, when we rolled down the window of the car, we heard no noise. Did you hear a noise from it? Was it between 5:30 and 6:00 Wednesday evening? I remember my husband saying when we saw it, "That's not a plane—no plane can stay still like that." And it did just bob up and down. He said it wasn't a helicopter, for it made no noise. He rolled down the car window and stuck out his head. I said, "Get your head in, for if it is a UFO it may zap us up." We laughed and said if we told anyone, they would take us away in white jackets. We thought it may be from the air force also, but we doubted it. Please let us know if yours made noise.

Still another report was one that had happened a year earlier and I only mention it because those new photographs taken in Shoreline Park were a year old. The headline was, MOTHER AND SON REPORT SEEING OBJECT FROM BAY BRIDGE.

"Jean" and her son were driving north on the Bay Bridge in the late afternoon when an object appeared to be hovering over the water in a circular movement. They saw windows and figured it could be a new design from Eglin AFB. Now, having seen the UFO photos, they wanted to report what they saw.

Later that evening the news lead-off story on WKRG-TV 5, the local CBS affiliate was: "A photo expert says pictures of a reported UFO could be the real thing. The story and photos prompted at least half a dozen people to say they've seen it too."

The coverage went on to interview Curt Shields, a professional photographer who deals with special effects in his business but "does not believe this is a case of trick photography."

Shields said, "I'd have no trouble duplicating this photo [photo 2] with some sort of Christmas ornament or something like that. But when you go to this photo [photo 1], where it is behind a tree, that's another matter. You start getting into something that would take several steps and quite a bit of knowledge."

WEAR-TV 3, the local ABC affiliate, also dealt with the UFO story that night. They talked with other photographers.

Christopher Stark studied the photos and said, "This is very, very clean and clear. Polaroid pictures are very hard to manipulate. You don't have an enlarger, you can't superimpose it."

Joe Turner, *Sentinel* photographer, said, "I saw the photograph of the object behind the tree limb and ruled out the possibility of superimposition. Then there was corroboration by other witnesses."

Mark Curtis, WEAR reporter, concluded by saying it is possible to create such pictures with photographic techniques, but it requires so much detailed work that experts agree it is highly unlikely that these are fake. And they say the other accounts of witnesses are too similar to dispute the pictures. I wondered what the experts would have said if they had seen the November 20th and December 2nd photos.

It seemed like each time I looked at the newspaper or turned on the TV news, the UFO was being discussed. Later that night *Sentinel* editor Duane Cook and Don Ware, the state representative for MUFON, appeared on a local call-in television show.

Frances and I watched the program and listened as they again asked for the person who had taken the photos to contact them somehow. They promised anonymity and said it would greatly help their investigation.

When the show was over, Frances and I discussed what we should do.

We wanted to help the investigation. After all, we had good reason to learn as much about these visitors as we could. But I wasn't ready to get more involved, and Frances agreed with me.

There were things that had to be considered first. I had to weigh the benefits to the investigation versus the risks to my family. How would telling MUFON affect our already changed lives? I went to bed that night still unsure of exactly what I would do.

DECEMBER 4, 1987—FRANCES'S ACCOUNT

Ed and I had gone over and over the pros and cons of coming forward. At breakfast we finally decided that Ed would call Don Ware of MUFON and tell him that the first five photos had been taken in front of our house. He intended to stick to his story that they had been taken by a friend, Mr. X. Ed wouldn't call until after he had made the morning rounds of his job sites.

While Ed was gone, I did my housework and wondered if we had made the right decision. We would be helping the investigators, but I hoped that they'd also be helping us. This experience had gone beyond just a simple sighting. Maybe we could learn something from the MUFON investigators that would help us understand and deal with what was happening to us.

Around eleven Ed came in to pick up some plans to take to one of the job sites. While he was there, he phoned Don Ware. Ware asked if he and another investigator could come over in the afternoon. Ed said yes, as long as they were gone by the time our daughter and her friends came in from school.

Through with my housework, I went in to take a shower. Ed rapped on the door, telling me he had to leave and that he would be back for lunch.

Later, stepping out of the tub, I faintly heard car doors closing. I thought, darn it, here I am dripping and naked and the doorbell's going to ring. But it didn't. I decided it must have been someone at a neighbor's. Then I thought I heard voices.

I pulled on my robe and hurried through the bedroom. There was no longer any doubt in my mind. I could hear voices, men's voices. Why hadn't they rung the doorbell? Through the dining room I made my way to the foyer, tying the sash on my robe as I went.

At the foyer doorway I stopped. Two men stood on our front walk, their images distorted by the beveled-lead glass in the door. Who were they? And what were they doing? I could see that the door was locked, but still I was frightened. It wasn't normal for them to stand there that long and not ring the doorbell.

I stepped back around the corner into the dining room. If only I could hear what they were saying, or see them clearly. Maybe I could from the dining room window. The blinds were open. I had boldly crossed the room before; now I got down on the floor so that they wouldn't see me.

On my hands and knees I crept to the window. Water from my hair ran down my neck, chilling me. What was going on? I inched up until I could see out the window. Nothing. They were out of my sight and I couldn't understand a thing they said.

Back I went, peeking around the corner of the foyer. They were still there. One of them had something in his hands. They were both pointing and waving their arms around. I still couldn't tell what they were doing, but it wasn't normal for our neighborhood.

I hesitated to cross the foyer to Ed's office. What if they saw my red robe through the glass in the door? I decided to go the back way. Dashing past the four-foot opening, I hurried through the living room and rec room to Ed's other door.

Once I was in Ed's office, I carefully edged one blind slat open. I could see one man's back. The other was still out of sight. Their words were nothing but mumbles. Either they were naturally softspoken or they didn't want anyone in the house to hear them. I needed to get closer.

I tiptoed across Ed's office and eased along the closet wall that jutted out into the foyer. I still couldn't hear what they were saying, but maybe I could at least see what they were doing. My heart racing, I steeled myself to peek around the corner. What if one of them was looking in through the glass?

With that as my impetus, I exposed no more of my face than was necessary. The second man stood on the porch, his back at an angle to me. Through the glass, a wavy-looking copy of the *Sentinel* was visible in his hands. He was clearly comparing the photos of the UFO with our trees and what he saw before him.

I jerked back and hid in Ed's office. Who were these people? Reporters? UFO enthusiasts? What? If they rang the doorbell now, would I answer it? I didn't know.

Looking south through Ed's office window, I could see a dark-blue car parked at the extreme edge of our lot and, beyond it, a small reddish-brown pickup. If only Ed were home. But not knowing who these men were or what they wanted, I wasn't sure I wanted Ed there. If they saw him, they would know who he was.

Then, apparently satisfied they had found the photo site, the men headed for their cars without ever ringing the bell or knocking. I eased the blind back in place, steadying it so that it wouldn't swing and give me away.

Only minutes later Ed came home. I told him what had happened. As we stood in the doorway so that I could tell him where they had been, a small reddish-brown pickup drove slowly by. I couldn't tell if the driver was one of the two men I'd seen, but Ed agreed it seemed like more than coincidence.

DECEMBER 4, 1987—SITE LOCATION REVEALED

What Frances told me about the men bothered me. Not knowing who they were, I didn't know what they might do with what they'd learned. If they were reporters, would they call me? Or was it possible I'd be watching the news and hear my real name connected to the photographs?

I decided worrying wouldn't do any good, so I had lunch and got ready for Don Ware's visit. Ware had been glad to hear from me, telling me knowing the site of the photographs would be a big help to the MUFON investigation. That made me feel a little better about what I'd done, but only a little. I couldn't help wondering just where this first step I'd taken would lead.

At this point I still wasn't ready to come forward with the fact that I was the photographer, much less all the rest of it. It was hard enough to get more involved, just as Mr. X's messenger. The things that had happened to me were bizarre, totally unlike anything I'd gone through before. And if the UFO voice could be believed, it wasn't over.

But I had a business to run. There were contracts under negotiation, plans to draw, half-built houses to finish, and new ones under way. There was also my community involvement and commitments to fulfill. The last thing I needed was for anyone to know that I was Mr. X. I tried to convince myself that I could keep that a secret. Like it or not, though, I knew that the time might come when I'd have to tell the whole story. But not yet.

That afternoon Don Ware and Charles Flannigan came to the house. They took measurements of the distances from where the pictures were taken to all the fixed objects visible in each shot. Then they calculated the heights of the important objects.

Their professionalism impressed me. These two weren't kooks. Although they believed, as I now did, in the existence of UFOs, they had their feet firmly on the ground. Facts and proof were what they were looking for.

I told them a bit more about Mr. X's feelings during the sighting and how the craft had appeared to him. I didn't get into the blue-beam stuff. If they suspected I knew more than I was telling, or that I might be Mr. X, they kept it to themselves.

Not long after my daughter got home from school, they finished. They left a form for Mr. X to fill out detailing more about his sighting and asked me to try to convince him to talk with them personally.

That night WKRG-TV again flashed the familiar photograph (photo 5) on the evening news broadcast. I videotaped it all. Dr. Frank Palma, astronomer, was interviewed and opened his comments with, "There's no doubt that people are seeing a number of things."

Dr. Palma examined the photographs and said he could tell what it was not, but he didn't know what it was. "It's an unidentified flying object. It's a very fascinating picture, and frankly I just have to say I don't know what it is. It's one of those mysteries."

He had immediately looked for evidence of a hoax, trick photography, or evidence that it was a hot-air balloon. He didn't find any.

Dr. Palma summed up with, "There wasn't any evidence that I could see of any kind of support of this object."

The excitement of all the TV news reports led to questions and more questions. Most of the questions started with "why." The others were "what." Mainly—what is it? Hubcaps thrown into the air was a favorite. Reflections photographed off a window was another natural. Everyone was trying to find the answer, including WEAR-TV 3 news anchor Sue Straughn.

On the late news the night before, Sue had made an absolute statement that she knew what and where the UFO was. She claimed that she would reveal the secret the following night on the regular nightly newscast. Needless to say, I tuned in.

I'd wager they had a record number of viewers that night. But the UFO update report came and went with no revelation from Sue. It didn't really surprise me, not if she thought it was some fixed, man-made thing in those photographs. Still, I was a little disappointed, so I watched the late-night broadcast too—just in case.

They ran the same short tape about the UFO, then Sue announced the results of the telepoll they had conducted about the UFO. The question had been, "Do you think UFOs have an earthly explanation?" The results were close; 51 percent of the callers said yes, 49 percent no. Then she turned things over to the weatherman, Bob O'Brien.

He asked her to disclose what the UFO was. Sue refused and tried to move on, but Bob wouldn't let her. He proceeded to run a tape of what Sue had told co-workers she thought was the UFO.

The tape showed the Pensacola Beach water tower, from every angle possible. It even showed it from across the sound in Gulf Breeze. Of course the water tower didn't look anything like the UFO, from any distance.

The tape ended, and they switched to Sue, whose smile looked a bit strained. For the rest of the program she had to endure more than a little good-natured kidding.

It was a cute tape, and I laughed at it myself, although I did wonder how on earth anyone could think the water tower was the UFO. It gave me something serious to think about too.

People who didn't want to believe the UFO was real, for whatever reason, would come up with any kind of explanation for what it was. I figured I'd better start getting used to the idea that some people would never accept the truth. And some of their explanations would be harder to believe than the truth. I'd just have to deal with that.

DECEMBER 5, 1987—FIFTH SIGHTING—DIFFERENT CRAFT

The newspaper and television news reports had the town in an uproar. I felt better knowing that others had seen the UFO. But the UFO was wearing me down. I had thought it was over and finished, only to have it almost grab me from my own backyard.

My daytime thoughts wandered from fear to trying to make friendly contact. But how to be friendly when it was one-sided? All the UFO wanted to do was order me around, carry me off, and examine me. They needed to understand that I had rights.

I did fantisize about being the only one to befriend the UFO. But mostly my thoughts were serious. I worried about when and if it would show up again.

I was unusually nervous the night of the 4th. Nothing really happened. No voices or sounds in the night. But still I didn't sleep well. I was restless as the night passed into the third morning since the visitor on the porch.

The red number on the clock radio glowed 5:30 A.M., only five minutes later than when I had last checked. Time seemed to be passing slowly. I should have still been sound asleep, but my thoughts were jumping back and fourth between a construction-site schedule and the UFO.

We would usually sleep later on Saturday mornings and give Frances a break from the early-rising routine that greets her on weekdays. She was breathing evenly beside me, and I lay there trying not to toss or turn. The last thing I wanted to do was disturb her.

I stared at the clock, waiting for the numbers to change, willing myself not to move. My muscles were slightly tight, the way they get just before you have to roll over to another position. Finally I had to move.

Easily I turned onto my left side and laid my right hand gently over Frances's fingers near her cheek. She is the best part of my life. Always there when I need her, and always there for the kids, no matter what her sacrifice.

The sight of her lying there in peace seemed to calm my thoughts. Maybe the UFO had done what it came to do. Maybe it was over. I wanted to hold Frances and tell her it was over. *No, let her sleep,* I told myself.

Trying not to rouse her, I slipped out of bed, aware that she always seemed to know when I was getting up. She turned and wiggled deeper into the covers. I picked up my bathrobe and tiptoed out of the room. I didn't have anything really pressing me as far as my business was concerned, I just couldn't lie there anymore with my thoughts whirling and my muscles wanting to move.

In the kitchen I started to make some coffee but changed my mind. Frances takes care of the kitchen, and I couldn't find the coffee. I didn't want to bother her by banging pots around, so I just sat at the breakfast bar and looked at yesterday's paper.

I glanced up at the clock. It was nearly six. About five hundred feet across the soccer practice field behind my house, the sun was breaking the horizon over the high school. The darkness lifted from the east, and the back field began to show more clearly. I noticed an object hovering above the ground, very close to the school. I jerked from the bar stool and pressed my nose to the window.

Damn! The UFO was there, below the tree line. It was different, really different. It was bigger. I could hardly move. Not that I was frozen in fear. It was just so incredible to see. I shook my head to clear my thoughts and make my body function.

The gun and camera were on my nightstand. As I rushed into the bedroom and grabbed them, Frances stirred and said something. I was already moving back out the bedroom door, running to the kitchen, and couldn't hear what she said.

I went out the back door and to the end of the pool. I stood behind the wooden windscreen, leaning back against it for a moment to steady myself. I took a deep breath and held it while I spun around and aimed the camera. I braced myself and pushed the shutter button (photo 12).

The UFO had lifted higher and was hovering, still, above the trees near the school. Then the UFO voice came to me: "Do not resist. Stay where you are. You are in danger. We will not harm you. . . . Zehaas.''

I turned and ran back to the house, thinking, *Won't harm me, my ass. Right! I know all about your blue light and I'm not interested. I know what it can do.*

I hadn't said anything, but the voice answered, ''Zehaas [this was more of a sound than a name], we have come for you.''

The UFO hovered slowly across the field, once again very low to the ground. By now I figured that everybody on my street would have seen the UFO. Surely somebody had called the police.

The voice: ''No.''

No? No what? Nobody had seen them? Nobody had called the police? No, don't run away?

I watched them from under the big porch roof. No way was I going to budge. I should have taken more photos, but I was afraid to cover my eyes with the camera. Afraid to take my eyes off it as it moved closer. Finally I pointed the pistol at the UFO.

I yelled, ''I'll shoot!'' My voice didn't come out right. Again, ''I'll shoot!'' The words echoed as if they were in a pipe.

The voice: ''No. Step forward.''

''Screw you! Come and get me.''

Flash. . . . They were gone. Again straight up.

I went back into the house, quietly closing the door behind me, questions racing through my head. What the hell did they want from me? Why all these cryptic messages? When would this all be over?

The UFO voice actually seemed to be calling me by name, not my name but ''Zehaas,'' whatever that was. The voice was clear when it said, ''Zehaas, we have come for you.'' What the hell was going on?

The insinuation was that the UFO occupants had named me, maybe like a pet, but that was outrageous and more than I could accept. My mind whirled with confusion and I felt sick to my stomach. This had to stop, or if not, I had to get help.

DECEMBER 5, 1987—FRANCES'S ACCOUNT

I got ready for bed the night of the 4th, hoping for better things. For the past two nights sleep had been slow in coming and not all that restful. The creature and the UFO were my constant companions.

The new witnesses, especially the one with the photos, were encouraging. But they couldn't override my concern about our late-night visitor. My greatest fear was that it would come back. That idea made getting a good night's sleep impossible. It was becoming harder and harder to get up each morning when the alarm went off.

Although the next day was Saturday, I couldn't sleep late. Dan had to get up early to go take College Board achievement tests. With all that had been happening, I worried about how he would do on the exams.

He had so much on his mind, with college decisions, tests, and schoolwork. I hated that the UFO had added to the pressure. Dan swore it wasn't bothering him that much, but knowing how I felt about it all, I found that hard to believe.

Laura's grades had already taken a dip. With the UFO such a big part of our lives, her studies were all but forgotten. I wondered if I should talk to her teachers, but that would mean telling them about the UFO, and I was afraid that would upset Laura even more. As I climbed into bed, I vowed to make the time to tutor her in math and work with her on spelling.

Our bedroom was still dark, sometime later, when I blinked my eyes open. The alarm clock hadn't awakened me. A faint glow from the school's security lights leaked around the blinds on the French door. After a few seconds I could make out the shapes of furniture.

Half asleep, I saw Ed walking toward the door to the hall. He was dressed in his robe and had something I couldn't see clearly in his hands. I asked him where he was going, my sleep-thickened tongue slurring the words. He didn't answer.

Drugged by that deep, heavy sleep that makes it almost impossible to keep your eyes open, my benumbed brain failed to register that anything was wrong. I had been dreaming about Costa Rica, and the UFO was still forgotten.

My lids drifted shut again. I forced them open, but lost the battle to awaken. My last thought was that Ed had to call one of his subcontractors early, then he would come back to bed.

Later the alarm went off. I quickly silenced it, not wanting to disturb Ed. It was a struggle to wake up. I stuck my left foot out from under the covers hoping the cold air would bring me fully alert.

I wanted just to roll over and go back to sleep, but I needed to be sure Dan was up and getting ready to go. Maybe once I got him on his way, I could slip back into bed for a little more sleep before Ed woke up. I looked to the other side of the bed. Odd; Ed was already up and gone.

Suddenly I recalled what I'd seen earlier. My heart stuttered a few beats, then raced. Had it come back? For the moment Dan was forgotten. I jumped out of bed and, barefoot, went looking for Ed. I found him in the kitchen. He showed me the latest photo, filling me in on what had happened, what he had heard.

"Why didn't you wake me up? I don't like you facing that thing, especially alone."

I wasn't angry at him. I was worried about what could have happened. I was also upset that it had come back yet again.

We agreed we shouldn't mention this latest sighting to Dan, not yet. He needed his full attention on the tests he would be taking, not on some UFO that seemed intent on disrupting our lives. I left Ed to go see if our son was up and dressing.

After a light breakfast Dan left. Ed and I sat at the breakfast bar and talked about how our lives had changed since the 11th of November. We still had all the routine things to do, which had often left us tired enough. With the added element of the UFO, we were becoming exhausted.

Still sleepy, I told Ed I was going back to bed to try to get a little more sleep. It was now full daylight. I doubted the UFO would come back. Ed decided my idea was a good one and joined me. Two hours later we were up again, wondering what would happen next.

DECEMBER 10, 1987—MORE WITNESSES

For the fourth week in a row the local weekly newspaper ran something about the UFO. Reading about it always set questions tumbling in my head. Some of those that came to mind were: Why was the UFO showing itself to me? Just why does it have telepathy with me? Why can I hear it hum when it's around?

The only reason I could think of related to the first sighting on November 11, 1987. Somehow, during that failed abduction, I received a type of "connection" while in the blue beam.

The hum I hear when the UFO is around is the same as the hum I heard in the blue beam. Therefore I believe the UFO had to connect with my brain in order to talk to me. It made that linkage in the beam. When the UFO dropped me and disappeared, I believe it left that link, that odd hum, with me. Whether intentional or not, the "connection" remained.

Those thoughts brought up other questions. How long would the hum be with me? And what would get rid of it? Those I couldn't answer, so I continued reading the *Sentinel*. The first thing that caught my eye was a statement MUFON had released to the press:

> "Preliminary evaluation, prior to the photogrammetric analysis, is an unknown of great significance because of the quality of the five photographs and the reputation of the independent witnesses."

The *Sentinel* also contained a photograph of photo expert Marie Price examining the Polaroids. The accompanying article concluded that

The pictures have been closely examined and to this date, the authenticity of the photographs has not been disproven.

Duane Cook still had possession of the photographs and made them available to many experts. I learned later that he had even taken them to the Jet Propulsion Laboratory in California. The photos had been handled so much that the condition of the originals has been affected. There are smears and big palm prints on some, scratches on others.

Throughout the investigation, most of the reported sightings had come from the Santa Rosa/Escambia County area, but now, according to the *Sentinel*, "Jane" and her husband from Citronelle, Alabama, had come forward with their story:

This couple owns about 20 acres of mostly deer land, with two ponds on the property. On the night of November 19 "Jane's" husband was outside when he suddenly saw an object idling in the sky over one of the ponds with a beam of light shooting to the ground.

He ran inside to get "Jane" and when they returned the object had moved over to dry land, then returned over the pond.

Then, her husband shined a flashlight toward the object and it disappeared.

This couple may have also seen the blue beam in photo 11. Citronelle is about eighty-five miles northwest of Gulf Breeze.

The *Sentinel* continued;

Back in Florida last Wednesday, about 6:45 P.M. "Darlene" and a friend were driving north across the Bay Bridge. They looked over to the right by the Cordova Mall area and saw a whole ball of light pop up from behind the trees.

"It was round, but we couldn't see any windows or anything," said "Darlene." "We weren't close enough."

At first they laughed, thinking "there's a UFO," but as the object remained motionless the scene began to take a different tone.

Then, the light popped down again, then shot back up— remaining idle until the two had crossed the bridge.

I haven't talked to these two, so I can't say what they saw. The UFO I saw is capable of rapid movement and of idling or hovering almost motionless for long periods of time.

I sat in my office for a long time after reading the paper. I thought about all the things nobody else but my family knew anything about. The other photographs, the creature, the abduction attempts. I wondered if there might be other witnesses suffering and being harassed. Surely I was not the only person experiencing this dogged determination on the part of the UFO.

Should I tell MUFON or the *Sentinel* editor or somebody what was going on? What if the next abduction attempt succeeded? I would continue to resist the UFO's attempts to capture me, but how long could I keep up my guard? I didn't know, but I feared that if it did not end soon that I would not be able to hold out.

DECEMBER 17, 1987—SIXTH SIGHTING— THE LIQUID

1:00 A.M.

Before going to bed each night, Frances and I had developed a nervous routine—reviewing how long it had been since the last encounter. Each night without an incident was celebrated with hopeful conversation.

Frances smiled and turned her eyes toward me. "This will be twelve in a row."

Twelve nights and no problems. Not much sleep either. But we were beginning to believe that "it " was gone. I closed my eyes with that hope foremost in my mind.

Two hours later a noise shook me from a deep sleep; at least that's what I thought at the time. Most of the events of that night were clear in my mind and Frances also remembered the same things. However, several months later I began to remember more than I had recalled at first about what was happening when I woke up. But even at that time I still did not remember several other important events of that morning.

A year later Bob Oechsler and Dr. Maccabee learned from studying the serial numbers on the photos that the sequence as I had remembered it was incorrect. In particular, Mr. Oechsler discovered that the photo that I called 17 actually preceded the one that I called 16.

Their discovery prompted me to undergo hypnotic regression with a clinical psychologist, Dr. Dan Overlade, to recover memories that had been suppressed. The information gained from that regression, including the discovery that I took one photo (the "real" 16) that was subsequently lost, has been incorporated into the story of that night as presented here.

Two hours after going to sleep there was a tremendous white flash that

89

filled my head. My eyes were closed, and the sensation was of a complete "white-out" inside my head, not of some external flash.

I shuddered and managed to open my eyes. Standing at the side of my bed were three dark figures, exposed only by the traces of light from a streetlight filtering through the nearby window. My vision was very blurred, and I strained to see the figures. They were motionless and looked into my face. Several other shadows moved toward the foot of my bed.

I tried to yell, "Hey, what's going on here?" but my voice did not respond to my moving lips. As I opened and closed my mouth, trying to yell, I started to sit up. The figures turned quickly, but deliberately, to leave the room.

Struggling to sit up, I thought of trying to grab one of the figures. Suddenly the noise, which I had remembered and reported earlier, exploded in my head. A strange dizziness swept over me and I fell forward face down onto the foot of the bed. I tried to shake it off, but couldn't seem to get my balance.

For a moment I lay there and listened. The sound was in my head, but so loud that it seemed I could hear it with my ears. It was just as if I were standing at the base of a thunderous waterfall.

I felt Frances pulling on my left arm as I tried to get up. She was saying something, but all I could hear was the roar of crashing water. Her grasp was determined and her face seemed distorted as I fell off the side of the bed. While I struggled to stand, the noise began to fade. I could hear Frances faintly saying, "What is it? Ed, what's wrong?"

Her voice was hollow and kind of echoed through my head. I could still hear the "waterfall," but I could also hear some odd sound that had the same tone as the UFO voice. It sounded like the high and low tones of music being fast-forwarded on a reel-to-reel tape recorder.

I stood at the foot of the bed, with Frances next to me. *Breathe deeply,* I told myself. I straightened my back and raised my head. I was getting really pissed. Grabbing the camera, I started out the bedroom door, telling Frances to stay there. She didn't listen.

I strode into the kitchen. Framed in the kitchen door window, I saw the UFO hovering about 150 feet away. It was much too close, and I was afraid to show myself through the glass.

By now Frances knew I was going out to get a picture, no matter what she said. But I saw no reason to be stupid about it. There was a way out so that "it" couldn't see me—through the laundry room door on the side of the house.

Creeping out that door, I was able to slip under the back porch. From there I crawled over to some pampas grass. I was in my underwear, but don't remember feeling cold, even though it was maybe 40 degrees outside.

The UFO was to the north, just within the edge of my view. It began to rise and fall smoothly, and to glow and fade. It would rise about ten feet and glow bright orange, then descend again and fade to a pale orange that was hard to see.

From my left it drifted directly in front of me and hovered there—very still and "picture perfect." I shot photo 13. The flash went off, but this time I knew it would. I did flinch down, but the UFO made no noticeable change.

For a few moments I lay on the ground with the pine straw poking my bare skin. Then, back on my knees, I pulled the film and slipped it under the elastic waistband on my boxer shorts. Behind me the French door leading out from the rec room opened slightly and Frances called to me. I answered something, but was absorbed in watching the UFO move away.

It stayed about thirty feet high. Suddenly a bunch of smoke or steam with some kind of liquid came out of the bottom of the power source. Later that day I retrieved a plastic butter tub the kids had left out. It was full of bubbling liquid. I saved it for future analysis.

By now only a minute or so had passed. I ran up the terrace to the pool deck and hid behind a windscreen. The UFO was moving farther east, away from me, and closer to the edge of a wooded area. About four hundred feet from me the UFO still throbbed on and off with the orange glow.

Was the UFO having trouble? Was it going to land? Great. Great. Great. The glow disappeared at the tree line, and I jumped up from my knees. Had it landed? Maybe it would be there in the morning.

I strained to see through the darkness. The school security lights back-lit the trees, and I could see nothing on the field. Quickly I thought, *I should call the police.* I started back to the house while looking over my shoulder at where it had disappeared.

It was there. I knew it. More than anything I wanted the UFO to be sitting, helpless, in the field. That would wipe out any doubts, answer the questions I couldn't, and eliminate the chance I'd be called a nut. It was too dark to see, but I knew it was there. Wasn't it? Before I called anybody, I had to be sure.

I started to run out onto the back field but stopped when I realized it could all be a trick to get me out into the open. That thought set my heart to pounding. I retreated to safety behind the wooden windscreens at the end of the pool. From there I watched the darkness for about a minute, not moving.

It had to be there. I'd make the call. Again I started for the back door. The glow reappeared. I ran back to the windscreen and raised the camera. Not yet looking through the viewfinder, I stared at the UFO. I couldn't believe what I saw.

This was *not* the same UFO. Its shape was different. It looked bigger. It glowed white and was lifting off the ground. Again it stopped very still, and I could see the grass field glow beneath the power source. I snapped photo 14. No flash; the cube was used up. As before, I pulled the film and slipped it under the elastic on my shorts.

I did a lot of running around—from one windscreen to another and up and down stairs. Finally, I ran on over to the kitchen door. When I got there, the door popped open. Frances stepped outside.

I whispered, "What are you doing?"

She whispered back, "What are *you* doing?"

Frances continued whispering, and the UFO was moving slowly toward the house again. I didn't really care about the flashcubes, but I wanted her inside, so I asked if she'd get them for me. She went in, and I took off for the back right side of the yard. I stopped at the fence, under some small oaks. The UFO was headed in my direction.

As I watched through the chain-link fence, on my knees and as close to the tree cover as possible, I felt something bump my shoulder. I think I yelled and fell into the fence saying, "Holy shit, what are you doing here?" How Frances had managed to get back to me so fast I'll never know.

She pushed a flashcube into my hand and said, "Take the picture, fast."

The two previous photographs had slipped from under my elastic waistband and threatened to drop out the leg of my shorts if I should stand. I quickly pulled them out and stuck them into Frances's hand.

The UFO came at us faster than you could follow it. One moment it was four hundred feet away. The next it was overhead. How could they move like that? I shot photo 15 as it stopped and was still in an agitated state. The UFO is blurred, but the tree in the foreground is clear.

Three weeks later when I gave a full accounting of this event, I incorrectly reported taking photo 17 next. The correct sequence places photo 16 next. My brain must have hit "overload" because I didn't recall this next part until I underwent hypnotic regression almost a year later.

In the order of events as uncovered by hypnotic regression, I pulled the film (photo 15) and pushed it toward Frances while yelling, "Let's go. Let's go. Run . . ." I darted across the thirty feet to the terrace steps leading to the pool level. Frances should have been directly behind me as I hurriedly shot a photograph. I ran up the steps and pulled it out of the camera. I pushed this photo under my elastic waistband. After the sighting was over, this photo was not found and I had no memory of even taking it.

The UFO was slowly sliding over the roof of the house. I jerked to a stop, aimed, and shot photo 16. Then I discovered that Frances was not behind me. I cried out to her, and suddenly a commanding voice rocked into my head.

"We are here for you."

Again I yelled for Frances as I pulled the film from the camera. I tossed this picture onto the wood deck at the back porch. Bang! The "white flash" filled my head and I seemed to be falling. Next my eyes tried to focus but were blurry, and I remember being very cold.

Without warning I hit headfirst into the chain-link fence next to Frances. An unknown amount of time, yet to be completely accounted for by hypnotic regression, had passed. For over a year I had no recall of ever being away from Frances. She was still kneeling where I had left her and staring into the sky.

Dizziness swirling through my head and my stomach tied in a knot, I managed to look at her and say, "Are you okay?"

She answered with a low, emotionless, "Yes."

This was odd in that Frances never answers a question with a single word. Being disoriented myself, I ignored this minor detail and followed her gaze into the sky.

The UFO was rocking back and forth at least thirty feet above the sheltering oak trees. Though I hadn't been keeping count of the exposures, I noticed there was no "pull tab" sticking out of the camera, which indicates there is film ready to shoot. The film pack was empty.

Frances still held three exposures in her hand, with the plastic bag containing the flashcubes and film lying on the ground at her knees next to the fence. I retrieved a pack of film, loaded it, then managed to aim the camera at the UFO that so clearly dominated Frances's attention.

The UFO's bottom pulsated with energy, but there was no sound. The sight was overwhelming. The air felt heavy, and the hair on my arms was standing up. I squeezed the shutter button and the flash flooded the area as I took photo 17.

Frances yelled something to me or to the UFO, followed by, "Did you get it? Let's go! Run. Run."

I grabbed her by the arm and sprinted toward the house. We reached the back porch, and the UFO slowly glided over the house about as fast as an average walking speed.

Frances tripped and fell onto the wooden deck near the screened-porch door. I stepped back out from under the porch and lifted the camera to take another photo, just in time to see the UFO's bottom ring brighten before it flashed and was gone. It disappeared before I could take the photo.

The blue beam could have had us at any time. We were in the open. Later we thought that if they had shot me with the beam, then it would have gotten Frances also. She was next to me, holding on, and that may have stopped the UFO. Or had they already accomplished what they had come for?

December 17, 1987—Frances's Account

Somehow I had found the energy and enthusiasm to go Christmas shopping. The kids had only one more day of school before Christmas break. I was looking forward to those two weeks. Once I didn't have to get up early to get them off to school, I'd sleep late. I needed to.

Dark circles had taken up permanent residence under my eyes, and no amount of makeup could hide them. Several of my friends had asked me if I'd been sick. I just said I hadn't been sleeping well and let it go at that. I could hardly give them the whole explanation.

It had been twelve days since the last sighting, and I hoped and prayed it was all over. For the first time in three years we'd be staying home for Christmas. The kids had parties planned, and I wanted everything to be calm and normal. At least as calm as it can be when thirty teenagers are running around, watching movies, and having a good time.

I got ready for bed, my hopes high, but not unrealistic. We had gone twelve days before between sightings, only to have our belief that it was all over shattered by the reappearance of the UFO. Maybe this time it would be different.

One good thing had come out of this. I was so tired each night that I fell asleep faster than I ever had before. Unfortunately it wasn't a deep sleep, so I felt less rested than I had when it had taken me most of an hour to fall asleep. As I climbed into bed, I said a silent prayer for an uneventful night.

Later the shifting of the water bed woke me. I opened my eyes just in time to feel, more than see, Ed pitch forward across the foot of the bed.

"Ed, what is it?"

He didn't answer, he just lay near my feet. Dear lord, what was wrong? I scrambled out from under the covers. Had he had a heart attack? Fainted? What? I was across the bed in seconds, tugging at Ed's arm. I tried to turn him over so that I could check his pulse and breathing. I couldn't budge him.

Ed tried to get up. He looked as if he were dizzy, then he staggered and fell. I asked again what was wrong; did he hurt? Still no answer. I didn't know whether he couldn't hear me or just couldn't answer.

By now I was on the floor beside him, so afraid. Ed struggled to stand. Although I wasn't sure it was a good idea for him to be on his feet, I helped him. His skin felt cold and clammy. And he was still off balance.

"Ed, please. What is it? Is it them again?"

It took awhile before he answered me. And then it was only to tell me to stay put. He should have known better. He was not going UFO hunting without me.

There was no crawling around this time; we marched boldly into the kitchen. The cold vinyl sent chills up my back. So did the sight through the glass door. The UFO hovered not far from our back fence. Ed and I watched it from the middle of the room, neither of us wanting to be too near the glass.

"I'm going out."

Ed's announcement didn't surprise me. I didn't bother to protest. I did caution him to be careful—to keep some kind of cover between him and the craft. And to use a different door.

He went out through the laundry room, and I watched him through the rec room doors. I could see him in the backyard, creeping around, doing a good job of protecting himself. Even so, my pulse raced and trickles of sweat slipped down my sides.

The UFO was doing these strange things, rising and falling, brightening and darkening, but I was more interested in Ed. He snapped a photo, and I opened the door and called to him.

"You've taken its picture, now come inside."

Either he didn't hear or he chose to ignore me. Seconds later, as the UFO moved away, a cloud of vapor poured from the bottom of the craft. I had no idea what it could be. But it might be poisonous. I called to Ed again. "Get in here."

He started up the steps toward me, then stopped behind one of the windscreens. Why was he so stubborn? I wanted to go out and drag him inside. Of course, I knew I wouldn't, and couldn't.

Suddenly the UFO just seemed to disappear. Not the blindingly-bright-and-then-zip-gone-away type of disappearance. It just seemed to fade to nothing. Had it landed? *Dear Lord,* I thought, *is it in trouble? Or are they coming out?*

Ed kept moving about, one minute looking like he was coming inside, the next stopping to watch the darkened field. I moved to the living room for a less obstructed view. Why didn't he just come inside? I nibbled on my bottom lip and waited.

Finally Ed headed toward the kitchen door. Then he suddenly turned and dashed down the side steps. *He's going to the field! Don't.* I prayed he could read my thoughts. I ran for the kitchen door, planning to scream at him to come back.

By the time I had the door unlocked, Ed was back up the steps. He started for the back door, throwing one last look behind him. The UFO reappeared. I tried to will Ed inside, knowing it would do no good to call, and waited.

The UFO lifted, and I could clearly see the reflection of its white glow on the grass. Ed raised his camera, but I saw no flash. Then he headed for the back door yet again. This time I stepped out to meet him. Maybe that would get him inside.

I scrunched up my toes on the chilly concrete, hard and rough beneath my feet. Ed seemed oblivious to any discomfort as he ran toward me. We exchanged a few tart comments, questioning each other's sanity. Then we noticed the UFO was moving toward us.

"Go get me some flashcubes, okay, baby?"

I hurried to Ed's office, grabbed the bag with film and flashcubes, and was back in seconds. He wasn't at the door anymore. I softly called to him, but got no answer. He wasn't anywhere to be seen in the upper area around the pool.

They took him! The thought flashed through my mind, and my knees gave out under me. I had to hold the doorframe to stay on my feet. No, they couldn't have. I wasn't gone that long. Ed was out there somewhere, behind something where I couldn't see him. Maybe he had gone out onto the field.

In seconds my mind sorted through the possibilities, discarding the *one* I didn't want to be true. He was safe. I made myself believe that and strained to see some sign in the darkness. A flicker of movement in the right back corner caught my eye. Ed! Relief replaced fear.

I hurried across the deck and down the terrace, my long nightgown sweeping debris from the steps. Pine needles pricked my feet, and I wished I'd taken time to put on my slippers. I touched Ed's shoulder and he jumped. I don't think he had planned for me to join him.

The UFO was moving slowly across the field toward us. Kneeling on the ground, the bag at my knees, I pulled out a flashcube and gave it to Ed. He handed me the photos he had already taken. Then suddenly, almost as if it had materialized from one place to the other, the UFO was overhead. Ed shot one photo as it stopped.

It wasn't until more than a year later that I learned, through Ed's regressive hypnosis, that there had been a time gap. According to investigators what I experienced was a suspension of time. I still have no recall of Ed being away from me or of his reloading the camera. In my mind only moments passed between the time he took the first photo and I said, ''Dear Lord, Ed. Look at that.'' The hairs on the back of my neck bristled.

I looked up into the glowing bottom of the craft in awe. What kind of beings were these? What type of civilization had such power? We were nothing compared with them. We were sitting ducks!

That realization hit me as Ed took another photo. The same thought must have occurred to him because he grabbed my hand and ran, jerking me along. We sprinted for the back porch. At any moment I expected the blue beam to engulf us. Instead the UFO hovered slowly along behind us.

Ed shoved me under the shelter of the porch roof. As I stepped up, my nightgown hem caught the edge of the wooden deck, entangling my feet. I fell to my knees, dropping the bag and the photos Ed had given me. Glancing over my shoulder, I saw Ed on the concrete deck, the camera raised as if he had just taken, or was about to take another photo.

''Get under here,'' I called to him, then turned back to gather up the photos scattered over the deck. The photos and bag in my hands, I stood up as Ed stepped under the porch roof with me.

We went into the rec room, and while Ed locked the door there, I went on to the kitchen to lock that door. I dropped the photos I had on the breakfast bar, and when Ed came in, he pulled another from the camera and added it to the pile.

Ed blasted me for coming outside. I reminded him *he* asked for the flashcubes. How else was I supposed to get them to him? By now I realized I had a headache, so I got a glass of water and an aspirin while Ed peeled the photographs. Then we took everything to our bedroom.

The photos spread over the bed, we put them in order. Ed seemed a little confused, but I was positive that the photo taken over the house was the last. In my mind it had to be because I had only run up the stairs once. Ed agreed with me, for, at this point, one trip up the stairs after I had come outside was all he remembered. It wasn't until a year later that we found that one photo was missing, and that the photo he took looking up into the UFO was actually the last one of this sighting.

We speculated about why they hadn't fired the blue beam. Then he told me what they had said about being here for him. We tried to figure it out. Ed said there was no inflection in the voice he heard, no way to tell by that. So, did they mean, "We are here for *you*" or "We are here *for* you"?

I had no idea. Either way, I didn't like it. Standing in the glow of the UFO—running from it—I had felt so insignificant, so out-gunned. Who were these beings? And why didn't they just make mass, open contact with earthlings?

From all we had seen, they weren't afraid of us. If it wasn't fear that held them back, what was it? There were so many questions I wanted answered. Something told me the only way I'd get those answers was through Ed. That meant closer contact with the UFO. I decided I'd rather have my questions go unanswered.

DECEMBER 22, 1987—PRELIMINARY INVESTIGATION

 ate in the day Donald Ware brought me a copy of the report he intended to file with MUFON. It contained copies of the first five photos, measurements of the site where they had been taken, and the information I had given them from Mr. X.

Donald told me to ask Mr. X to review the report for accuracy. There was a certain look in his eyes: The I-know-that-you-are-really-Mr.-X look. He didn't say anything more, just gave me the report and left.

I skimmed the pages, picking up a word here and there, then dropped the report on my desk. I'd read it later. Now I wasn't in the mood. I didn't want to get all the UFO information churning in my head.

Christmas activities were on the family's mind, and I tried not to talk about the UFO. Talking about it seemed to amplify its importance and overshadow what I wanted to be a happy Christmas season.

Only five days ago I had taken five photos by running back and forth across my backyard. These latest photos didn't answer any questions, they only made the questions worse. Why and how did the UFO look so different? Had I seen and photographed two different UFOs? But the biggest question of all was still, why me?

I had closed my office door so that I could wrap a present for my wife when a soft ring started in my head. This was different from the high-pitched ring people hear from time to time. This was a lower pitch, and it started to get louder until it became the hum I'd come to know all too well.

At first I sat at my desk and looked out the window, searching for any strange glow in the sky. Nothing. I left my office. I calmly crossed through the living room so as not to disturb my daughter, smiling at her as I passed. If I panicked, she would follow me and become even more frightened of the UFO than she already was.

I went on out into the backyard, steadied myself against one of the wooden windscreens, and watched the sky. The hum was really rolling now. I felt as if my brain was vibrating from the force of it. My son stuck his head out the back door and asked if I was okay. I tried to appear calm as I replied. "Sure. No problem. Just looking at the pool water. We need to vacuum the bottom." I knew that all I had to say was *pool vacuum* and Dan would disappear.

He went back inside, and I wanted to grab my head and scream. The hum pressed deep in my head. If it didn't stop, what then? Five minutes passed. The hum was like a siren pulsing with its high-low pitch. The last time the hum had done this, the UFO had dropped from the sky and the voice demanded that I step forward.

I was sweating. What if they were going to do this until I broke down? Nobody could live with this vibration constantly squeezing and throbbing in their head. I thought about getting in the truck and trying to drive farther away from it, but I realized I wouldn't even know which way to go.

Another four minutes passed, and suddenly the hum stopped. I slumped down and sat on the edge of the wooden deck with the dog at my feet. My shirt was wet and I could feel the sweat running down my back. I was cold and wanted just to go to sleep. The hum had lasted about ten minutes.

The next day I discovered that during this same time a man calling himself "Believer Bill" had taken nine photographs of three UFOs he had seen less than two blocks from my house.

December 23, 1987—Seventh Sighting— Three Craft in Morning

5:55 to 6:00 A.M.

I knew it couldn't go on much longer. My mind was made up. The next time I saw "them" I would try to get a picture and, no matter what, call the newspaper and tell them when, where, and *who*. Plus I would call the Mutual UFO Network and make a full report. They would know my name, but if I asked, they'd withhold it from the public.

I had begun my morning routine, checking my building schedule on a house soon to be closed out. That done I went to the kitchen. Walking past the half-glass outside door, I noticed leaves floating on the pool and stepped out to turn the pump filter on.

There they were. Three UFOs, each at the same level, hovering just over the tree line. I couldn't believe my eyes. A chill ran up my back and I shook my shoulders in an effort to snap out of the stare that had me frozen in place.

I looked at them, just sort of "hanging" there in the open. I decided they must have some kind of a screening-cloaking device, or else a lot more people would have seen them.

By the time I ran for my camera and returned to the backyard, one of the craft had lifted higher than the other two. I took photo 18. Immediately afterward the highest craft turned brighter and winked out, followed by the other two. It was almost as if they had waited for me to take their picture before they left.

The picture I took of the three UFOs increased the pressure on me to do something. But what? I had already hinted to the MUFON investigators, Don Ware and Charles Flannigan, when they measured the site of the first photos, that there was more happening than I was telling.

The question was, just how much did I intend to reveal? How far was I willing to stick out my neck, or reputation, to be more accurate? They knew nothing of the abduction attempts, the creature, or all the other photographs I had taken.

This was the day that I decided to come forward, go public, but only to Duane Cook and the MUFON people, and only on the latest sighting with the three UFOs. That was as far as I was willing to go at that point. But I knew that it was inevitable that the whole story would come out.

Already two television stations and another newspaper knew I was the "Ed" referred to in Mr. X's letter. Not to mention some of my friends who suspected. One of Dan's closest friends, Patrick Hanks, knew even more—he knew I was Mr. X. Not long after the UFO events had begun, Patrick was in our home on one of his frequent visits when the fact accidentally came out. Out of friendship and respect he agreed to keep what he had learned to himself.

So, I started to write down everything that happened for future disclosure, preparing for the day when everybody would know my identity. Surely with all those other photos nobody could deny that the UFOs, whatever they were, wherever they came from, were real.

I would write it just the way it was. Most of the story would be unbelievable, but then I did have the pictures. The "experts" would say what they would. The government experts would take their official position that UFOs don't exist. The open-minded would say "maybe." Some would believe because they wanted to believe. I believed because it happened. I didn't need to believe. I didn't even want to believe. But it *had* happened, and I couldn't change that.

Later that morning I called the *Sentinel* and asked for Duane Cook. I told him that I had an incredible picture of three UFOs in one shot, taken by me early that morning. Duane was very passive. I had just told him my big secret and he merely said, "Oh, really, can I see it?"

I had expected a lot more surprise from him. When I told Duane I was going to call MUFON so that they could make a report, he told me that Don Ware had already been to his office that morning.

It wasn't until later that I learned the *Sentinel* had received nine photos that morning. They were photographs of the same UFOs taken by "Believer Bill" the evening before, two blocks from my house.

Not long after my call to Duane, he, Dari Holston (also with the *Sentinel*), Don Ware, and Charles Flannigan arrived at my house to look at the photo of the three UFOs together over the woods.

There was a lot of debate over who should have the right to run the photograph first. Duane wanted the photo for the *Sentinel,* and Don wanted it for the next issue of the MUFON *Journal.* I felt like I was caught in the middle. There was agreement on one thing—everybody wanted the story out; it was just a matter of the best way.

The end result was that Duane would make halftone copies (copies in black-and-white specially designed for reprinting in newspapers) for Don to forward to MUFON headquarters for publication in their next journal. Duane would also be able to run the shot in his paper.

I told everyone I'd meet them at the *Sentinel* building after a quick lunch.

After lunch we all converged on Duane's layout room and waited while he made the halftones. With lots of time to talk with Charles and Don, I gained confidence in their character. They didn't press me, even though I'm sure they suspected that I was Mr. X.

Later, in the parking lot as everybody was leaving, I even hinted that Mr. X had several more photos that he might eventually share. Don and Charles drove off, leaving only Duane and me. Duane related the details of his recent trip to California to have my first five photos analyzed.

Duane and Dari had flown to see Dr. Robert Nathan, an expert on photo analysis who works for the Jet Propulsion Laboratory in Pasadena. As an independent investigator, not representing the JPL, Dr. Nathan had agreed to give the photos some personal time.

Duane described their trip in detail and then went on to say, "On his first cursory examination of the Polaroids, Dr. Nathan was generally non-committal, except to say that if they were hoaxes, they were very good.

"Using their horizontal-process camera, a giant version of what we have at the *Sentinel,* they took several shots of each Polaroid, at various light intensities, apertures, and shutter speeds to bring out different features of the originals. They also shot the two 35mm prints sent in by an anonymous reader after we printed the Veterans Day photos on November 19th.

"All in all, Dr. Nathan was very cordial and did assure us that he believed ours was not the only planet inhabited by intelligent life, especially in view of the billions of individual stars and star systems in the universe.

"On the other hand, as we left his office, he cautioned us not to expect too much from him, as it was his objective to find the flaws in the photos that would suggest a hoax. As a result, the best we could expect to get from him would be an admission that he couldn't find any irregularities in the photographs."

Months later Dr. Nathan made a statement in response to a reporter's question and was quoted in the *Orlando Sentinel.* "Robert Nathan has inspected the originals of the first four pictures. Nathan determined that they were not double-exposed."

I sent this quote to Dr. Nathan for verification along with a letter asking if he would rather not have his name disclosed in this book. I received no answer. Despite having more photos and my videotape at his disposal, Nathan has remained virtually silent. But as he promised, his objective was to disprove the photos. If he could do that, then he would have something to say.

DECEMBER 23, 1987—FRANCES'S ACCOUNT

Ed's early-morning photo set off fireworks, both at home and with the press and investigators. I tried to convince Ed not to show his photo, not to come forward. I felt like that would lead to the complete disclosure of our identity.

He argued that maybe if he acknowledged his part, at least that he had seen the craft, the UFO would leave us alone. I found his logic faulty—I doubted if the beings on the UFO cared what we admitted to the press or anyone else—but I finally agreed with his plan to tell Duane Cook and MUFON.

Later the people from MUFON and the *Sentinel* came to our house to see where the photo had been taken. I stayed in the kitchen, working on lunch, hoping all this didn't get out of hand.

At this point Ed had established guidelines that no one was to ask me or the children anything about what we knew or had seen. It was his idea to protect us from "interrogation," from having our lives disrupted anymore. So I just tried to keep to myself once everyone arrived.

Even so, I couldn't help overhearing at least part of what was said in Ed's office. It was shouted. Someone accused the *Sentinel* people of being greedy, of trying to find a way to make some quick money by selling the first five photos to the *National Enquirer.*

Someone from the *Sentinel* countered with, "We've lost money since all this started."

I felt sorry for Ed, caught in the middle of it all. Knowing him, he was trying to referee and calm everybody down. When they all tromped through my kitchen to the backyard, I tried to be invisible. I didn't really know who was who, and with the mood they were in, I didn't want to meet any of them.

Finally, after more arguing, they all left. Ed popped into the kitchen long enough to gobble down his lunch. Finished, he rushed off, telling me he would be back as soon as possible. "As soon as possible" didn't turn out to be all that soon. It was well into the afternoon by the time he got back.

Something told me this was just a taste of what would happen if Ed admitted he was Mr. X. and told the whole story. I wished we'd never gotten involved at all.

DECEMBER 24, 1987—PHOTOGRAPHS FROM ANOTHER WITNESS

When the paper arrived, I expected to see the new photographs taken by "Believer Bill"—all nine of them—along with the one shot (photo 18) I had taken and given to Duane. But Duane had chosen one of the best "Believer Bill" photos and ran it with mine as a comparison. My photo of the three UFOs was printed next to "Believer Bill's" photo along with his letter to the editor:

Dear Editor . . .

Well, here it is. I too have to join the believers because I have now seen a UFO (3 of them). Right there on Shoreline. I can't understand why nobody stopped as I did to watch them. I waved and pointed to everybody driving by but nobody stopped. It was only about 5 or 5:30 P.M., just getting dark. I was heading east on Shoreline, very close to where you can turn to the school. In the north (looked like over the high school) I saw three UFOs just over the line of sight of trees. I pulled over to the side of the road as other cars went on by. I watched for a minute or so and remembered that the kids had left a toy camera "Hot Shot" on the back seat floor. I had no idea how many shots were left in it, if any. (I have enclosed the camera with the pictures.) It was better than nothing and I got 9 pictures.

I never could get all three UFOs in the same shot. But the first three photos are shots of each. As they hovered around I could no longer tell which was which. They were white on the bottom when I first saw them. But as they came lower and I took the pictures, they became more orange. I started to run through the woods so I could get a closer shot but as I did and after shot #9 all three of them began to glow bright white and disappeared straight up. There was no noise. No rockets blasting. They just went fast and were gone in maybe two seconds.

If I remember right, the UFO in the paper last month looked like these. I'm not going to be hypnotized and all that crazy stuff so here are the photos. The experts can claim what they want. Claim they are trick photos but I'd like to see somebody take a trick photo with this toy camera. I'll keep the negs for my grandkids.

As you can see it got darker and darker as I took the pictures. But from the beginning to the end it was maybe 8 to 10 minutes.

Believer Bill

Two people had taken photos of the UFO other than myself. With all the sightings being reported daily, and now more photographs, how could anybody deny that something strange was flying over Gulf Breeze?

After reading the letter to the editor from ''Believer Bill,'' I had a feeling that the hum I had heard on the 22nd was related to his sighting. He had been only about two blocks from my house. But I didn't mention it because it was just speculation on my part. ''Believer Bill'' hadn't said anything in his letter about the date of his sighting.

Two months later ''Believer Bill'' wrote another letter giving more details, and I include it here:

Hi,
Sorry about taking so long but I don't want to be involved. I thought I said the date I took the photos in my letter but I guess I forgot. It was Dec. 22, just before 5:30 P.M. I took them over to the Mall for one hour service so I could see if the camera worked. I was disappointed when I saw the quality of the prints. The real thing was much clearer. I can't say exactly where I was standing while shooting the pictures. I was running around waving my arms trying to stop somebody to look. I was close to the Oyster Bar but parked on the roadside closer to the school. I stuck them into the *Sentinel* mail slot at about 11:00 that same night.

B. Bill

DECEMBER 27, 1987—EIGHTH SIGHTING— WITNESS SEES UFO AT MY HOUSE

8:15 P.M.

There may be more to this next sighting than there first appears to be. No photographs were taken, and there was no telepathy. But another person, Patrick Hanks, saw the UFO while at my house. Significant, because other people had seen the UFO at different locations about town, but until this day nobody except Frances and I had seen it while at my house.

Patrick is a college student, a friend of my son's. Over the years we have all grown close to Patrick, and he no doubt knows he is always welcome at our house. Many of the "games" that Frances and I organize for the teenagers have Patrick as a key participant. Patrick is quick-witted and always has a clever comeback to keep a conversation going.

Here is the transcript of a MUFON interview with Patrick Hanks done at our house:

One evening I decided to drop by Ed's because I knew what was going on with the UFOs. . . . I'd known since early on and I had spent some other nights over here earlier. About a week before that I spent some time over here. I knew what Ed was going through and I thought I'd drop by and see how he was doing. I arrived at the house about 8:15 in the evening. The door was answered by Ed's wife and she just . . . she said, "It's here," and she pointed toward the back of the house, and I immediately knew what she was talking about. So I headed through the house toward the back of the house. I got to about the middle of the living room and I saw through the windows the craft that we'd been seeing [in the local newspaper] all along. . . .

108

Q: What windows was that, ah Pat?

These that are right here in the living room.

Q: Straight right from the front door?

Yes, and looking out over the field where these other incidents had been seen. I looked through the window, and it was at the far southeast end of the field, just at about tree line. It wasn't real bright, but it was fairly bright . . . and just as I'd gotten here to see it, Ed at the same time was out at the pool pump. Ed had seen it and was heading in as I stood in the middle of the room watching. Ed came through the kitchen door and saw me, and as he saw me, it left. I was in such a position that I could see Ed peripherally and see he came through that walkway there [indicating the door between the kitchen and living room]. I was standing there [pointing to the area near the living room windows overlooking the backyard] and I saw it [the UFO] out there [back field].

Q: What did you think the object was when you first noticed it?

Well, I, I knew it was what Ed had been seeing because it was just, it was obviously that.

Q: Would you describe what you saw in as much detail as possible?

Okay. A craft, about twenty feet, or what we thought at the time was about twenty feet wide . . . straight edges, power source coming out of the bottom, light on top. It was the one we'd been seeing. It was . . . wasn't real bright, it wasn't very, very glowing or anything. I mean not to the point where it would probably wake up everybody in the world if they'd seen it. It wasn't as bright as daylight. But it was bright, it was glowing, it was hovering, and as Ed came in, it moved a little bit toward the southeast and then blinked out, it was gone.

Q: And that's how, how you last noticed it? Was it, would you recount that just one more time?

The way it left?

Q: Yes.

As I was standing here, and Ed saw me, it moved to the southeast and went out, just no light.

Q: Had Ed taken a picture before or after?

Of this incident?

Q: Yes.

No, 'cause he had been out at the pool. He was coming in to get the camera. When he saw me, it left. We assumed that maybe they knew I was here through Ed.

Q: Would you elaborate just a little bit about why you think that?

Because they supposedly had the ability to sense through Ed the things that are going on around him. They knew what Ed's thoughts are, feelings are, I guess, and so we just assumed that, see, 'cause the instant Ed turned the corner and saw me, it just left, and so we just sort of jumped to a conclusion through that.

Q: What do you think UFOs could be?

They could be anything. I mean they could be government, they could be us, they could be the Soviets. But I, I doubt it. I think they're probably alien life, from other planets.

Q: Why do you think UFOs are being seen now?

I don't think they've been, I don't think they're being seen now any more than they probably have been all the way along. But people now are just more willing to come forward or maybe they just understand that that's what it is as opposed to something else, a shooting star . . . something they've just seen.

Q: Have you ever observed a UFO before?

No.

The UFO had allowed Frances to see it. Now, for some reason, maybe accident, Patrick had seen it. Does the UFO know when I am alone, or can it somehow read my mind? Does it know when others are watching? Did the UFO *allow* Patrick to see it?

As Patrick said, it was about 8:15 P.M., and I had stepped out back to drain some water from the pool. There had been a lot of rain over the holidays, and the water level was above the pool skimmer.

When I leaned over to change the valve setting, I began to hear the hum. I stood up and quickly called to Frances without yelling. I wasn't sure if she heard me or not.

In the darkness I scanned the sky, and there it was. Low to the ground, maybe twenty feet high, and very close to the tree line at the high school. It was only slightly glowing, except for the bottom power source, which was very bright.

My eyes were fixed on the UFO for only a few seconds. I called for Frances again as I went for the back door, about twenty feet away. On into the house, and I saw that the kitchen was empty. I was going for my camera. As I rounded the corner into the living room, I almost walked into Patrick, who had just turned from looking out the living room window.

"I saw it . . . I saw it," Patrick whispered, with a lot of air hissing with his words.

Frances was on the other side of him, also looking out the window. She said the UFO had winked out as I came around the corner. We all stood at the window for a moment longer, and Frances explained how she had rushed to let Patrick in, hoping he would see the UFO too.

Patrick was very worried that MUFON investigators would barge in and upset his parents if he reported what he had seen. We went outside and watched the sky while Patrick explained that he would rather withhold his name from any reports. Again I could understand. How could I tell him to disclose his name when I still withheld mine?

December 28, 1987—Ninth Sighting—1-Minute 38-Second Video

Having made a commitment to write down all the events in my daily log, each night I would sit quietly on the back porch and write. Some nights I would be there for an hour or so, a lot of that time spent just sitting.

I wasn't really in deep thought or struggling with the problem of having a UFO make uninvited visits in the night. Sometimes I would just sit, too tired to consider the meaning of it all. Too aggravated by the disturbance to our normal family life even to talk. An hour or so of peace and calm.

I could hear the family through the kitchen window. They were fast to recover from each sighting, and they gave me strength. Especially Frances. She kept everything running, even when she was hurting more than all of us.

Her family was being torn apart by strangers. Strangers who came to investigate. Strangers from across town and strangers from other states. But the worst strangers, of course, were the ones who came in the night, dressed in shields. The ones who could come and go as they pleased. The UFO strangers, who could sometimes press a buzzer in my head as if to let me know they were here. But then again, sometimes they would just arrive unannounced, no hum, maybe trying to catch me off guard.

Tonight was one of those "no hum" visits. It was 8:00 P.M., and, as I said, I was peacefully writing in my log when I noticed an easy shadowy movement slide slowly from the back of the high school gym along the dark grass field, closer and closer toward my back fence. The grass field was dark green, and the textured shadow changed it to a fuzzy orange.

It was clear to me now that the UFO could conceal itself from sight.

112

The glow was there, but there was nothing above it. I had a clear view from ground to sky and I could see no craft.

Was it close enough to the ground to cast a glow and still be invisible to my eyes? Somehow they must change their colors to look like the sky or whatever background was necessary. By standing, I could see a complete panorama of the back field. There was nothing there but the glow, which continued to move closer.

I cracked the bedroom French door and called to Frances. She answered with a casual "I'll be right there." I waited a moment, standing in the door and watching the glow. It paused and turned a little brighter.

Then, as I was turning my head to call Frances again . . . wink, and there it was—the complete form about 10 feet above the ground and 150 feet away. It was a pale orange and hovered there, completely still.

Something touched me from behind, and I heard Frances whisper, "Call the police."

I answered, "You call the police and I'll get my camera."

At that moment the UFO disappeared. No glow, nothing. We stood together at the door and watched. The kids were busy with other things and so far undisturbed by Frances's absence.

Several minutes went by, and we assumed it was over. At about that time our daughter came calling, "Mom, mom," and walked into our bedroom. She saw us standing quietly and asked, "What's wrong?"

We told her the UFO had been there, but was gone, so she shouldn't worry. Again, at just about that moment the UFO popped back into view at about the same place it had left.

The message was clear to me. Call the police or anybody and "wink" it would be gone. It must have been reading our minds or had some kind of great listening device.

This time as the UFO hovered, it would tilt slightly back and forth, and now and then I could see a slit of orange glow appear at the bottom of the power source.

Frances and I held each other, with Laura in between us, and we watched. Laura wanted to know what the UFO was doing, and it was coming closer. We closed the door and I went for my camera. Frances turned out the lights in the house so that we could see out the windows and not be seen.

In the dark I found my Polaroid, but discovered it was out of film, and I had used up my extra pack the day before at a job site. Maybe there was time to get the video camera ready with the battery and a blank cassette.

I fumbled with the video in the dark and finally got it ready. My family was giving me a running play-by-play of what the UFO was doing. When I finally looked out the living room window to see, the UFO had hovered lower and the windscreens blocked my view.

Outside. I had to go outside. There was very little light outside; the porch lights lit up only the closest part of the backyard. I hoped the video camera would work in the low-light setting.

From the laundry room door I moved along the right side of the house. I was ready to dive under the back porch to escape the blue beam if the UFO came too close. Maybe it knew I was outside and maybe not. My heart pounded, and I was breathing hard and fast.

I reached the corner of the house and slowly looked across the back-yard. Nothing. Either it had winked out again or it was out of my view behind the pool windscreens. Down on my knees, I crawled between some hedges and the house.

The pool is terraced with large landscaping timbers, and I scaled them one at a time, never taking my eyes off the sky. When I reached the next elevation, the UFO came into view off to my right. Very clear to my naked eye, but much less so through the viewfinder of the video camera. Again its body was orange-colored, with a white top and brighter orange bottom power source.

I stood up behind a thick hedge and started filming. The UFO must have been over three hundred feet away and maybe one hundred feet high. The distances are so hard to determine when you don't know the size of what you're looking at. It seemed to rotate slowly and also would waffle back and forth as it traveled from south to north, my right to left. It would stop for a moment, briefly retrace its own airspace, and then continue on to the north.

Following it with the camera was not too hard, but there were a lot of branches and trees between me and the UFO. They were obstructing the view, so I stepped up to the next terrace level while I was filming.

The night was quiet, with only the sound of a distant train whistle softly pushing its way into the eerie scene of an alien craft silently displaying itself to a man and his camera. I was the man who didn't want this visitor but who couldn't resist these opportunities to record the visit.

The first fifty seconds of the video shows the UFO hesitate and move, hesitate and move, until it finally went behind a tree and completely out of my view.

Before it passed behind the tree, I heard some activity coming from the house and then I saw my son slip out the back French door and onto the porch. Frances was right behind him, and I think she had hold of his arm. I was distracted for a moment. When I again looked toward the sky over the open field, the UFO was back, this time traveling back the way it had come.

There was a lot of muted thumping and bumping going on behind me on the porch, but my eyes were fixed on the UFO. It looked very different, not physically, but the way it glowed. Almost as if it were in a disguise mode. The only parts visible were the bottom power source and the glow of the top light.

I filmed it again as it traveled soundlessly. It never seemed to move closer to me, nor did it seem to move farther away. Only a parallel path that somebody might easily overlook or dismiss as an unimportant light in the sky. Seeing it travel in this fashion made it easy for me to understand the ease with which it could move about unnoticed.

As the UFO crossed directly in front of my line of sight, still more than 300 feet away, it hesitated, then retraced its path. Then, with no noticeable change, it winked out.

This complete sighting, as I've written it, is recorded on the videotape. I've made the one-minute, thirty-eight-second video available to the media, and it has been studied by experts.

My thoughts are that this videotaped sighting could be the most important proof.

December 28, 1987—Frances's Account

Christmas had come and gone, and New Year's was just around the corner. The holiday celebrations had helped us through the past few days. I can't say the UFO had become a welcome part of our lives, but we had accepted the fact it was there and that it apparently intended to stay awhile. And we had also determined to go on with our lives as normally as possible.

Every new reported sighting helped. Knowing about those other people was good for Laura. She was still afraid of what the UFO might do to her father, but she no longer thought Ed and I were weird for having seen it. Although neither she nor Dan had seen the UFO, neither doubted its existence. Dan wanted to see it, Laura wasn't so sure. She said it depended on what the UFO was doing.

We had eaten dinner, and Dan was debating how he would spend his evening without dipping too deeply into his pocket. Laura was on the phone, the last minutes of her usage time ticking away as eight o'clock approached.

As he did each night now, Ed was sitting on our back porch writing in his log. I had cleaned the kitchen and was double-checking the supplies I'd need for the movie party we were planning for Dan's friends.

Ed called me, not sounding at all excited, so I told him I'd be there in a minute and wrote down the last few items I needed for the party. That done, I went to see what he wanted. I stepped out the door to see the UFO yet again. Ed told me to call the police while he got his camera, and it winked out.

Several minutes later Laura came looking for me. Only seconds after she arrived on the porch, the UFO blinked back in. Laura backed up against me. I put my arms around her. This was her first time seeing it in person. I remembered how I had felt, and did my best to reassure her.

Ed moved over closer to us. Laura snuggled between her dad and me. I could feel her heart beating, her rapid pulse and total silence telling me how dumbfounded she was by the sight of the UFO.

Finally, as the UFO drifted toward us, Laura asked what it was doing. I told her I wasn't sure, and Ed decided it was time to go outside. Laura raced through the house, calling her brother. The three of us converged in the darkened living room.

We watched out the window while Ed tried to find something to photograph with. The craft continued to hover and drift, while Ed worked to ready the video camera. An occasional swear word told us how his struggle was progressing. By the time he joined us, camera in hand, the UFO had dropped all but out of sight behind the windscreens.

I knew that Ed was going outside, even before he said so. Dan wanted to go with him, but a firm refusal from both Ed and me ended that. Laura begged her dad not to go out.

"I'll be all right, sweetie. Just stay here with Mom and Dan. Dan, help take care of your sister."

Ed went outside. We couldn't see him, but after a minute or so the UFO reappeared, higher and to the right of where it had been. I hoped Ed was getting good film for the risk he was taking.

Laura kept fretting about the blue beam shooting down and snatching her dad. I told her that everything would be fine, putting conviction I didn't feel into my words.

Dan went into the rec room and said he could see his dad through the French doors. He asked again if he could go outside.

"No. And that's final."

I had turned to look at him. When I looked back outside, the UFO was gone. None of us had seen it disappear. Dan had been looking at me, and Laura's attention had alternated between the two of us.

As I searched the darkness for some sign of the UFO or Ed, I heard the deadbolt on the French doors click. With an order for Laura to stay put, I ran for the rec room. Dan stepped out the door and I grabbed for him.

"I told you no."

"What if Dad needs me? With two of us out there, maybe they won't come after him."

"Your father is perfectly capable of taking care of himself. He doesn't want you out there to worry about. Now come inside."

Dan resisted my attempt to pull him back inside. A slender six-footer, he's all muscle. I knew I'd never physically overpower him, and he seemed determined to go to his father's defense. I resorted to whispered threats, hoping not to bother Ed.

"If you don't come inside right this second, the party's off and you're grounded."

He still refused.

"Dan, your father's counting on you to take care of us while he's out there. Don't let him down."

Dan hesitated, then preceded me back through the door. By now the UFO was back, though much harder to see. Laura gave her brother a hug he didn't want, telling him she was glad he was okay. Dan endured, muttering that he'd have been okay outside. We continued to watch the UFO until it suddenly winked out.

We waited, our eyes on the sky, wondering if it would come back again. Finally Ed came in and we watched the video. Having seen the "real thing," the tape was anticlimactic, but still impressive.

Now that it was over, the kids, Laura especially, were talking a mile a minute. Since the UFO hadn't done anything threatening, she wasn't quite as frightened of it as she had been before. Dan was simply fascinated.

Ed and I hoped that this nonaggressive behavior was now the norm. I could handle the UFO popping in and out as long as it didn't try to hurt any of us. I couldn't like it, but for however long it took this craft to decide to go away, I would endure. I would have to.

JANUARY 4, 1988—COMPLETE REPORT COMMITMENT

My encounters with the UFO were slowly spreading to more and more newspapers. Mostly the reports were splintered, out of order, and sensationalized. Misquotes seemed to be the norm, with exaggeration a close second. In one article I read that "I had an implant in my head" and that the aliens were somehow in control of me.

It was clear that the complete, uninterrupted accounting had to be reported. It was also very clear that an article in a newspaper, no matter how credible the paper, was not the best format. The brief clips presented during the local television news were very limited in presenting the facts due to lack of time. I realized I was going to have to count on the nonprofit UFO research groups.

I had an obligation to tell the story, the whole story. But I also had an obligation to protect my family, not only from ridicule but also from the UFO's unknown intentions. I wanted the story completely on the record in the event something should happen to me. After all, what was the UFO planning? Maybe a sudden flash of the blue beam as I left the house or got out of my truck.

If they would just fly over and calmly remove the hum from my head, then I would be willing. I would go out into the open and get it over with. I was tired of watching the sky and looking over my shoulder. Tired of being afraid. Tired of fighting something I didn't know how to fight.

How long could I be a nightly prisoner in my own house? And what was all this stuff about Zehaas? The UFO said I was in danger . . . Zehaas. Was that Zehaas with a capital Z, as in something named Zehaas?

118

Or maybe that was a Zehaas on my back porch with the silver rod. Was that a warning that I was in danger of the Zehaas? Maybe everything . . . maybe nothing.

I just knew I had to get the story out. As incredible as it sounded, it had to be told . . . a kind of insurance policy.

JANUARY 12, 1988—TENTH SIGHTING— THE ROAD SHOT

Reporting the sightings in detail was the best solution, other than the UFO landing or leaving the area for good. Trying to hide from the UFO at night, and even watching the sky as I drove around town during the day, had been breaking me down. On top of that, having to worry about my neighbors or investigators discovering my identity and being branded a nut was too much.

Now that the MUFON investigators had agreed to withhold my name and help me as much as they could, all I had to worry about was the UFO. My routine seemed to be returning to normal and I was hoping for a continuation of this peace and quiet. The nights were less agitated, and in some ways confidence was building in me again.

I knew the truth. "They" do exist. We are not alone in the universe. Of course, that makes the assumption that these UFOs are from somewhere far away. Far away, maybe, but how do we know? They could live in those super crafts and park them in secluded areas of the world. It's just that we always think that UFOs come from another part of the universe. My guess is that they do come from another world.

I had decided the telepathy aspect could be very interesting if I could talk to them instead of just receiving cryptic phrases. But they didn't seem to be interested in small talk, so if all they wanted was to undo the hum or take back the telepathy, great. They could have it.

The only reason to keep the hum, if I had a choice, was to increase the chances of exposing them. They were fast, but didn't seem to be violent. They were advanced, but not so smart. If they were trying to capture me, they were doing a pretty bad job of it. There had been plenty of opportunities during the December 17th sightings. (A year later I found out that they had succeeded.)

Why didn't they understand that all they had to do was ask me to talk? No more cat-and-mouse. Even if I took a picture of one of them, many people would still not believe it, so they didn't have to be afraid of me for that, or for any other reason.

The best I could hope for was to have the UFO go away. Stop tormenting me. It just didn't make sense. Was I part of some kind of master plan? If I was, I wanted out.

At about 5:00 P.M. on January 12th, MUFON investigator Don Ware called to say he had looked for the location where "Believer Bill" had taken the pictures on Shoreline Drive. Fifteen minutes later I called Don back to tell him that I had just heard a hum. It was brief, almost the same as on January 5th. It was very loud but faded in about twenty seconds.

Earlier that day I had been completing a house and had worked most of the day pushing the subcontractors to finish up loose ends so that I could meet the customer's move-in deadline. My mind had wandered as I locked up the job site and headed home. I should have checked on the power meter to see if it was operating, but it slipped my mind. It was important to the next day's work load to have the 220 power ready to service the A/C system.

It was getting late when I finally remembered this detail. There was no choice; I had to return to the job and check the power. There was still light in the sky as the sun reflected off the bottom of the clouds. All I had to do was drive out to the house site and, without getting out of the truck, look to see if the meter had been installed by the power company.

I drove about seven miles out Highway 98, a major four-lane highway connecting Gulf Breeze and Fort Walton. Several times I thought of turning back, going home, but didn't. Instead I made the turn onto County Road 191B, Soundside Drive.

The sun was setting and cast long shadows of pine tops across the narrow road, which curves through a pine woods thick with underbrush and black jack oaks. I pressed the gas pedal and rounded a curve. Everything turned bright white. The hood reflected a brilliant flash. Some of the "light" came through the windshield and hit my arms.

I yelled, "What the hell!?"

I really screamed, and at that moment, flash! Again I was being hit with a white beam. Almost like a flashcube going off inches from my eyes. It was extremely bright and left my eyes trying to refocus on the road. Within seconds, I realized I couldn't feel my arms. The sensation was the same as when your foot goes to sleep and you feel all those pin pricks. But this was stronger, more like when you try to stand on that foot and it really hurts.

The "pin pricks" started at my elbows and quickly covered my arms and hands. Then a reverse nonfeeling traveled back the other way. From my hands to my elbows I had no feeling. I had to look at them to know they were there.

Still accelerating down the road, I knew I was in trouble. The truck swerved from side to side and was almost out of control because I couldn't watch the road curves and watch my hands control the steering wheel at the same time.

Only seconds had passed from the first flash of light. From overhead, and coming from behind, the UFO passed straight down the road in front of me. It stopped and hovered in the middle of the road, about five hundred feet from my truck. I was still going about forty-five miles an hour when I put on the brakes and swerved to the left. My idea was to make a giant U-turn, off on the left side, cross the road, up on the right side, and flee in the opposite direction back to the main highway.

It didn't work. As I left the paving to the left side and onto the grass shoulder, my hands couldn't control the turn, and all I was doing was driving closer to the UFO, which was still hovering in the same place. I hit the brakes hard and came to a stop about 200 feet from the UFO. (Later it was measured to be closer, about 180 feet.)

Everything was happening very fast, and my first thought was to reverse the truck, but the UFO distracted me as it undulated with a brilliant glow reflecting off the road. It slowly rocked back and forth. One moment the power source was a large oval, the next it was a small slit.

My arms were still without feeling. My thoughts were on protecting myself. No way would I go with them peacefully, but what if they shot that white flash straight into the truck? Would it knock me out completely? Would my whole body go numb?

For a few seconds I stared at it. No change; it just hovered. I remembered my shotgun behind the seat and tried to reach it with my right hand. No feeling. I reached behind the seat but couldn't feel if I was touching anything. By sliding to the left, opening the door, and then pulling the back of the seat forward, I could visually guide my hand to pick up the shotgun.

When I looked back toward the UFO, it had lifted higher and seemed to be moving closer. I leaned across the seat to retrieve the camera, which had rolled over between the passenger seat and the door. By bracing my left arm on the steering wheel, I managed to shoot photo 19. I pulled out the film, preparing for another shot, when I noticed that the UFO was definitely moving closer.

I panicked, afraid the white flash could hit me in the truck cab. Out of the truck and onto the ground I pushed myself in a gasping rush. I was scared, and my chest heaved as I hyperventilated. I was trying to crawl under the truck. The camera was slung on my left wrist, and I dragged the shotgun with my right hand.

When I looked forward, down the road, the UFO wasn't there. I was halfway under the truck when it hit again. Flash? My legs stung and went numb from the knees down. I dug into the grass with my elbows and finally managed to make it to where my head was below the oil pan.

Again looking forward, I saw the UFO hovering once more above the road. I tried to get the camera lined up on the UFO, but the truck was too low to allow my elbows enough room to hold the camera upright. I took another shot and saw the UFO slowly begin to rotate. Then came the hum, really loud.

A voice: "You are in danger. We will not harm you. Come forward."

As I think back now, I remember that these instructions made no sense. "You are in danger. . . . Come forward." No way; they were going to have to drag me out from under the truck.

A blue beam flashed from the UFO to the road. Five times it shot down. Each blue beam deposited a creature on the road close to the UFO. I began to yell obscenities. I wasn't yelling at them or at myself, but just out of shock. Each time a creature was left standing there, I yelled. Each one stood waiting and was joined by the next.

Finally all five began to move in lock-step toward me. Each one had a silver rod. They moved the rods up and down in their right hands as they marched down the middle of the road. They were two hundred feet from me, and I knew I could not stay under the truck. I started backing out, thinking that the creatures would be on me at any moment.

When I stumbled into the driver's seat, they were about halfway from the UFO. They didn't seem in a big hurry, but I was. I threw the truck into reverse and backed across the road. Finally, without looking back, I fled.

My arms and legs were still dangerously numb, and driving was almost impossible. When I reached the main highway, with all its traffic, I pulled over and rubbed some life back into my arms.

I had been estimating the diameter of the UFO to be about forty feet, but clearly this UFO was only about as wide as the road. When I found the photo of the first shot on the floor of the truck and saw that it had turned out, I was excited, even though the second shot only showed the back of the truck tire.

JANUARY 12, 1988—FRANCES'S ACCOUNT

When Ed returned home from his trip out to Soundside, I knew something was wrong as soon as he came in the front door. He staggered. Knowing he wasn't drunk, I felt sure that something else had happened. I helped him to our bedroom, and he told me about his encounter with the UFO.

Everything we had experienced to this point had been frightening enough. This was terrifying. Why wouldn't they leave him alone? Why this dogged determination on their part to get him?

Ed lay on the bed; I massaged his arms and legs, and we talked about this latest episode. These beings were obviously far advanced, at least scientifically, but they seemed to have lost their sense of compassion, assuming they had ever had any.

This experience with the UFO had altered so much in our lives, changing the way we thought about ourselves as humans, our abilities and strengths, and what we believed about alien life-forms. Yet, to keep our secret, we had to try to act as if nothing had happened, giving others the impression that we were still the same old Ed and Frances.

Didn't these creatures know how the things they did affected our lives? Maybe they did and they just didn't care. Or maybe they couldn't understand why we reacted the way we did. After all, how much thought do we humans give to the sometimes devastating effect our actions have on lesser animals? Personal concerns pushed such thoughts aside.

We tried to think of some way of fighting back, of protecting Ed. I made him promise me there would be no more late trips alone to job sites or anywhere else. From then on, if he had to go out like that, I wanted to go with him. There didn't seem to be anything else we could do, but we could refuse to let the UFO make him a captive in his own home.

JANUARY 13, 1988—MATERIAL-SEIZURE WARRANT

The next morning there was still a noticeable tingle in the back of my legs as I leaned forward and got out of bed. It was deep inside my calf muscles. But other than that, and an anxious night rubbing my arms and legs, I was physically okay.

Frances was up and taking care of the school morning routine. We had not disclosed the "roadside" event to the kids. Trying to shelter them was top on my list of priorities.

Soon the kids had left for school and I had eaten my breakfast. While Frances showered, I went to my office. In the peace of the morning I could think through what had happened. Maybe the UFO wasn't out to harm me, just as its message had said. But what they had done was completely contrary to that.

My first instinct had been to protect myself, and if it happened again, I would do the same. My speculation that the UFO just wanted to take back the hum was fast disappearing. What I had experienced was an attack. They had blocked the road and, with the white "flash," forced me to stop. When I didn't "come forward," they had come after me with five creatures armed with silver rods.

Had they managed to hit me directly with the white flash, I would possibly have been helpless. Those five creatures could have just walked up and carried me away. No witnesses to tell what had happened, only my truck left abandoned on the side of the road. Surely the police would have suspected foul play, but what could they have done?

Still, the question remained, why me? If they had captured me, would I have been returned? It was clear to me now that my only defense was people. The UFO always seemed to catch me alone. Therefore lots of people, always have people with me. No more solo trips down lonely roads. If the UFO wanted to catch me, it would have to do it in front of witnesses.

My mind jumped back to the word *Zehaas*. "You are in danger . . . Zehaas." What could that mean? At that moment I was interrupted by the doorbell, which was not that uncommon at that hour, 8:30 A.M. Assuming that one of my subcontractors needed some last-minute instructions or a set of plans, I opened the front door.

Standing very close to the door were two large, official-looking men who promptly began to step into the foyer as they flashed some identification cards. I was taken by surprise and stepped backward. The man on the right unbuttoned his suit jacket and exposed a very large pistol in a holster under his arm. The exchange went something like this:

"Are you Edward Walters?"

"Yes," I answered.

"I'm Agent McKathy with Air Force Special Security Services. This is my partner, Agent [some name that I can't remember]."

Of course I should have paid more attention to their names and their identification, but as they were talking, they were also barging into the house. As they entered my office, Agent McKathy said, "We know you have some photos of a UFO. This is a material-seizure warrant to confiscate the photographs and negatives."

The paper they handed me had bold lettering across the top, MATERIAL SEIZURE WARRANT. Inside was a lot of legalese that I only got a glance at before the second "agent" took it back. He demanded. "Where are the photographs?"

They both looked over my desk and across my bookshelves. I was quite stressed to have these two "officials" demand my private property. Agent McKathy jabbed his finger toward my face and said, "Don't try to hide them from us."

As calmly as I could, I denied having the photographs any longer, even though I knew the photos were in the closet next to one of the agents. They demanded to know where they were. The only thing that came to mind was the *Miami Herald*.

"I gave them to a reporter from the *Miami Herald*. He was here a few days ago doing a story."

The men were very rude, but finally left with a threat that I'd better not be lying or they would be back. They walked away and I shook my head in disbelief. Had I really just been threatened by the military? Our military? How did they know who I was? Only a few people knew I was the photographer. Had one of them talked?

I had never thought I would be threatened by the government. The military must have known what was going on. How could they not know? How could a UFO cruise around our skies and be unknown? But they didn't have to use strong-arm tactics to get my cooperation. With the right attitude I would have told them anything they wanted to know and would probably have turned over the photos too. Their methods surprised and angered me but couldn't overshadow what had happened the night before.

The roadside event, with photo 19, was still the main item to deal with, so I called Charles Flannigan to arrange a meeting at the site and give him the details of those brief, but terror-filled minutes. I would fill him in on the agents when I saw him.

On the phone Charles asked me to bring another sample of the liquid I had seen fall from the UFO during the December 17th sighting. When I opened the container, the liquid was still bubbling slightly.

At 4:00 P.M. I arrived at the location where I had driven off the road the night before. While waiting for Charles to arrive, I sat quietly and relived the experience. When he drove up behind me a few minutes later, I shuddered with a flash of disbelief. If I hadn't had the photograph showing the UFO, this would be very hard to explain.

We located the tire tracks in the grass where I left the road. Using the photograph, we could tell approximately where on the road the UFO had been hovering and measured this to be 190 feet from the camera to the UFO. Charles took several control photographs and measured the width of the road.

Still more tire tracks showed where I had slammed my truck in reverse and backed in an arc across the road and off the other side into the sand. My tires had dug into the sand and grass as I accelerated forward and away from the five creatures.

Shortly Charles finished his on-site report, and we returned to my house. There I gave him a drawing I had made of the UFO and one I had done of the creature. I also told him about the "air force agents." Charles told me he would check into it.

JANUARY 13, 1988—FRANCES'S ACCOUNT

The episode with the "air force agents" left me wondering just whom we could trust. A staunch conservative, I didn't like to think our government would treat its citizens in such a high-handed manner.

There was some speculation among the MUFON investigators and the local press that the men hadn't been who they claimed to be. One theory had the two being UFO enthusiasts who would go to any lengths to obtain the photos. I found that impossible to believe. How would they have known who we were and where to find us?

Another idea was that they were after the photos for personal gain—either they worked for some publication or they wanted the photos in order to sell them to someone who would publish them. While I found this hard to believe, I had to concede it was possible. There were various newspeople who knew what we had and, conceivably, where to find us. But even knowing what greed can make people do, it was still difficult to accept that explanation.

I even found myself wondering about the MUFON people we knew. Had they been behind the attempted seizure? It didn't seem likely. While Ed insisted that the originals now remain in his possession, that was only to try to protect them from further damage. He had agreed to allow the investigators access whenever they needed it and permitted copies of the shots to be made.

Which brought me back to the premise that these men had, in fact, been representatives of the U.S. government. I hated to think that that was the truth, but it seemed the most likely explanation.

We had felt pressured enough: now something else had been added. Each new problem chipped away at our dwindling sense of security. As the days went by, it seemed as if we had less and less control over our lives. I knew Ed too well to believe he would tolerate that for long. I didn't know how he would try to fight back. I only knew he would.

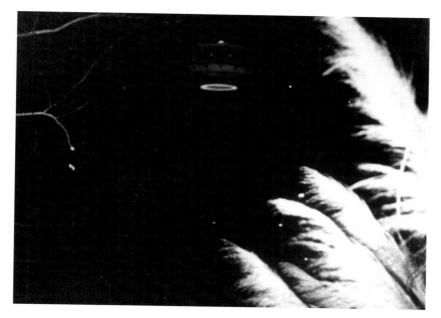

Photo 13

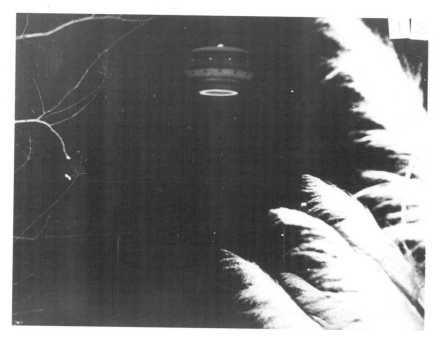

Photo 13, light-blasted and enhanced for detail

My sixth encounter in thirty-six days occurred on December 17, 1987. Just after I took this photo, the UFO expelled a cloud of mist and a strange liquid fell to the ground. The UFO was only about one hundred feet away and not very far off the ground. There were many small lights around the bottom that are hard to see in the photo.

Daytime photograph at the location of photo 13

This photo was taken at the same location as photo 13. The buildings are about five hundred feet away.

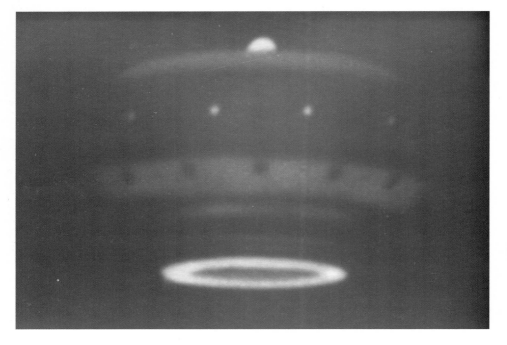

Photo 13, light-blasted and enhanced for detail, enlargement

The enlargement, *above*, shows the orange ring that is also described by many other witnesses in and around Gulf Breeze.

Photo 14, reduced original   *Photo 14, light-blasted and enhanced for detail*

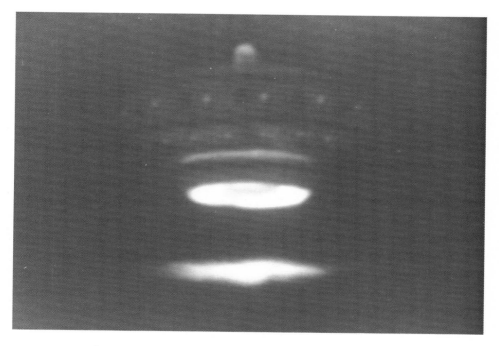

Photo 14, light-blasted and enhanced for detail, enlargement

On December 17, Frances and I saw the UFO disappear into a wooded area near the high school. I thought that it must have landed. I started to run across the field to get closer when it rose and hovered just above the ground. In the enlargement, some small lights can be seen between the ''power ring'' and the central body.

Photo 15

After the UFO lifted into the air, it moved quickly toward Frances and me, then came to a sudden stop, causing the blurred image in the photo.

Photo 16

Running for shelter, I stopped for a second and managed to catch a shot of the UFO as it slowly passed over our house. It was very close at this time, only about seventy feet away.

Photo 17, reduced original

Photo 17, light-blasted and enhanced for detail

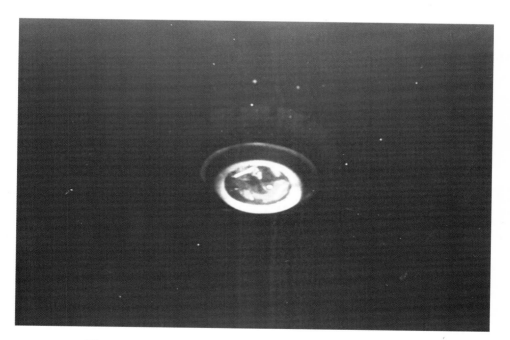

Photo 17, light-blasted and enhanced for detail, enlargement

Frances and I huddled on the ground beneath an oak tree and watched the UFO hover above us. Inside the "power ring" was a twisting, throbbing mass of what I call a silent energy storm. We discovered many months later that at one point during this encounter, Frances and I had been separated, though we have no memory of this.

Photo 18

Photo 18, light-blasted and enhanced for detail

Just before 6 A.M. on December 23, 1987, I looked out over the field behind my house and saw these three UFOs clearly in the morning glow. They were hovering over the trees about two hundred feet away from me. I ran for the camera. After I took this photo, the UFOs flashed away one by one. They seemed to move straight up, but so quickly it was impossible to follow them with my camera.

Photo 19

Photo 19, light-blasted and enhanced for detail

On January 12, 1988, this UFO came from behind me as I drove to one of my construction sites. It passed over the truck and a white flash flooded through the windshield and numbed my arms. My truck went out of control. I managed to stop at the side of the road and saw that the UFO was now blocking it. My arms were stinging, but I managed to shoot this photo before I crawled beneath the truck to evade another strike of the white flash. Five beings were then deposited on the road.

Photo 19, light-blasted and enhanced for detail, enlargement

Daytime photograph at the location of photo 19

According to Dr. Bruce Maccabee, "With the wealth of foreground and background information it was possible to return to the scene and literally match up the tree branches along the horizon line and determine the camera location. The UFO's distance from the truck was 185 feet, which would make the width of the UFO 12 feet and the overall height of the UFO 9 feet. The width of the 'power ring' is 7.5 feet and the object is about 3 feet off the road."

JANUARY 16, 1988—ELEVENTH SIGHTING—TWO DIFFERENT CRAFT

2:00 A.M.

My decision to report all the facts was based on a family tradition: "The truth can never hurt you." I could only hope that the UFO phenomenon was no exception. These events were so outrageous that the truth seemed to bend under the weight of skepticism. But press on I would, and my family was behind me.

Earlier that day Duane Cook and I had speculated on how to change a confrontational event with the UFO to a nonhostile meeting. If we only knew its reasoning and purpose in following me, maybe we could figure it out.

The "why's" and "what if's" were no help when the UFO seemed to be determined to stun me with the blue or white beams. My options were few. Surrender and go with them—that wasn't for me—or resist, which didn't do much for me either.

We further speculated that there were twenty UFOs out there. The Spanish voice in the December 2nd sighting had said he saw twenty. Twenty UFOs? If so, since there seemed to be five or six of the creatures in each craft, that would be 120 to 1. Not bad odds if you're Superman. Superman I wasn't.

My family was holding up under the strain, and what a strain it was. First and foremost was the UFO, then the threatening "government types," and then the investigators who tried to restrain themselves but sometimes failed. Around the dinner table I tried a few UFO jokes to relieve the tension and show the kids that I was still the same dependable dad. Basically it worked.

Only four days had passed since the roadside "attack," and as I turned in for bed, I assumed nothing and expected anything. Just as long as the UFO stayed clear of my family, I had decided to stop having the .32 pistol nearby. I would try to think positively. This couldn't continue indefinitely. I would be open and inviting and hope for a more positive contact. But if they started flashing that beam around, then I would resist.

Lying in bed, with the blanket pulled closely around my shoulders, I began to hear a soft hum, a sound like that of a fluorescent light. The stillness in the bedroom was so defined that even if I said something or moved around, I imagined that the stillness would mute everything except the hum.

I sat up in bed and reached for the bedside light. There seemed to be no reason to lie there and wait. If the UFO was around, and I assumed it was, there was nothing to do but go look. My bedside light made Frances wake up and ask where I was going. This time I spoke clearly and was determined to show no fear.

"I hear the hum and I'm going to have a look."

Frances threw the covers off as I walked out of the room. With my camera in hand, I went to the back door and stepped outside. It was cold. My breath created a mist that reflected in the back-porch light. I was dressed only in my shorts, and soon my bare feet demanded relief from the freezing concrete deck around the pool.

My mind was locked into a deliberate line of thought. I stepped back into the house, where Frances was waiting by the door. She was whispering to me, but my mind was on contact—positive, constructive contact. I was going to make myself completely vulnerable.

I carried only the camera. No gun, no running or hiding. The hum still pressed against my forehead, but it was not controlling me. This was my decision. Somehow this UFO had to stop tormenting me and disrupting my family. I had to get it over with. Whatever was going to happen, let it happen now.

Back through the house, with Frances at my side, I reached the front door and without looking walked into the yard and stood next to my truck. Frances stayed in the doorway. Standing alone, I was exposed. Exposed to the night and exposed to whatever was in the night sky.

I waited, and watched for any movement, anywhere. The vacant lot across the street, with its overgrown bushes, held my attention in those moments I wasn't focusing on the various bright stars. I shuddered from the cold, and my teeth chattered. Whether from the cold or from the excitement, I shivered. But I was not afraid. I was ready.

"Come on, come on," I said under my breath. "Come on. I can't stay out here all night."

Moments later I noticed a particular star that gave off a reddish glow. It was different. So much so that I finally realized that it was closer and not a star at all. Immediately it began to descend. Straight at me, it was falling and growing in size.

I could see it clearly, and it was not like the other crafts. Very different, much smaller, and more of a traditional saucer shape. Not at all like the globe-shaped UFOs that appeared in the previous ten sightings. Another distinct difference was the transparent "energy veil" that glowed and extended about four feet below the circular power source.

The hum was still very softly pulsing in my forehead, and as the UFO came directly at me, I flinched and started to duck under the truck. Stopping still, the UFO hovered at about 150 feet overhead. I was startled as the hum suddenly increased.

Then, higher than the "energy veil" UFO, another UFO winked in, giving off a bright white glow from its power source. There was no time to try to think through what was going on. I shot photo 20. Within seconds the "energy veil" UFO slowly moved off to the east. Then, followed by the bright UFO, both craft raced away and winked out as they reached my vantage point looking toward the roof line of my house.

When I returned to the house, I noticed that the hair on my arms was standing up and crackled when I rubbed them. This lasted less than a minute.

This sighting confused me even more. I had been ready to get it over with, but they must have had something else in mind. What was going on? Two distinctive-looking UFOs had shown themselves to me and then quickly departed.

Were there the same creatures in both UFOs? The bright white craft looked similar to the past sightings, but what about this new "energy veil" UFO? What was it about me that caused these crafts to have such an interest?

Again the questions were growing. More questions and no answers. And always the one I wanted answered most of all. Why me?

JANUARY 16, 1988—FRANCES'S ACCOUNT

Over the past four days Ed and I had talked and retalked the UFO experience from beginning to end. There were so many frightening aspects to consider and no clear-cut answers.

The MUFON investigators had advised Ed not to display a gun anymore. They felt the UFO beings might regard this as a hostile act and were reacting accordingly. Ed and I had come to a similar conclusion. He had already decided that a change in his attitude might reduce the explosive nature of the entire event.

There had been no chance to try out this new approach, and I wasn't sure just exactly what Ed had in mind. So, when he turned on the light and told me he was going out to look for the UFO, I didn't know what to expect. I didn't expect him to boldly step out into the open, leaving himself exposed to an attack.

When Ed returned from the backyard, my questions, Didn't he think that was dangerous? and Wasn't he carrying this nonhostility thing too far?, went unanswered. For all the attention he paid me, I might as well have not even been there. He walked out the front door, leaving me behind.

Watching Ed standing out in the driveway waiting for whatever might happen, I wondered about this man I had married. What was it about him that fascinated these creatures so? I didn't have long to contemplate the answer. What I had taken to be a bright, reddish star dropped to hover above Ed and the truck.

My heart stuttered, then raced. This was not the UFO I had seen before. I hardly had time to make note of the differences before another UFO dropped into the scene. Ed took a picture, then both UFOs zipped over the house, out of my sight.

What were they up to now? Now that Ed had dropped his defensive stance, they seemed to have changed their minds about what they wanted. They could have taken him, but had not. Was it because I was there? Was this all some kind of test? Were these two UFOs on the same side, or had one chased the other away? Instead of getting the answers we had hoped for, we were piling up more questions.

JANUARY 17, 1988—INTERNATIONAL DIRECTOR ARRIVES

The UFO visits seemed to have no pattern. There had only been four days between the last sightings. There was no way to predict when it might return. If only it were clear what the UFO wanted.

Don Ware and I had been discussing these unknowns a few days earlier when Don advised me that Walter Andrus, the international director of MUFON, was following this case closely and would like to set up an appointment with me. Walter wanted firsthand information to better decide the merits of the sightings. I agreed to meet with him.

Walter drove from Seguin, Texas, where the MUFON headquarters are located, and arrived in Gulf Breeze on Sunday morning. With Walter were six other investigators. Introductions were quickly made, and we began reviewing photographs and my account of the events.

As always I tried hard to answer the questions as straight as I could and at the same time tell my feelings and the speculations that went through my mind. Most of these investigators had already listened to the detailed reports I had given them during the session of January 7, 1988.

The original Polaroid photographs are fairly dark, so we huddled around the very strong light from a slide projector. The 500-watt bulb showed details in the UFO pictures that were too dark to see even in the sunlight. We also used a large magnifying glass to study details that are unclear in all the reproduction pictures. Of course there is a huge difference between seeing the UFO firsthand with the naked eye and seeing the darker, more distant image on film.

The question was asked as to whether I would consider myself well read on UFO phenomena. I replied that I had not read any UFO books and had been exposed only to the normal media information about reported sightings. But, like most people, I had seen various Hollywood-type movies about aliens and space travel. I further explained that during the course of these sightings and events I had refrained from reading any books related to the phenomena. For instance, when I described the blue beam, I had no idea that there were other cases involving blue beams. I didn't learn about those until later.

One investigator asked jokingly if he could sleep in a corner of my living room so that he might be fortunate enough to see the UFO. Another asked if there were any rental houses in the neighborhood where he could set up a radio contact with me. But most of the questions involved where did this or that happen? I gave my permission for them to take photos of any and all areas they felt were necessary.

As I answered their questions, I realized that an important facet of letting the complete story out was how it was released. If all that had happened was not told clearly and with detail from the beginning, the story became splintered and difficult to understand. For instance, somebody might wonder why I had been able to take so many pictures if they didn't understand about the hum. I knew I needed to think about how the public should be told.

After several hours my interview with the international director and his investigators was over. The next day Walter Andrus gave a statement to the press, which was published in the *Sentinel* under the following headline:

MUTUAL UFO NETWORK INTERNATIONAL DIRECTOR
VISITS GULF BREEZE, BELIEVES PHOTOS AUTHENTIC

By Walter H. Andrus, Jr., International Director
Mutual UFO Network (MUFON), January 18, 1988

The series of UFO photographs taken by a resident in Gulf Breeze attracted nationwide attention by investigators from the Mutual UFO Network who met on January 17th with the photographer to view and analyze the evidence presented. Donald M. Ware, the MUFON State Director for Florida, who resides in Ft. Walton Beach, was so impressed with the case that he invited Walter H. Andrus, Jr., the International Director of the Mutual UFO Network, with world headquarters in Seguin, Texas, to participate in the investigation personally.

"After interviewing the photographer-witness and examining each photograph taken since November 11, 1987, continuing through January 16, 1988, it's my opinion that the details in the photographs are incredible. This is one of the most amazing UFO cases that I have investigated in the past 30 years in the United States. Samples of the photographs have been delivered by Duane Cook to the topmost authority on computer enhancement of UFO photographs for further evaluation of their authenticity.

"I advised Mr. Cook, Editor of the *Sentinel,* that the photographs show many different views of some type of aerial device in far greater detail than most UFO photographs in the MUFON files. Photographs can be faked through several processes known to the investigators in the Gulf Breeze investigation. As further confirmation of the authenticity of the photographs being evaluated, the witness made a videotape of the same or similar craft from his backyard after he ran out of Polaroid film. It is very difficult to fake a videotape or motion picture film.

"When evaluating the authenticity of any UFO photograph submitted to the Mutual UFO Network for analysis and evaluation, the credibility of the photographer is even more important. I drove 1500 miles round-trip from Seguin, Texas (near San Antonio), to meet with the local UFO witness. The witness/photographer was evaluated as a sincere, truthful and successful businessman who could destroy his personal reputation in the community if he was perpetrating a hoax. No evidence was disclosed that this Gulf Breeze citizen was involved in anything deceptive. On the contrary, he impressed each of the investigators by his sincerity in sharing very openly his experience.

"Over the years, newspapers and the electronic news media have sometimes exploited UFO witnesses due to the interest in UFOs by the public. The photographer, in this case, has cooperated with MUFON investigators, however he wishes to remain anonymous so as to protect his family and his own reputation from public ridicule, that is frequently prevalent in any community. I feel that it is imperative that the witness's private life and that of his family be respected and protected. Duane Cook, Editor of the *Sentinel,* was commended by me for his diplomatic and sensitive reporting on this important case in order to protect the confidentiality of the witness and his family's well-being. The citizens of Gulf Breeze should have some respect for the photographer because he has endangered his professional reputation and subjected his family to cruel ridicule by disclosing very significant scientific information in the ongoing search to solve the mystery known as unidentified flying objects.''

JANUARY 17, 1988—FRANCES'S ACCOUNT

Another of our chances to sleep late was sacrificed to the UFO. The seven MUFON investigators arrived early Sunday morning. Ed had barely finished a quick breakfast and I was still in my bathrobe, when they all crowded into Ed's office.

I thought about going back to bed, but quickly discarded that idea. I didn't want to be curled up asleep and have the entire investigative team tramp into my bedroom for an on-site inspection of where Ed had seen the first creature. Instead I dressed, made the bed, and put in a brief appearance in Ed's office to let all the investigators know that I did exist. At this point Ed was still insisting that I be left completely out of their questioning.

After leaving Ed's office, I went back to the kitchen. I sat down at the breakfast bar to read the newspaper, and fatigue overwhelmed me. I had to get some sleep, somewhere.

The rec room and living room sofas were out; both were too ''public.'' I opted for the guest room, although it was a mess, having become the catchall storage space for everyone's unnecessary, but treasured junk. Even the fold-up Ping-Pong table had been wheeled in there. I didn't care. I climbed over the arm of the sofabed—the Ping-Pong table blocked normal passage—and lay down. The drone of men's voices from Ed's office next door helped put me to sleep.

Several hours later I awoke. The investigators were gone and Ed had been searching the house and yard for me, wondering where I had disappeared to. I told him I hoped the MUFON investigators didn't think I had been intentionally avoiding them. I had just taken advantage of the opportunity to make up some missed sleep.

JANUARY 18, 1988—MUFON SURVEILLANCE

Don Ware called and asked if investigator Bob Reid could come by later in the day and pick up some negatives, especially the one showing the blue beam. I agreed but reiterated my position that all the rights to the photographs were under my control and that MUFON should return all the negatives when the investigations were completed.

Bob Reid arrived later that evening with some equipment and a set of walkie-talkies. The idea he presented was that he would be on watch nearby in the neighborhood. If I heard the hum, I would call him, and he would, he hoped, videotape and photograph the UFO. It sounded like a good idea to me.

Bob is very personable. He quickly makes you feel like you have known him for a long time. He is very well read and especially knowledgeable on the various aspects of the UFO phenomenon. According to Bob, there always seems to be something that materializes to discredit, or at least to introduce uncertainty about, most good UFO-sighting reports. We wondered what might be misinterpreted in my case. For several hours we talked about it.

I tried to give Bob an idea of my personal life and history to see if anything appeared odd. I told him about my special relationship with the teenagers of Gulf Breeze, a relationship of trust and a lot of fun. They know that I can always be counted on to host a get-together. Many a weekend I have organized treasure hunts and pool parties for these young friends to enjoy. I enjoy it as much as they do.

The games we play are often really silly. I might get everyone out in the road and give each one a candle. Then I light the candles and say the

137

first one around the block wins. They don't win anything—they just win. No rules—they like that—just make it all the way around. If somebody blows your candle out, you blow out theirs. One night the kids stayed in the road for hours trying to make it around the block.

There was one game I called sacred kings. It's a card trick embellished with a lot of ceremony, candles, and hocus-pocus to make it seem supernatural. This particular game can be especially scary at night in a darkened room.

Bob was quick to recognize that these games could be interpreted in the wrong way and possibly twisted to insinuate that the UFO was nothing but a big game. I had never looked at it that way, and I would never deny my activities with these young people. I'm proud to be a creative host and have been asked to record all these get-together games for others.

Recently I installed a ten-foot video movie screen in my rec room for movie get-togethers. All-night movie-thons are the latest happening at my house. The best part of trying to stay awake with the kids and watch movie after movie is that the sleepier we all get, the funnier it all becomes.

My concern for the youth of our town springs from my teenage years growing up in a small town much like Gulf Breeze. Teenage boys and girls are easily attracted to mischief, as I once was. Regrettably, as a teenager, I was involved in an unhappy episode with some high school friends and, as a result of protecting their identities, served a short sentence. That incident is core to my concern for and attention to my children and many other young people and has surely influenced my efforts to work with them. I told Bob that no matter what anyone tries to make of it, as long as the kids want to have their parties at my house, they'll be welcome.

As we continued to talk, Bob expressed interest in how my family had come to live in Costa Rica. There was nothing mysterious or secretive about it, so I explained it to him.

When construction money dried up in late 1974, Frances and I decided that if we were ever going to have an adventure, this was the time to do it. We took our savings and, on the advice of her uncle, bought a coffee farm and moved to Costa Rica. Fortunately for us, the price of coffee began to rise soon after our purchase.

Our farm sustained us happily for over four years. But Frances and I realized that while we were all having a broadening experience living in a delightful foreign country, Dan and Laura were missing out on some of the holiday traditions we had grown up with. Our childhood memories of Fourth of July fireworks, trick-or-treating, and the Easter Bunny were fond ones. Would our children one day wish they had those same memories to recall? Neither of us wanted them to feel like expatriates in their own country, so we reluctantly decided it was time to move back to the United States.

After a little more discussion Bob began his "camp out" surveillance. Later that night he was joined by Gary Watson, another field investigator. Together they maintained a twelve-hour watch from dusk to dawn. Their intensive surveillance lasted for about nine days.

JANUARY 21, 1988—TWELFTH SIGHTING— WITH REID ACCOUNT

10:20 P.M.

The latest question before me was if I would agree to a special news documentary designed to show the photographs and detail the events in a half-hour prime-time spot on our local ABC station. I was reluctant to agree to anything that would put my family in the public eye and cause them hardship.

Don Ware had already talked to the news director at WEAR-TV 3, and he was ready to proceed. All they needed was my approval. Everyone reassured me that the show would be a serious and unsensationalized treatment of all that had happened. Finally I agreed, but was still unsure about the possible aftereffects.

The documentary was still on my mind at 10:00 P.M. on the 21st when I checked in with Bob Reid on the walkie-talkie. He was on watch duty about a block away with a clear vantage point toward the rear of my house. Bob was ready with his cameras and only needed me to say, "I hear something."

Again, at about 10:30 P.M., I called on the walkie-talkie to tell Bob I had an item I wanted him to deliver to Don Ware when he returned to Fort Walton Beach the next morning. I would walk over to give it to him in a few minutes. In order to reach Bob's location I had to follow a dirt path that skirts past a neighbor's house and out into the city hall's large parking lot.

Bob had set up his equipment behind the apartment complex that borders the parking lot. An eight-foot-high chain-link fence separates the two. To reach Bob, I had to walk all the way around the fence and double back behind the buildings, covering more than twice the straight-line distance between us.

140

This route is dark, and at night it's a bit eerie. As I followed the dirt path, only two hundred feet from my front door, I began to hear the hum announcing the alien presence. For a moment I considered retreating to the safety of my home, but I decided to go on. I ran through a small patch of woods, with trees on both sides of me, calling to Bob with the walkie-talkie.

"Bob, get your camera. Bob, get your camera, I hear it."

Bob's laconic reply, "I see it," seemed unnaturally calm under the circumstances.

The hum got louder. I was scared and ran faster, trying to reach the edge of the woods. Being in the darkness of the trees and having the UFO someplace close made me breathe heavily and begin to shake. My voice had tightened, and it was hard to whisper into the radio. "You can see it?" I asked incredulously.

Bob, "Yeah, but I think it's a plane."

"No," I said, "this is no plane."

"Yes, it is. It's a plane coming from the west."

I couldn't see the plane and I couldn't see the UFO, but it was there, somewhere; I could hear it. As I ran, I spun around looking through the openings between the trees. I tripped but caught myself on the chain-link fence as I came out of the path and into the clearing near city hall. Bob was still saying he could see a plane when I looked up and saw the UFO. High and very bright, it was in the south.

I yelled into the walkie-talkie, "Look to the south! It's next to that brightest star. Look south!"

I couldn't see Bob, but he must have been looking the wrong way. The UFO stayed there for just a few more seconds before it winked out. The hum got louder and louder as I hurried around the parking area that serves the apartments. When I finally reached Bob, he was watching the sky and had his video camera going. But he hadn't seen the UFO and he couldn't hear this hum that seemed loud enough to wake every resident in the entire apartment complex.

I remember a lot of excitement and the overwhelming feeling that the UFO was going to pop in and zap me at any moment. I sat in Bob's van for shelter and watched the sky while the hum faded. It had been only ten minutes or so since I had left my home, but I was physically and emotionally drained.

Bob told me that all along he had been watching a low-altitude airplane that was approaching from behind me in the northwest. At first only its yellowish landing light had been visible, and he was already studying its slow progress toward the Pensacola airport when I first heard the hum. Bob's preoccupation with this airplane kept him facing almost directly opposite the direction in which the UFO appeared. As the northwest was also the same direction I was coming from, it was very doubtful he would have noticed the "new star" that winked in high in the southern sky for only a few seconds.

This brief sighting disappointed Bob. The UFO seemed to have disappeared just as he got oriented to the direction in which I was looking. We discussed the frequency of the sightings and any possible pattern that the UFO may have established.

We noted the similarity in the time of the interrupted sighting on December 27th at 8:15 P.M. and the December 28th videotaped sighting at 8:00 P.M. We decided there was a chance of a sighting the next night at about the same time, 10:30 P.M., like tonight's. With that thought in mind, we planned an even more careful surveillance for the 22nd.

Here is Bob Reid's first-person account of his stakeout and this event:

When Ed asked me if I would provide a short first-person account of my nine-day "Gulf Breeze UFO stakeout," conducted during mid-January 1988, I said of course I'd love to. Little did I know how difficult it would be to keep my focus limited to just this narrow (and relatively unimportant) aspect of one of the most significant and well-documented UFO cases ever recorded. Part of the difficulty is because the stakeout didn't achieve the results we hoped for. But it wasn't a totally wasted effort either. Failure to attempt a stakeout under the circumstances would have been valid grounds for criticism by those who make it a point to second-guess any investigation they did not personally conduct—Plus, we almost got one!

During our first meetings with Ed, we (Don Ware, Charles Flannigan, Gary Watson, and I) had proposed that one or more of us conceal ourselves in the vicinity of Ed's house with cameras so that we might confirm this apparent alien attention he and his family were getting. Ed welcomed the idea but, not yet knowing us very well, he wanted assurance that our presence and activities would in no way draw attention to him or his family. We agreed that this meant concealment at some distance from his home. Ed, in return, agreed to help.

On 18 January 1988 I bought two 3-watt citizens band walkie-talkies at Radio Shack and that evening took one of them, with a battery-charger unit, to Ed in Gulf Breeze. This we'd decided would improve the chances that our stakeout would be a success. The plan was that Ed would give me a quick radio call as soon as he "got the hum" and that I'd be there ready with long lens and video. I stayed at Ed's until well after midnight that night, rehashing the details of previous sightings and refining our plan. The stakeout was to begin the next evening, the 19th of January.

I returned to Gulf Breeze in the morning to talk with Lynn Hunsley, manager of the Sailwind, an apartment/condo complex that sprawls lazily along the southern edge of the Gulf Breeze High School property. Mr. Hunsley, a retired U.S. Navy flier, was quite interested in the pictures and articles he'd seen in the *Sentinel* and said he'd be happy to help our investigation in any way he could. Yes, it would be okay to park my van in the back parking lot next to the fence. There I would be away from the lights and noise of street traffic and adjacent to the school grounds. And although pine trees occluded my line of sight with Ed's house, I would have an almost clear view of the northern horizon, to include the sky above his place. After checking out my proposed vantage point I returned to Fort Walton Beach to set up my van, rest, and await the evening of my first stakeout.

A word here about the setup I put together for this mission. Removing the rear passenger seats from my minivan, I replaced them with a pad, pillow, and sleeping bag. Alongside were laid out my 8mm mini video camera (similar to Ed's), 35mm still camera with 70–210mm zoom lens (ASA 200 Kodacolor film, lens preset on infinity at 1/60 sec and aperture 3.5), 7 × 50 binoculars, small battery-operated tape recorder, flashlight and compass. Also had a metal detector, although I didn't have much idea what I might need it for. If I slept, it would be with my clothes on so that I'd be in instant readiness to respond.

The walkie-talkie, the key factor in my plans, was to stay on all night. It was plugged into the cigarette lighter, with antenna protruding through a gap at the top of the front passenger-side window. Ed and I planned to make a brief check of our radio contact sometime early in the evening, then he'd shut his down (put it on the battery charger) until he had need to call me. Thus there would be no way I could establish contact with him during the night. This was consistent with the agreement we investigators made not to permit our activities to bother Ed or interfere with his home life any more than was absolutely necessary.

The pattern of Ed's previous "photo opportunities" indicated dawn (0500–0600) and dusk (1645–1745) to be the most likely times for sightings, with the possibility that something might appear at any time during darkness. My personal circumstances, unfortunately, did not permit the fifteen to sixteen hours a day required to cover this entire period. Later Gary Watson would cover the early evening until I could get there, but for this first stakeout there was no coverage until I arrived on the scene at about 2145 hours (9:45 P.M.).

Ed soon made his prearranged radio check to confirm my presence and that the radio was working okay. Then he shut down. The night of 19 January was as long as it was uneventful. Occasional bits of other folks' radio conversations kept my ear alert, and there were lots of aircraft lights. I soon became familiar with normal air traffic patterns in the southeastern part of the Pensacola terminal area. But nothing appeared in the sky that was in any way anomalous. And Ed never called.

Back again next evening; Ed's lighthearted radio call told me he again had no premonition of activity. We exchanged a little banter before he shut down, but that was all I heard from him for the night. Still nothing in the sky except for routine air traffic. It became an idle game to watch as landing lights of aircraft approaching the Pensacola airport metamorphosed from "hovering orange UFOs" in their head-on, almost stationary base-leg appearance to normal aircraft as they slowly wheeled left for final approach. Knowing how reports of strange things seen in the sky often encourage preoccupied people to look skyward for the first time, I wondered how many of the current flurry of "me too" reports in Gulf Breeze might really have just such a prosaic explanation. These thoughts didn't discourage me, though. Misidentified landing lights would be a pretty doubtful explanation for Ed's photos!

Thursday, the 21st of January, and I was back at the Sailwind at 2130 hours (9:30 P.M.). It seemed an awfully short interval since I'd left the identical parking spot at 0615 that morning. I suppressed any thoughts that this whole thing might be a grand exercise in futility, but it did seem possible that if we had many more nights like these last two, this stakeout business would soon be as interesting as watching a dripping faucet. Perhaps the "visitors" sensed my budding ambivalence, for they saw to it that this would not be a dull night. And though the stakeout would continue for another week or so, this was to be the only night when anything even approaching the phenomenal happened.

Soon after I was set up, Ed called on the radio. All was quiet, and he was going to busy himself with things around the house. He wished me a successful night. Actually I suspected he was feeling a little guilty about being the cause for so much apparent waste of time and effort. This suspicion was reinforced a few minutes later when he came back on the air to say he was coming over to bring me something. Don Ware had asked Ed to have negatives made of some of his more important photos so that copies could be made for the MUFON report and for distribution to other investigators. Ed was bringing me one of these negatives so that I could deliver it to Don.

At this stage of the game Ed was still a little apprehensive about being out in the open where he was not protected from the sky by some sort of shelter. His experience with the beams, especially the white one that had numbed his arms and legs nine days earlier while driving on Soundside Drive, had left him leery of being very far away from a roof of some sort. (We later joked about rigging him some sort of headgear with a metal garbage-can lid attached for him to wear while walking around in the open!) Knowing this, I asked if he wanted me to drive over to his place to pick up the negative. No, he didn't think there'd be any problem. He'd just walk it over. There seemed a hint of forced bravado in his voice, but I didn't argue. Anyway, if this cross-country jaunt did result in activity by Ed's "friends," I planned to be ready with the video camera to record it all for posterity. I really doubted there'd be much chance anything would happen. He'd have the walkie-talkie with him, and I'd be able to monitor his progress if he got into any sort of trouble.

Straight-line distance from Ed's house to my location was probably a quarter of a mile or less, but intervening fences made it necessary that he travel at least half again this distance to get to me. Being familiar with the pathways and having plenty of ambient light, Ed elected to travel without a flashlight. This meant that I could not follow his progress visually, although at the midpoint where he reached the Sailwind fence he would, for a short way, be able to see my van's location there at the back of the parking lot. He gave me a call saying he was going out his front door and would be with me shortly.

I stepped outside the van into the chilly night air to await his arrival. In a couple of minutes he gave me a call to say he was leaving the hard-surface road and taking up the pathway along the schoolyard's western boundary. He was obviously stepping out and making good progress. About this same time my eye caught sight of a "false UFO" low on the horizon to the northwest. Though this one was brighter than some, experience told me this was just another aircraft's landing lights. I watched it idly. Next communication from Ed was about a minute later, and it made the hair stand up on the back of my neck.

It was a voice urgent and frightened that now came over the radio. Unfortunately I didn't have any kind of recorder going, so I don't have the exact wording, but the gist was that he had suddenly gotten a strong hum and knew the craft was in the area someplace close. His radio transmissions came rapidly now; his voice tense, but barely above a whisper. I could "see" his almost frantic activity as he pushed ahead, all the while looking around for the familiar but dreaded object he knew was generating this hum inside his head. He was moving through an area of trees; he wanted me to look around to see if I could see anything in the sky. I glanced to the northwest and the "landing-lights UFO" was still on "base leg," a very slowly approaching orange ball. Could this be the craft Ed had been photographing in some new configuration? Ed had now passed the midpoint of his route, so there was no turning back. He called again to ask if I saw anything. I tried to keep my voice calm. I said I saw a light, but I didn't think it was a threat. It was behind him in his direction of travel and didn't seem to be closing very rapidly.

There were a few seconds of silence, and when his voice came on again, it seemed to have gone up another octave in pitch. Sounding almost frantic now, Ed confirmed that he, too, could see it. And yes, that pinpoint in the sky was the alien craft; that was exactly the way it looked the last time he had seen it (at 0200 the morning of 16 January in his front yard). I was still dubious; for one thing I wasn't even sure Ed could see "my" light from where he was. Trees should have blocked his view. Nevertheless, I raised my video camera and was fumbling with the knobs when Ed radioed that the object had just blinked out. I looked, but mine was still there. In fact it was just now starting its left turn to final, and I could begin to make out wing-tip lights and a rotating beacon. By now Ed had hurried around the fence and was coming into view at the far end of my parking lot. Chagrined, I turned the camera toward his approaching figure and let it roll.

Ed almost trotted as he closed the distance. He was wild-eyed and in a state quite different from his usual jocularity. He was swearing oaths and seemed to be sweating despite the chill of the night. He gestured vigorously at a point high in the southern sky, diametric from the direction I'd been facing. The object had been up there. There, next to that brightest star, he said. He pointed at Sirius. It had been within a hand's breadth of Sirius and was of at least equal magnitude. And although it had blinked out before I could locate it, he said that the hum was still in his head. In fact the hum seemed to be getting louder. ("Can't you hear it?" he asked me incredulously; it seemed to him it should have been waking up everybody in the whole Sailwind complex.) Ed was sure the craft was still in the area and still posed a threat to his person. I motioned for him to get into my van, as the side door was wide open. He didn't hesitate.

And that's the end of the stakeout story. I kept the video going a while longer just in case, but of course nothing materialized. The hum started to diminish almost immediately and soon was totally gone. Just as quickly Ed's strange sense of agitation dissipated and his humor returned. Within fifteen minutes he was almost back to normal. Another quarter hour of small talk and he was ready to trek back over to his house. I was slower in recovering from the effects of what I'd witnessed than he apparently was. I was really concerned. Didn't he think it would be best if I gave him a ride? Wasn't he afraid the craft would come after him again on the return trip? No, he didn't think there would be any problem, and anyhow we had radio contact. "I'll give you a call when I get there," he promised. With that Ed struck out for home. Eight or ten minutes later he called me from his front doorway to wish me good night. "Good night, my man," I replied. True story, folks, about one of the bravest men in the world today.

It would be easy to imagine that the dramatic transformation Ed underwent that January night was just that—imagination. I think maybe I wish it were, but the video record proves otherwise. Ed's torment in the Sailwind parking lot was the real thing, just as real as are his photographs and his graphic descriptions of the aliens and their incredible capabilities. It's time the world started taking these things seriously.

JANUARY 22, 1988—HELICOPTER CIRCLES HOUSE

About 8:00 P.M. I checked in with investigator Gary Watson via walkie-talkie. Gary was on watch from the back field, where he awaited relief from Bob Reid. Bob was scheduled to spend the night on watch from his van.

The 10:30 P.M. possible sighting time was getting closer and had been discussed over the walkie-talkies with hopeful expectation. Knowing the two investigators were hoping that the "return theory" would be successful, I walked over to join the watch with my Polaroid and video cameras at my side.

While we waited for Bob to arrive, Gary and I commented on what seemed to be heavy air traffic that night. I was more than a little curious about all the activity myself. Our neighborhood is strictly suburban residential, and at 10:00 P.M. to have helicopters and jets crossing over our sleepy bedroom community was very unusual.

Soon after Bob Reid arrived, a large military-type helicopter circled over the back field, passing directly over my house. At first Bob and I dismissed its arrival as a coincidence and watched it make a wide circle and again approach from the north. If there was to be a chance of a sighting at 10:30, then this helicopter circling around was not helping.

Again the helicopter made a wide circle and headed directly for us, passing over our heads at between five hundred and one thousand feet altitude and on over my house. By now we were a bit uneasy about this strange development, and I even concealed myself near some small oak trees. Both Bob and I started filming the lone helicopter. Over and over again the pattern was repeated at precisely the time we had discussed on the walkie-talkies that the UFO might arrive. Six complete circles over my house, then the helicopter flew off to the north and out of our sight.

Never before, and never since, have I seen that much air traffic over my house. The natural question is, did the military, or somebody else, pick up the walkie-talkie transmission about the UFO possibly showing itself at 10:30 that night? Was it just too big a chance for the "authorities" to take, that several investigators with cameras in hand might record the appearance of the UFO?

Bob maintained the vigil and walkie-talkie link all that night, but nothing else materialized. Not even a hum. Did the helicopter "scare" it away?

Several days later the *Sentinel* reported that the UFO had been spotted on this same night, January 22nd, at 8:00 P.M. over a subdivision called Polynesian Isles near Highway 98 about four miles east of Gulf Breeze. Here is their report as recorded by Diana Hansen:

> Three local youths were playing basketball at the canal front home of Scott Zepp. His friends, Mark Turner and Clark Allen, had come over to spend the night. The boys were keeping a close watch on the time since they were to call some girls at exactly 8:15 P.M.
>
> Fourteen-year-old Scott was the first to notice a "strange" craft hovering about 100 yards away just a few feet above the tree line northeast of the house toward the bay.
>
> He alerted the other boys, who all turned to see the same thing. "First we saw red lights moving around in a circular motion," Scott reported, "then they changed to white lights."
>
> They all stood mesmerized for what seemed like a couple of minutes. Then one of the boys pointed out a "ball" on top of the craft. There was no sound from the craft itself. Mark and Scott estimate the size to be "a little larger than a helicopter."
>
> In a smooth and swift motion the craft moved closer to the boys and hovered at a distance of "about 50 to 60 yards for about four seconds." Just as quickly it moved back out to its original position.
>
> At about that time, the craft began to emit a white beam of light. The intensity of the light grew steadily until, as Mark remembers it, "It looked like the headlights of a car shining right at us . . . it almost looked like daytime around us." The blinding light obstructed their view of the UFO.
>
> The fear finally started to set in and the boys rushed in to get

Scott's mother, Beverly Zepp. By the time she got outside, the craft had moved out over the bay. However, Mrs. Zepp was able to see there were circulating lights around the bottom.

"We watched it until it started to move out over the bay," said Mrs. Zepp, "then I got them all in the car and we drove over to the road that runs along the bay in Whisper Bay." They continued to watch until the UFO disappeared from sight.

The boys feel certain that what they saw was not an airplane or helicopter. But the thought of a UFO does not really frighten them. Mark wonders, "With all the other stars and planets in the universe, doesn't it seem like there would be somebody besides us?"

JANUARY 23, 1988—MYSTERIOUS RADAR BLIMP

The suspicion of a military "investigation," or at least knowledge of the UFO phenomena in our area, was reinforced by the front-page photograph of a radar blimp (see inset photo following page 256). The *Pensacola News-Journal* printed the photograph with a caption describing the blimp as "mysterious."

Eglin Air Force Base public-affairs specialist George Roberts described the blimp as a research project on radar reflection. Roberts advised the media that the blimp, tethered to a ship anchored in Pensacola Bay about two miles from Gulf Breeze, would be in the area until late February.

As of mid-April the blimp was still doing "research," and as more and more UFO sightings were reported ten miles to the east of Gulf Breeze, the "research" blimp was moved to that area.

JANUARY 24, 1988—THIRTEENTH SIGHTING—ENCOUNTER VIDEOTAPED BY COOK

The official dedication and open house of the city's newly completed recreation center had been a big success. I had attended the ceremony and had enjoyed visiting with several city and county officials. There was no mention of the UFO, and that was fine with me.

It rained most of the day and was still sprinkling a fine mist when I left the recreation center. Some golden oldies were playing on the radio, and I sang along as I drove the few blocks back home. When I pulled into our drive and parked, the truck was silent but for the occasional gust of wind blowing the misty rain.

I could hear a very soft hum that had been covered up by the radio. I sat and listened. The hum was so soft that the slightest movement of my body on the vinyl seat cover made it fade. I sat and waited. It was about 5:15, getting late but still daylight. I waited and listened.

If the UFO showed itself, I was ready to run for the house and grab the walkie-talkie. Gary Watson should be on watch at any moment. He was due at 5:30 P.M. The hum continued to fade in and out, and I rolled down the window to see if that had any effect. I just got wet.

The UFO apparently doesn't care much about the weather, or it would have chosen a warmer, drier day to tempt me with the hum. I was tempted. Tempted to go out and get it over with, let whatever would happen, happen.

Somewhere in or above those gray clouds that hung so close to the ground was a UFO. A UFO that was waiting for me. Intentionally or unintentionally, a UFO that was humming to let me know it was there. A craft like no earthly craft, which for some reason would not go away.

152

Why follow me? Was the UFO allowing and staging these photo opportunities, as some of the investigators had suggested? That was hard to accept. Surely if the UFO wanted somebody to take its picture, it would certainly have chosen somebody with a decent camera. I would suggest a network camera crew member or maybe tourists on an airliner bound for Hawaii. They would take more photographs than I could take in a week.

The temptation was strong to try to set up the opportunity to have the UFO filmed. Just a little while longer and Gary would be at his normal position for the evening watch. Bob Reid was scheduled to join him later. I needed their help if I was going to get this over with and not hide from the UFO any longer. I wanted somebody to film whatever happened if I confronted the UFO.

Through the rain I dashed across the driveway to the front door, and at that moment the hum surged louder. I ran into my office, grabbed the walkie-talkie, and called for Gary. No answer. I called for Gary again several times and heard only static in return. Frances, overhearing my calls to Gary, asked what was happening. Though the hum was constant and strong, I decided not to upset her by telling her.

Despite my attempt, Frances knew from looking at me that something was wrong and insisted I stay in the house. But I couldn't. I wanted to expose the UFO and at the same time get rid of the hum. The walkie-talkie was blank and I couldn't wait, so I called Duane Cook to ask if he would help me. He readily agreed.

Taking my Polaroid and video camera, I drove to the *Sentinel* office, where Duane was waiting. We planned to drive to a secluded area in the hope that the UFO would show itself. There was a brief delay as Duane and Dari Holston discussed whether she should come along with us. I had little to say. With my head humming like a hand massager, I just wanted to go and get it over with.

Finally only Duane got into the truck with me, and we drove east on Highway 98. The traffic was heavy with evening-rush-hour congestion. The hum continued pulling at the front right side of my forehead. I had to make myself listen to Duane's words as he tried to figure out the on/off/standby controls on the video camera.

I managed to answer him, "Yes, that's okay. If the red light's on, that's okay."

The windshield wipers smeared the rain and road film, making driving even more difficult. Duane may have been concerned about my impaired condition but only said, "I'm surprised they would pick overcast."

I didn't care about the weather. Not only could I hear the hum, but I could feel the UFO's presence. I kept insisting, "Duane, it's here. That SOB is here."

The UFO was somehow pulling on my forehead, fading in and out. I tried to explain the feeling to Duane but could only insist that the UFO was near. Then the pressure increased, and the UFO voice said, "In sleep you know."

I was scared and yelled out loud, "Oh, damn, damn, it just said something. Oh, damn, it's here." I repeated aloud, "It just said, 'In sleep . . . in sleep you know, in sleep you know,' "

Duane continued to videotape and had started to say something when the hum dug deep into my skull. I yelled and pleaded for "this thing to get out of my life."

My head, my mouth, my face were tingling. "Oh, damn, I don't know if I can drive. Duane, does my face look like it's moving? Is my face moving?"

Duane answered, "No, no, it's all right. It's still. Does it feel like your skin is crawling? No, it's okay, you're looking good."

We continued to drive, and I had to make myself stop looking up and out the side windows and watch the road instead. It felt like the UFO was right on top of the truck and was reaching into the cab ready to pull me from the wheel. My right eye began to press outward.

"Is my eye moving? Is my eye moving?" I leaned over to look in the rearview mirror.

Duane answered as he tried to look into my face, "No, I don't think so."

But I could feel something. My right eye felt like it was coming out of its socket, and the hum grew stronger. Duane was staring at my face and tried to reassure me, his voice, as always, calm and steady.

"You're okay, your eye is stable."

A rush of speed swept through my body. I looked at the road and thought we were speeding out of control.

"Duane, are we going too fast?"

He quickly replied, "No, no. You're doing just fine."

The hum decreased, but my face still throbbed. I was afraid. These sensations had never happened before during any of the other incidents. There was a twisting pull that reached from my forehead, through my neck, and down into my stomach.

The traffic cleared the further we drove. The hum was still with me, but much lighter and I tried to explain to Duane what I had been feeling.

I was getting worried and complained that this idea to go out after the UFO may not have been a good one. Duane wasn't ready to give up, and asked about the voice.

"It was just like a knife sticking in my brain," I told him.

I felt if there was to be any chance of seeing the UFO, we had to get off the main highway. Duane was quick to suggest Soundside Drive, but I wanted no part of going someplace that deserted. Plus I had already seen what had happened on Soundside Drive when the UFO lowered the five creatures. I wanted this trauma over, but not like that.

The hum began to press harder again. I wondered out loud if the UFO knew that Duane was with me.

"If it's reading your mind, it does. But as long as it knows I'm not a threat—that's what it needs to learn."

My stomach knotted, and I started to talk out loud to the UFO. Maybe I could explain that I needed Duane to help me. I needed Duane to film what was happening. As I spoke, a pain shot from my head to my stomach, and I almost vomited.

The rain had slackened, and Duane suggested that we turn off the highway on any one of the roads that led toward the country club golf course, which was off to our right. As we approached a turn-off road, I noticed my face was numb.

"I don't like this. I don't like this." I had to force myself to continue driving.

If the UFO wanted to take back the hum, sever the mental connection, I was ready. I would stand out in the road and only ask that they allow Duane to record whatever happened on film. I was scared, but I wanted it over. As bad as this was, having an unwelcome visitor pop in and out and never knowing when I was safe, was worse. It was better to have an ending.

We continued to drive along, and I was afraid for Duane. I had known I was in trouble, but now I had involved him in my dangerous confrontation. I told him my fears.

"This was a bad idea. Duane, you might be in trouble too. Maybe we should take you back. This is bad. This is bad."

"If you think I'm in trouble, then find a place to park. You can stay in the truck and I'll go to a distance and tape and watch, or else I'll stay in the truck and you go. . . . I don't think I'm in trouble."

We were now on a road with very few houses and mostly the golf course on both sides. The yellow glow of street lights reflecting on the rain-streaked windshield added to the difficulty of watching for the UFO.

I could still feel it close by and urged Duane to keep looking. I was looking for a place to stop.

Suddenly my heart raced and I knew something was going to happen. I eased the truck over to the side of the road, at the same time calling out, "If you're going to do it, come on. Okay, okay, okay, come on."

The hum grew louder, and I warned Duane once again that he might be in trouble, then I stepped out of the truck. I was in the middle of the road. I was exposed. Duane got out also, still filming me, but stayed close to the truck as I paced back and forth across the road.

"Okay, I'm ready. Here I am."

Again I called to Duane to be careful, and he responded, "Don't worry about me."

My stomach cramped, and I yelled, "F—— this! I want it out of my life. Duane, they're here. Come on, SOB, let's do it."

My left hand burst with pain. Then a crushing pain rushed from my right forehead, across my chest and down my left arm and leg. I was driven to the ground and screamed to Duane.

"They're here, Duane, they're here."

They were using my own nervous system to hurt me. I screamed again, wanting them to do whatever they had come for.

"I'm not going to do this again. This is it. I'm not going out like this anymore. You better do it, I'm not going to do this again. Come on, come on, SOB."

The hum eased and in a moment stopped. I was still standing in the road. The misty rain wet me, causing me to shiver. I walked back to the truck. Duane had already climbed back in because it was beginning to rain a little harder. When I opened the door, I could see he was still filming.

I was disappointed that we hadn't filmed the UFO, but maybe the torment and that strong surge of pain had ended the hum. Maybe the connection was broken. I glanced up, across the sky, and announced that I would not be back. Suddenly, about two hundred feet behind Duane, and maybe six feet high, the UFO winked into view. I yelled, "Oh, f——, oh s——, there it was."

I jerked the camera up to my face but I didn't line up the viewfinder on the UFO. I never saw the UFO through the camera. I just aimed in the general direction and hit the trigger. The flash went off for photo 21.

When I lowered the camera, there was nothing in the sky. The UFO was gone.

All that time Duane had spent out in the rain filming, and they did this. Why hadn't they let him see them? I was outraged. All the torment, then this. I charged around the truck and into the roadside brush, yelling at the UFO. A few minutes later Duane called me over to get the camera and see if I had photographed the UFO.

"I can see why you manage to get these photos," he told me. "You are fast."

Duane took the camera and the film. After waiting the sixty seconds for the Polaroid film to develop, he peeled the backing off to expose the photo. I doubted that I'd gotten anything but there it was, the UFO, clearly visible. Duane noticed the difference in this photograph even in the dimly lighted truck. Across and above the UFO were streaks of light. The craft had been caught in action, moving up and out of sight, while the shutter was open.

Luck had been on my side with this photograph. Even if the UFO was orchestrating these photo opportunities, as some people had suggested, the circumstances of this sighting were such that I hadn't been confident anything would show up on the film.

While we looked at the photograph I realized that my hands were tingling. They felt very strange, but Duane could see nothing wrong with them. I dismissed it as a reaction to all the excitement.

Several more times I called out to the UFO, "Come on, you SOB, I'm not doing this again." Then I asked Duane again if he had seen anything.

"I'm sorry. I was filming you, and when I reached for the door handle, I fumbled getting the door open is what it amounts to. If I had had the window open to start with, maybe."

We tried to figure out exactly where the UFO had been, relative to Duane. It had appeared in just about the only place where Duane could not have seen it. Had he managed to turn around fast enough, the panel between the side window and rear window would still have blocked his view. Plus the UFO was so fast that it was only visible for a few seconds. All this torment from the UFO and my witness had not seen it.

Duane said, "I know one thing. I saw you shoot this picture. And this is the picture that I saw you pull out of the camera, and I peeled."

"That's good, isn't it?" I wanted some consolation for all we had been through.

Duane responded with a certain amount of emphasis, "You bet it's good."

"You needed to see!" I protested.

Duane was fast to overrule me. "It's more important that you shot it, and I saw you shoot it, and this is what I saw you shoot. This is better than if I had seen it and you had not gotten the picture. I would have loved to have seen it too. It's my loss that I missed it, not yours. But I can flat guarantee anybody that I saw you take this picture.''

We decided to take another shot from the same position as a control picture. Like the one I had taken before, this one showed the carry rack atop my truck. But this time the sky was empty.

I was exhausted and beginning to relax from the fear, the fear that both Duane and I had been in mortal danger. Duane reassured me, insisting there was no history of people being killed by a UFO. He said he had never felt himself in danger.

We calmly continued to review what had happened, with me emphatic that "I'll not do that again.'' I thanked Duane for coming with me. I would never have done this alone. If I *had* been alone, they might have taken me, and there would have been no witnesses.

I thought of Frances. She was waiting for my return. She hadn't wanted me to go and had tried to convince me to wait for Gary or Bob. Knowing she would be worried, I needed to get back home.

Duane and I made some notes on exactly where we were on the road so that the MUFON investigators could see the area later. We then returned to Duane's office and agreed to meet at my house later, along with Bob Reid, to watch the videotape.

Later Duane wrote a complete report of the events he witnessed, and it is included in Appendix 2.

January 24, 1988—Frances's Account

During the hour or so that Ed was gone, I fed Dan and Laura, excusing their father's absence by saying he had been called away by a customer. Not long after the kids had retreated to their side of the house, Ed came back. He was upset, and it took him a while to tell me all that had happened.

Duane and Bob Reid would be coming over soon to watch the tape. Laura would realize something was going on. Not wanting to frighten her, Ed gave Laura a very watered-down version of what had just occurred. We sent her off to her room, then Dan and I watched the video with Ed.

I hated it. Watching Ed tormented by some unseen force was almost more than I could handle. When it was over, Dan promised to keep his sister occupied when the others came. Shaken by what he had seen, he understood why we didn't want her exposed to it.

While we waited for Duane and Bob, I made Ed promise me he wouldn't go out like that again. Just because the MUFON investigators wanted all the information they could get was no reason for him to take that kind of chance. It was ridiculous. Let them find someone else to be their guinea pig, not my husband.

Bob Reid arrived, as did Duane. Dari Holston was with him, and she had something to add to the night's events. She and Ann, another *Sentinel* employee, had secretly followed Ed and Duane when they had gone out earlier. Once they went off the main highway, Dari had turned off her headlights to ensure that neither Ed nor Duane would know they were there.

The women parked about six hundred feet down the road from Ed's truck when the men stopped to await the UFO. A pine thicket hid Dari's car, but it also blocked their view when the UFO popped in. Dari told us all she had seen was an indistinct orange glow through the trees.

I watched the video again with the others. It was less shocking the second time around, but still upsetting. Bob took notes throughout, asking questions when the tape was over. One of his questions was to me. He wanted to know what I thought of all this.

Ed reminded Bob of MUFON's agreement not to bother the children and me with questions. I told Ed that maybe it was time for him to stop protecting me from talking to people who, for all their questions, seemed to have our best interests as a genuine concern. Ed agreed, so I told Bob exactly what I thought. How I hated it. How I didn't understand why it was Ed they seemed to want. How I wished none of it had ever happened. Bob didn't say much, and I wondered just what the MUFON investigators had to say about us when they were together.

The men went into Ed's office. Dari stayed in the living room with me, and we talked about other things. I didn't really know her, but it was so good to have someone there who knew all that was happening and who tried to take my mind off it.

JANUARY 25, 1988—HOPE FOR ENDING

Frances and I rehashed the incident of the night before until we rationalized that the UFO must have done what it had planned to do. The videotape showed that something very strange had had control of my nervous system.

I had wanted to keep Dan and Laura from seeing the torment I had undergone, but it was neither practical nor possible to keep it from them. The image of me kneeling in helpless pain enraged my family, but we all knew there was little we could do to fight back. Therefore we wanted to believe that the UFO was gone, that the torment was over.

Later that night I went over to the MUFON watch car to talk with Charles Flannigan, Gary Watson, and Bob Reid. These men were very supportive, but I felt that their efforts were probably in vain. The UFO seemed to know when and who was watching. If the craft was still around, and I hoped it wasn't, I didn't think it was going to show itself to this group.

As we talked, there was a lot of speculation about the UFO making it possible for me to take these pictures. If it was true that the beings were letting me do it, then why had they said that photos were prohibited on the second sighting back on November 20, 1987?

There were other unanswerable questions. Why had they shot me with the white flash on the roadside on January 12, 1988? Why had they tormented me just the night before while Duane videotaped the incident? Why keep coming back? And the ever-present "Why me?"

It was suggested that the UFO kept returning to me just because I was so stubborn. When it said, "No pictures allowed," I took pictures anyway. When it said, "Step forward," I went the other way. And then there was the question of abduction.

160

The investigators asked if there was anything I could remember that seemed strange. Any strange recurring dream? In other words, was it possible that I had been abducted in the past? The idea they suggested was that the UFO could block your memory of an abduction and the event could only be remembered under regressive hypnotism.

I told them of a dream I'd had several times, but I made light of it, as if I thought it were nothing. Actually this dream was very vivid and occurred at least once a week.

The dream would begin with me rising high in the sky and looking over a coastline. I could see the sandy beach with waves breaking on the shore. Sometimes I would recognize the beach but most often not. Then I would quickly descend and pass beneath the water into the ocean. I would gasp for air, in fear of drowning, but as I went deeper and deeper, I realized I was inside a container with a large diamond-shaped window. Through the window I could see the water and fish. Shortly thereafter I saw a lot of bubbles passing in front of the window, followed by rising sand, which soon completely covered the glass. That's all I remember of it.

I didn't tell them all the details or the frequency of the dream. Nor did I tell them of the other times in my life when an unexplained loss of time had occurred. I didn't want to encourage the MUFON investigators to think anything other than what I wanted to be true—that last night had ended the phenomena.

When the investigators saw I didn't intend to pursue that line of thought any further, they brought up another question. Was it possible the UFO had landed on the night of December 17th when it had suddenly gone black, not far above the ground, then later reappeared in the same general area? I didn't know. I hadn't seen it land. They thought it was worth looking into.

It was late in the evening as Charles and I walked across the back field for a preliminary look at the area where I had seen the UFO black out and appear to land. We saw no immediate evidence of a disturbance to that corner of the field, but since we were using flashlights, we realized a thorough daytime inspection was necessary.

As we returned to Charles's car, we noticed a dried-out circle of grass about one hundred feet from the area under suspicion. Directly east of my house, about four hundred feet from my fence, this dried area appeared to be a perfect circle about ten feet in diameter. We made note of its location so that Charles could further examine the site later that week in daylight.

The next day Frances and I walked over to the area, which showed clearly in the daytime, and shot some pictures of what looked like a thirty-foot circle of light-colored grass with a ten-foot circle of dried-out grass in the center (photo 24A). I reported back to Charles, who told me he had also taken some photographs earlier that same day.

Charles notified Tom Roche, Santa Rosa County civil defense director, who checked the area for radioactivity. Later Mr. Roche reported that no radioactivity was detected at the site.

On February 3, 1988, a field agent for the Center for UFO Studies (CUFOS) tested the site for various other abnormal characteristics. Here is his preliminary summary:

> Basically we just looked over the area and there wasn't anything out of the ordinary but the coloration change of the grass. It appears to be drier with hardly any green grass, as opposed to outside of the circled area where the grass seems to be a little bit greener. . . .
>
> But as far as salinity meter readings, moisture content of the soil directly underneath the grass, abnormal magnetic readings, none of that is there. There is no deviation in the pH factor, which gives you an indication of whether there is any excess alkalinity in the soil, which is a strong indication of anything abnormal.

He also took samples of the grass and soil from within and outside of the circle, "Just in case we later learn of anything unusual."

As the spring weather encouraged new grass growth, the unexplained circle remained clear.

JANUARY 25, 1988—FRANCES'S ACCOUNT

Ed went over to tell Bob Reid and the others that he wouldn't be coming out again if he heard the hum. If the UFO wanted him, it would have to come and get him. I was glad he wasn't going to go out to confront the craft again, but I wished he wouldn't stay so long whenever he went to see one of the investigators "for just a minute."

His minutes usually lasted for an hour or two. During that time I couldn't reach him—he always took the walkie-talkie with him—and I had no idea if he was all right or not. This night was no exception.

As I waited for Ed to come back, I worried about what he had said about the UFO having to come after him. What if it did? What if this ordeal wasn't over as we hoped?

There had been a creature on the back porch once. What would it have done if Ed hadn't gotten up with the gun? And what was to prevent them from coming back again if that was what they wanted? Could they get in even if the doors were locked? Would it hurt them if we shot them, or would it just make them mad? I didn't know.

JANUARY 26, 1988—FOURTEENTH SIGHTING—TOWEL INCIDENT

My family was still very shaken by the video of the torment I had suffered on the road two nights before. They needed some breathing room and a lot of time to recover. So did I.

I was still trying to convince myself the contact was over, that the UFO had done what it wanted. It *had* to be over. Having the UFO jumping in and out of the sky over the house was taking a toll on our nerves.

Even if the phenomenon was over, I still had to deal with the after-effects. First there was the documentary that Don Ware had arranged with WEAR-TV 3, the local ABC affiliate. It was to begin the next day, when Charles Flannigan would come by, pick up some photos, and take them to the television studio to begin the shooting.

I was having heavy second thoughts about doing anything that might keep my family upset. Certainly it would be better just to drop it all. The investigators had enough photo evidence, and more and more people were reporting seeing the UFO. We all just needed a break, and now that it was likely that the UFO had finished with me, this was the time.

I called Don to tell him of my decision to cancel the half-hour documentary. He did not see it my way at all. Don felt strongly that the story should be in the public eye. The more public, the better. His reasoning was, the more widespread the story, the harder it would be to cover up.

Of course Don wanted the documentary to focus on the UFO and the photographs of it, but I argued that, without a doubt, it would lead back to me. He promised that my name would be withheld, but this is a small town, and already more people than I wanted to knew my identity. I insisted that we delay until the following Monday so that I could decide what to do.

Peter Neumann, WEAR news director, had been talking directly with Don Ware about the documentary. I had known Peter for several years and considered him a friend. He's sharp and has that certain keenness of wit that makes him a respected public figure. I knew he would be able to see both sides of the problem, so his advice was important.

Early on the evening of the 26th, Peter came over to talk to me personally about the documentary. I explained my problems, and he was quick to tell me that first he would give me advice as a friend and second as a businessman. Peter wanted to put the needs of my family first.

I shared the photos and videotape with him so that he could see firsthand what had happened. Peter agreed that the delay in shooting the documentary was a good idea, and we said we'd talk it over again the following Monday.

Later I was preparing to take a shower as the family was settling down for the night. My thoughts were still tossing back and forth on what to do next. Maybe the pain in my head during the "torment on the road" event had been the removal of the telepathy. Maybe it was over. Maybe I could have a normal life again. As I soaped down, I let the hot water spray over my back and neck and prayed that it was over.

Frances banged on the door. "Ed, it's here, it's here, hurry."

I froze, and my heart throbbed. "No, come on, no way!" I yelled.

Out of the shower and through the bathroom I ran naked. I grabbed a towel as I went through the door into the bedroom. I was dripping wet and really mad. How could this be happening? When I reached the kitchen, Frances was squatting at the edge of the open door.

"Look out, there it is. Get down."

I could see the UFO moving slowly from north to south toward the house across the open field. It was the smaller UFO with the transparent energy sheet that I had seen on January 16th. No hum, and the dog was barking like crazy.

Damn it. It was back. Why? Why do this to me? I walked straight past Frances through the door and stepped out onto the pool deck. I yelled at the UFO, which was one hundred feet or so from our back fence.

"What the hell do you want?"

There was a rush of air in my head.

"Zehaas . . . We are here for you."

"Damn it, land or get the hell out of my life!" I yelled, out of control.

It was cold out, and I was almost naked, but I didn't feel anything but anger. I raised my hands and said, "If you want me, then let's get it over."

"Zehaas . . . in sleep you know . . . we are here for you."

"Bullshit! I'm not going anywhere with you." I raised my voice even louder. "Go torment somebody else."

"Zehaas . . . sleep and know."

Instantly the craft winked out. It was gone, and I stood there. Suddenly I was cold.

JANUARY 26, 1988—FRANCES'S ACCOUNT

Just before dark Crystal started barking. I stepped outside to see what was wrong. A man was walking around on the back field. In the poor light I couldn't see who he was, but there was a silver van like Bob Reid's parked on the outdoor basketball court, and I decided that that was him on the field.

I slipped back inside before he saw me, afraid he might want to come over and talk. I was just so tired of it all. Sometimes I felt as if we were under siege, and not just from the UFO. The MUFON people with their walkie-talkies and surveillance made me feel as if we were being watched all the time. Lately the phone had been "clicking." Don Ware said it could be bugged.

Peter Neumann was in the office with Ed when I went in to tell him about Bob. Ed said something about the investigators looking for a landing site. As I walked into the office, Peter had been telling Ed he would give advice on the documentary first as a friend, then as a newsman. I felt that we could trust Peter, and it was a relief to have someone like him to advise us about this. MUFON kept putting pressure on Ed to give them pictures, statements, everything. I knew they had a job to do and were interested in proving the authenticity of the photos and sightings, but they kept forgetting how emotionally wrenching this was.

We had tried to maintain as normal a life as possible for Dan and Laura's sake. But it wasn't easy, and having the investigators in and out of the house all the time didn't help. More than anything, I hoped and prayed we had seen the UFO for the last time.

The two men continued to talk in Ed's office on into dinnertime, so I fed Dan and Laura and told them to finish their homework. I waited to eat with Ed once Peter had gone. As we ate our reheated meal, Ed told me about putting off the documentary. I was surprised at how relieved I felt. So far this experience hadn't received that much news coverage, but a half-hour prime-time, even if it was only local, was something entirely different. I wanted us to be sure we knew just what we would be letting ourselves in for before we said yes.

After dinner Ed went back to his office. I fed the animals, cleaned the kitchen, and went to the living room to read for a while before bedtime.

Around 9:30 Ed walked through, saying he was going to take his shower. I told him I would read a little longer, then get ready for bed myself. A few minutes later Crystal started barking. It wasn't her panicky bark, just her nuisance bark.

I got up to go quiet her. Stepping through the back door, I looked up and saw the smaller, second-type UFO. It was low over the back field, to the northeast. My heart racing, I ran to tell Ed. He was already in the shower. I pounded on the door and shouted that "they" were back and to come quickly.

Ed yelled back. Sure that he heard me, I dashed out of the bathroom. Seeing Ed's camera on the dresser, I grabbed it and ran back to the kitchen door. The UFO was still there. I opened the door but was afraid to go out. I didn't even like to stand in the doorway, so I squatted down, thinking I would be a smaller target.

Crystal kept looking back and forth from the UFO to me. Bracing myself against the doorframe, I snapped a photo (22). The flash startled me and set the dog to barking again. She ran over to where I huddled, just inside the door.

Ed came into the kitchen, a towel wrapped around his waist. He said something about he had "had it and this has to end," as he started through the door.

"Don't go out there!"

"I just can't take this anymore. I want it over." He stepped past me, brushing the dog aside, and strode out onto the pool deck.

While I watched in horror, Ed just stood there, facing the UFO. The craft moved closer to him, then stopped and just hovered. No beams. No anything. Ed shouted at the craft, then raised his hands as if daring it do something. Not knowing what the UFO might do, I quickly took another photo (23). After a few more seconds the UFO shot straight up and disappeared, at least I guess that's what it did. It was just suddenly gone.

Ed came back inside, and we held each other, trying to figure out what exactly it was the UFO wanted. Sometimes they seemed intent on abducting him. Yet when given the chance, they didn't. What were these cryptic messages? What would Ed know in his sleep? Was it something they thought would make him less resistant, perhaps even eager to go with them?

The occupants of the UFO were obviously capable of communicating with Ed. Why didn't they just come right out and say what they wanted? Ed might not have agreed, but at least we would have understood why they were doing this to him.

FEBRUARY 1, 1988—WEAR-TV 3 DOCUMENTARY

WEAR-TV 3 was ready to start on a detailed accounting of the sightings and related events. They only needed me and the photographs to begin the work on the half-hour documentary. The news director, Peter Neumann, had assigned the project to an investigative team. They would prepare the documentary, as well as brief introductory reports to be shown on the evening newscasts one week before the documentary aired.

On the way to the studio with the photos in hand, I was nervous about the possible exposure of my family. The documentary was a super way to let the public know what was happening in the sky over our heads, but it could backfire on my family and me. Peter insisted that I would have veto power over any material I was uncomfortable with. Had he not been there with his steady professional assurance, I would never have agreed to the program.

When I arrived, the camera crew was ready to start shooting video of the Polaroid pictures. Their excellent equipment made the UFO show up clearly. I stood at the door watching the work proceed and after the first hour realized that this might take all day. The camera crew carefully mounted each photograph on a black background and took several timed exposures along with a closeup exposure.

Since I didn't intend to appear on camera, I made a point of talking with the reporting team so that they could get a firsthand feel for what had happened and was still going on. WEAR reporter Hope Buffington had been reading about the UFO phenomena in general and was very excited to see the original photographs.

She related the huge number of phone calls the station had received after their first broadcast of the November 11th event. WEAR reporter Mark Curtis also told me of other reports of people seeing the UFO. I made a mental note to follow up on those reports.

My agreement with WEAR allowed the release of the documentary to other ABC affiliates, thereby spreading the word. These other stations would have the option to air the news segments. The half-hour show was also made available for ABC network use. This wasn't a money deal; this was just news, and I felt I was doing the right thing treating it as such. The general public needed to know what was flying around in the sky. The only thing I asked to receive in return for helping with the program were copies of the tape.

The steady work continued into the afternoon. Soon it was time to work with the December 28th video I had taken of the UFO flying back and forth to the east of my house. Everybody was anxious to view the tape and use their transfer and enlarging equipment to study the UFO.

The video equipment studio was cleared of nonessential personnel; only the five technicians, the reporting team, and I remained. First they played the tape as I had shot it—just plugged it in and watched the screen as the UFO hovered across the sky. The craft traveled from right to left, occasionally stopping and going back a little to the right before it would continue left again. Clearly visible in the foreground was the bush I had hidden behind. Toward the extreme left, as I followed the craft with the camera, the UFO passed behind a pine tree, then disappeared from view.

The room was silent as people stared at the screen. This was what they had really wanted to see, the UFO clearly moving across the sky. Even though it was shot at night, the craft was there and everybody was stunned. They played the one-minute thirty-eight-second tape again and again. Each time they watched the tape they would blurt out comments like, "Look how fast it moves," or "No sound from the UFO, but you can hear the wind in the trees and a train whistle in the distance."

The last forty seconds of the tape showed the UFO moving from left to right, but with only the glow of the bottom "power source" and the lighted top "dome light." In this darkened form, it was easy to see how the UFO could fly in the night sky unnoticed if it chose to. In this guise the craft could easily hover over the bay or sound with nobody paying any attention. As everyone studied this darkened look of the UFO, it continued across the screen, and then, as the camera stayed on, the UFO just winked out.

The technicians promptly made a three-quarter-inch tape. They then increased that to a one-inch tape, on which they could show much more detail by slowing it down. The equipment they had could slow the motion down to one-sixtieth of a second. The sight of the UFO in slow motion, especially with its color enhanced, brought a startling discovery that everybody in the room watched over and over: Beneath the UFO the glow of the power source showed a pulsating leading edge that seemed to be spinning around and around. Some of the comments were "Oh, my god, look at that" and "What kind of energy could that be?" Seeing is believing, and nobody questioned what they saw.

The details of the UFO, exposed by their technical equipment, pleased and surprised me. Some of the details I had seen before, but they hadn't shown in the photographs until they were enhanced. But the apparent rotation of the energy ring had been invisible to the naked eye, and its discovery fascinated me as much as it did everyone else.

The WEAR investigative team devoted weeks of research to presenting an evenhanded report. Mark Curtis was the principal on-the-air reporter. Here are some brief comments by Mark as reported in the *Sentinel:*

> "I think it is the most fantastic story I've worked on," he said. "It is so unusual. This kind of thing usually happens in someone else's backyard, not your own.
>
> "I have devoted a lot of time to this story, by the sheer number of calls alone." Mark receives between thirty to fifty calls a week concerning the UFOs, from people reporting sightings to skeptics and people who are just plain interested.
>
> He went on to say there are very similar pictures and accounts of UFO sightings from Georgia, California, and Australia. "Pictures of a small round craft with small round windows," he said. "There have been calls about a big ship, earlier on. Primarily people have seen the smaller crafts."
>
> As far as "Ed's" experiences are concerned, which have been reported on by the *Sentinel* many times, Curtis says they are very consistent with other accounts.
>
> Curtis and his co-workers have spent hundreds of hours researching and investigating this story, and he has become increasingly curious. Sightings are still being reported.
>
> Curtis is excited about being a part of what experts say are the most well-documented UFO sightings of all time. He will be a part of history and part of a news story that is quickly spreading across the nation.

FEBRUARY 4, 1988—POSSIBLE LANDING SITE

Day after day was now dominated by various UFO-related events and meetings. The "landing site" investigators wanted to review the photographs again to bring themselves and new members up-to-date. Budd Hopkins was due in town on Monday, and an editor from a book publisher was about to arrive. I had received several letters from authors, addressed to me through the *Sentinel,* asking if they could write my story. I was just trying to deal with all the confusion one day at a time.

There was very little time to think about a book, but apparently a book would have to be considered. The MUFON investigators were among the first to mention it, and they thought it was a great idea. What better way was there to tell the complete, accurate story? The out-of-town newspaper coverage was being poorly handled. There was much too much emphasis on the sensational angle, such as the blue beam. Inaccurate, or outright false, information would be printed by one paper then picked up and reprinted by another as the truth.

Frances and I discussed the book idea, trying to see it from all sides. The ramifications of a book were many. First and foremost, I would have to give up my anonymity. There was no other way to do it right. Neither of us was sure we wanted to take that step.

The investigators had warned us that once our identity was known, UFO enthusiasts could become a problem. If we wrote a book, we would be leaving ourselves open to a real invasion of our privacy. Even though we wanted the story told, and told accurately, we weren't positive we were ready to make that sacrifice, no matter how much it might help the UFO investigators.

172

Telling the story, the *whole* story, was something else we had to think about. We didn't know where this would take us before it was all over, but things the investigators had said made us wonder if there wasn't more for us to consider besides the current events. They had hinted at possible past events that had been blocked from my memory. I didn't know if I agreed with them, and I wasn't sure I wanted to try to find out, but it was something we had to think about if a book were to be given serious consideration.

Later that night Frances and I reflected on a part of the January 24th event in which the UFO voice had said, "In sleep you know."

The ramifications of that simple, cryptic statement, when coming from a UFO via telepathy, were very hard to handle. The insinuation was clear. Somehow in my sleep I would know something. I suspected that this message had some connection with the way I had learned to sleep, the way I could, within a few minutes, become completely relaxed and fall asleep.

Many years ago I learned I could relax my whole body by thinking of a dark cloud first touching my feet and gradually moving up my body. As it moved, very slowly, each part of me would relax until the dark cloud reached my head and my brain faded into sleep.

Through the years I had felt my conscious mind succumb to the dark cloud and I began to shortcut the routine of following the cloud up from my toes. Just before falling asleep, I would think a peaceful thought, and soon I had conditioned myself to fall asleep quickly just by thinking the same thought.

As the years passed, I began to think two words just before going to sleep. They could have been any two words. I chose ones that I liked, the idea being that my mind and body were conditioned to relax and sleep at the mention of these two words. If I happened to be unusually anxious, worried or ill, my "sleep words" seemed to brighten my spirits the next morning.

Frances and I continued to seek an answer, trying to find any link between the UFO message and my sleep habits. The next observation was my memory recall in the mornings. Just before saying my sleep words at night, I sometimes concentrated on an important unanswered question or some problem. In the morning I would awaken with a clear understanding of how to resolve whatever had been on my mind the night before.

There have been times when I have solved problems beyond my normal ability, and I attribute that success to letting my subconscious recall the solutions hidden from my conscious mind. That old saying used when somebody has a problem or a decision to make, "Let me sleep on that," certainly works for me.

This sleep method of mine is quite likely a form of self-hypnotism, and I don't claim that it is anything extraordinary. I'm sure most people could do this if they wanted to and had the patience to condition themselves to begin to relax and sleep this way.

The UFO message "In sleep you know" seemed somehow to tie together with my ability to recall information from my subconscious.

The investigators suggested I use my sleep words method to uncover any information about the UFO locked in my mind. I was reluctant, even skeptical, because I doubted there was any information to be gained. However, I tried. To my surprise, my memory released a few puzzling phrases.

Now my curiosity was piqued. Was there more? My personal need to know forced me to pursue that possibility. I made many attempts to recall other UFO memories by using my sleep words. More enigmatic phrases were the result. I kept a complete log of these "in sleep you know" memories for future study, hoping one day to find answers to the questions they raised.

The investigators advised me that the technique of regressive hypnotism could possibly answer some questions. They urged me to meet with Budd Hopkins, who was coming to town on the following Monday.

Mr. Hopkins, the best-selling author of *Missing Time* and *Intruders,* had gained recognition as the leading expert on the phenomena of UFO abduction. His use of regressive hypnosis with possible abductees had many times unlocked events hidden in their subconscious memories.

I knew nothing about abduction case studies, nor had I read either of Mr. Hopkins's books, but the investigators felt that I should meet him. Apparently they had strong suspicions that during some of my sighting incidents I might have been abducted.

After talking it over with Frances, I decided I would meet with Mr. Hopkins, hoping he could help me understand what this UFO was doing and why me, but I was uncertain about being hypnotized, especially with the sightings continuing. My mind was so occupied with the daily fight to keep my family safe, I could think of little else.

FEBRUARY 4, 1988—FRANCES'S ACCOUNT

Although there hadn't been another sighting, the week since I had taken the two photos on the 26th of January had been anything but dull. Dan's last college application was finally completed and mailed. Laura's science fair project no longer occupied half of one kitchen counter. With that, and the college materials gone, we had a whole breakfast bar again.

The morning Ed had gone to TV 3 to begin work on the documentary, I had some PTA business at the school and couldn't go with him. He had come home telling me all about what they had seen when the video was shown in slow motion. Not only did the bottom light seemed to rotate, but it was obvious that the UFO hadn't gone up, it had winked out. I wished I had been able to be there with him to see it.

We slept late the morning of February 3rd and so missed the excitement when MUFON had an investigator dressed in a radiation suit out in the back field. He had a Geiger counter and was testing the "landing site." The verdict was "No radiation."

I was pleased about that, since Ed and I had been over there on January 27th taking photos with a borrowed 35mm camera. Ed had had me stand in the middle of the circle to be a size comparison. It was bitingly cold, and I had wanted to hurry back into the house to get out of the wind. I never once gave any thought to the possibility that the ground I was standing on might be radioactive. It wasn't the type of thing that I was accustomed to having to worry about.

All we had wanted when this started was to warn our neighbors about the UFO and find out if anyone else had seen it. Now we were being asked to give serious consideration to doing a book about what we had been, and still were, going through. The idea came as a surprise and I wasn't sure we wanted to come forward in that kind of forum telling all that had happened. But it seemed it was a proposition we would have to think about.

The times that Ed and I had where we could just sit and talk had grown more and more infrequent. When we did have a few moments, we seemed always to find ourselves mulling over questions about the UFO. I missed our old discussions about what we would do one day when both our children were in college—our often fanciful plans to travel and see the world. The events since November 11th had already changed the present. How would it change our future?

FEBRUARY 7, 1988—FIFTEENTH SIGHTING—BLUE BEAM AND FRANCES

On Sunday morning, February 7th, Duane and Dari came over so that I could see what Duane had written for the next edition of the *Sentinel*. Neither he nor I had disclosed any information, except to MUFON, about the January 24th event, when I had been tormented in the road. The videotape taken of me shooting the photograph of the UFO made this sighting especially important.

Now Duane planned to go public with the story. His article was surely going to rock the town to its roots. The spectacular nature of the event would shock most of the newspaper's readers, but Duane wanted to tell what had happened, and I agreed.

I read over his accounting and concurred that what he reported was detailed and correct. Then we talked about the "in sleep you know" message from the UFO. We still couldn't completely figure that out and wondered when and if the UFO would return.

By studying the times and days that the UFO had shown itself it became obvious that there was no pattern. The days between the sightings were random, and every method I used to calculate a possible return seemed to be farfetched. The shortest time between return visits was one day, and the longest was twelve days.

It had been twelve days since the last sighting, and I mentioned that that had been the longest time between sightings so far. We all nervously smiled and said that tonight would be the night, but no one was really serious.

The rest of the day involved visits by an investigative team to further study the "landing site." They had gotten permission from the county

176

school board to take soil and grass samples from the area. I went to the field with them, and they promised to give me a copy of the analysis results. The report by Max E. Griggs, extension agent, and the University of Florida were later forwarded to me.

That report studied the possibility of physical (for example, lightning), chemical, or biological causes that might kill Bermuda grass. Tests were conducted on the soil that eliminated many possibilities. The geometrically perfect form of the circle was also taken into account. A general conclusion was reached that toxic chemicals or exposure to an energy source, requiring mechanical precision, had killed the grass. The complete report is included in Appendix 2.

That set of investigators had gone, but others had called throughout the day. Most of my daytime hours were overrun by UFO reports and questions, and my nights were spent on guard for any sound out of the ordinary. The house construction plans and drawings to finalize were piling up. I had to struggle to find time to work.

On this February 7th, I had been in my office since dinner, totally concentrating on my drawing board. The family was quiet. I could hear the TV in the kitchen where my daughter was finishing some homework. Suddenly she yelled, "Daddy, Mommy's calling you." Again, she called, her voice animated. "Hurry, Daddy. Mommy wants you."

My first thought was that Frances had seen the UFO. I jumped up from my desk, and as I ran out of my office, grabbed the Polaroid, which was ready with film and flash. I expected to see both Frances and Laura in the kitchen as I turned the corner from the living room. Laura had opened the kitchen door and was standing three or four feet inside looking out.

I quickly said, "Where's Mommy?"

Laura looked out the door and started to point. I stepped in front of her and saw Frances running at full speed from the steps near the swimming pool toward the kitchen door. She was yelling.

"Watch out, watch out! It's back there."

Her eyes were open wide and her hair flew wildly back and forth as she ran. A few seconds had passed, and I started out the door with an eye on the sky behind her. There was nothing there in my field of vision but a clear, starlit night. I could only see to the east with the house blocking my view of the south, the direction from which Frances was running.

This was all happening extremely fast. As I stepped even with the doorframe, a blue beam shot down at an angle across the door and hit the concrete pool deck at the bottom of the step. My reflexes made me jump back and raise the camera to my chest. I hit the trigger, and the flash went off as Frances dived into the house just to the right of the beam (photo 24).

The panic and terror was impossible to describe. I slammed the door behind Frances and pulled Laura to the floor, where Frances lay gasping for breath.

"Are you all right? Are you all right?" I asked in a loud whisper, pulling on Frances's arm.

Frances wheezed, "Get Laura. Where's Dannie? It's out there."

Most of the window blinds were open, and we were afraid to stand up. We were terrified that the beam would shoot through the uncovered windows. I crawled toward Dan's room and found him surrounded by homework, lying in bed undisturbed, his radio headset on. He hadn't seen or heard anything. But when he saw my face and I told him to get down on the floor with me, he was with me in a flash and ready to fight. He said, "We can't let that thing get away with this. That's Mom. Let it shoot at me. Let's do something."

Of course there was nothing we could do but stay down, out of sight. We sought refuge in the hallway to the master bedroom, the only place without a window. Huddled together, we debated what to do.

The small sounds in a house that are always there now sent chills of fear through my body. Laura, frightened by what she had seen, was holding me around the arm. Dan wanted to get up and fight back. He had less respect than the rest of us for the UFO—the bravery of youth.

After about five minutes of complete silence, trying to figure out what was there, if anything, I decided we should get in the van. We crowded to the door leading to the garage and one at a time crept into the van. We locked the doors and were ready to start up the van and back out of there if necessary.

In the darkness I could see the gleam of tears down Frances's face. All we could hear now was our own quiet breathing as we sat on the floor of the van and waited. At one point Dan wanted to sneak back inside and get the shotgun. I overruled that idea.

Realizing I still had the camera by the strap, I pulled the film and waited sixty seconds. In the dim light we couldn't see much of how the picture had turned out, but as we passed it around, at least we were talking and everybody seemed calmer.

About ten minutes had passed, and we had all begun to recover from the panic. Then I heard the hum. I was quiet and said nothing to alarm my family. Only a few seconds of hum, followed by the voice: "Do not deny us." A pause. "We are here." Followed by, "Remember."

I tried to act normal and listen to what Frances was whispering to Dan, but hearing the voice must have made me change expressions. Laura, sitting closest to me asked, "Daddy, what's wrong?"

"Nothing, sweetheart, I'm fine," I whispered.

Gradually we realized it was over and we started to stir. Dan and I decided to go back into the house and check it out. We didn't just want to walk into a group of little UFO guys waving silver rods, so we carefully checked each room, each closet, behind the furniture, and under my bed. No sign of anything.

For the rest of that night we stayed together. We talked for hours and finally, one by one, fell asleep on the sofa and beanbag chairs in the rec room.

FEBRUARY 7, 1988—8:30 P.M.— FRANCES'S ACCOUNT

We were awaiting a call from Budd Hopkins announcing his arrival in town, but it was after dinner and we hadn't heard from him. I was late feeding the animals and told Laura I would help her finish her homework after I fed the dog and cats.

As always, I fed the cats on the screened porch first, then went out through the laundry room to feed Crystal. She was impatient, pouncing at her food when I set the dish just under the edge of the porch. As I turned to go back up the steps into the house, a blue beam flashed down between me and the door, blocking me out. Leaves and bits of gravel swirled around and within the beam.

Terrified, I screamed for Ed, not knowing if he could hear me even though the door was slightly ajar. Looking up, I saw the glowing underside of the UFO, the beam emanating from somewhere outside the center ring. The sight of the beam, not the force of it, stunned me. I hesitated a moment before I turned and ran toward the pool steps, yelling for Ed as I ran. I pounded up the steps and saw the kitchen door standing open.

Camera in hand, Ed appeared in the doorway as I rounded the deck at the shallow end of the pool. Before he could step outside, a blue beam shot down to my right, blocking his exit. Intent on getting inside, I didn't slow my headlong dash. I didn't have time to think about what I was doing. I simply ran. Scrunched up, away from the beam, I darted past it into the house.

Ed slammed and locked the door behind me. After a quick exchange of words about the UFO, Ed went to get Dan. I sent Laura with her father. Then, on my hands and knees, I started checking the door locks. I crawled into the rec room and locked the French doors to the porch, then remembered that the laundry room door not only wasn't locked, it wasn't even closed.

Both the inside and the outside lights were on. I could see nothing out of the ordinary. Still, I didn't want to go to that door with its glass upper-half. Just on the other side of it was where the first beam had come down. I hesitated, my heart racing, fear making my palms cold and clammy.

"Get hold of yourself." I muttered encouragement to myself and crawled over the piles of dirty clothes I had sorted earlier in the day. Turning the passage lock, I shoved the door closed and clicked the dead bolt in place. The doors secured, I hurried back to join the others.

Once Ed decided the house wasn't the safest place to be, we quickly made the move to the van. Its close confines seemed to reassure us. Soon our silent panic gave way to nervous chatter. As we passed the photo around, I told them about the two beams.

Later Ed and Dan reentered the house. Laura and I sat and waited, our arms around each other, her head on my shoulder. Minutes passed before they returned with the welcome news that there were no creatures to be found and no evidence that they had been there. Apparently it was over.

Ensconced in the rec room for the rest of the night, we talked. I retold what had happened, this time with my latest thoughts on the subject. With time to think it over, I had come to the conclusion that the UFO hadn't tried to get me with the blue beam. I had been an open target from the time they shot the first beam until I ran through the kitchen door.

"If they had wanted me, they could have had me."

Ed didn't disagree with me: he just wondered, "If it wasn't taking you they were interested in, then what did they want?"

We concluded that they had wanted to make a point. But what was the point? Had they just been showing their power, or was there more to it?

I felt as if they were saying, "See, we could have taken her, but didn't." What I couldn't decide was why. Was it an attempt to convince Ed he could trust them? Or was it meant as a threat, a warning of what could happen if Ed didn't respond the way they wanted?

I voiced my opinions, knowing it was all speculation. Then Ed told us what he had heard in the van, and we realized there could be a connection. Maybe the UFO beings had decided Ed needed more than just the telepathic message to understand that they wanted him to do more than just photograph their crafts. The question was, what was it that they wanted him to do?

FEBRUARY 8, 1988—BUDD HOPKINS INTERVIEWS

Several times during the past week I had talked to Budd Hopkins by telephone at the suggestion of Don Ware. Budd, who lives in New York City, was scheduled to visit a family nearby in connection with the abduction cases he studies and reports. I was flattered that he planned to take time out of his business trip to come by and talk with me.

Upon his arrival Budd explained the theory behind the abduction phenomena. He withheld most of the details so as not to influence or confuse the details of the events unfolding in my life. The basics were all he gave me.

A typical abduction case usually starts with a UFO sighting, followed by a loss of memory during the abduction, and ending with little, if any, recall of the event other than finding yourself at the original point of abduction with several hours unaccountable. It is that telltale sign of missing time that often first alerts investigators that an abduction has taken place.

As much as I tried to recall some missing time, or a time when "something was wrong" but I didn't know what, I did not succeed. I was reasonably sure that I had not been abducted during any of the sightings starting with November 11, 1987. Prior to that date I had never really paid much attention to strange dreams, dreams that Budd now told me could be clues that indicate an abduction memory stored in the subconscious.

Budd still felt strongly that abduction was a possibility, so we carefully reviewed the facts of the sightings and tried to uncover any missing time. (As of this meeting, although my notes were good, I had not yet begun writing down the moment-by-moment details of every sighting incident. Months later, while writing the December 17, 1987, sighting I remembered many more details of that early-morning incident than I could remember while reviewing the sightings with Budd.)

The first sighting was at 5:05 P.M., soon after Frances had gone to the grocery store. I estimated that the event lasted only about eight minutes from the time I took the first picture until I lay on the roadway gasping for air. Frances returned only a minute or two later as I was gathering up the photographs from where they had fallen. Her trip had taken about fifteen minutes, and when we went into the house, the time schedule was normal. No missing time.

The second sighting had begun at about 4:55 P.M. Frances had gone with Laura to the football stadium and I was due to meet the high school band at about 5:30 P.M. to walk to the stadium with them. By the time the sighting was over, I was still about on time arriving at the band room. Again, no missing time, so no abduction.

The third sighting was late at night, 3:00 A.M. I went into the backyard with the gun and the camera, but the UFO showed itself for only a few minutes before winking out. Frances and I sat up and talked about it until almost 3:30. Shortly after 3:30 A.M. the creature arrived on the back porch. Again the event lasted only a few minutes before we witnessed the UFO disappear. This time we sat up the rest of the night and are sure that at no time were we blacked out and abducted.

At this time, talking with Budd and the other investigators, I believed that without exception there was no sighting that I suspected to have involved an abduction. Even the attack on the road with the five creatures beaming down and coming after me had happened quickly.

The national news had just been coming on when I left. By the time I returned home, the local evening news was still on the TV. With the attack at 5:45 P.M. and my arrival back home about 6:20, that allows thirty-five minutes to make the round-trip. The round-trip drive normally takes thirty minutes, leaving five minutes for the event. No missing time for an abduction.

On and on I remembered the events having no missing time. The conclusion was, if I had ever been abducted by the UFO, then it happened in my youth.

After Budd and the others left, Frances and I talked about the possibility of an abduction somewhere in my past. I thought about the three unusual occurrences at difference times of my life that I had rationalized away, with no thought of a UFO connection. All three involved missing time that I had accounted for in one way or another.

The first incident had happened when I was seventeen, and I had explained it as a bad dream. The second, when I was twenty-five, I had passed off as a hallucination due to lack of sleep. The third was when I was thirty-three, and I had justified it as a possible heatstroke.

Talking with Budd had opened our minds, and we recalled these events, seeing them in a different light. This new possibility of abduction was very unsettling. I decided to hold back on discussing this with anyone but my wife for a while. There was so much going on that I could not face the idea of deeper involvement with the UFO, especially on a recurring basis that spanned most of my life.

FEBRUARY 8, 1988—FRANCES'S ACCOUNT

Laura called as soon as she arrived at school to remind me I was supposed to be there to help with starfish dissections. I dressed in a hurry and rushed to the school, with no time to eat. I decided it was probably just as well. I had taken chemistry in order to avoid dissecting anything. This year I had already helped with earthworms, was about to do starfish, and still had frogs to face next month.

I arrived home after staying at school all day to find Ed's office full yet again. Budd Hopkins, Charles Flannigan, and Bob Reid had all been there since about 1:30. I apologized for not having been home when they arrived and sat down to listen to their conversation.

It didn't take long for them to bring me up-to-date. Then one of them asked me about the blue-beam incident of the night before. I recounted what had happened in the briefest terms possible, finding my heart once again racing as the events came back to me.

Mr. Hopkins seemed to sense my distress and turned the conversation to generalities of the cases he has worked on. His gentle, soft-spoken manner calmed me, and I felt I had found the key to his success with the abductees he studies: It appears that he genuinely cares about the people with whom he works.

I stayed in Ed's office for about an hour, fascinated by what Budd had to say and answering his questions about our experiences, then I had to excuse myself to help Laura with her homework and start dinner.

When the investigators started to leave, around 5:00, I took time to say good-bye. Budd promised to call in the morning after he had thought over all we had told him and had formed an opinion on how best to handle this.

After they left, Ed and I talked over some things from his past that had taken on new meaning after what we had learned during this meeting.

Chill bumps rose on my neck as I considered the possibility that Ed had been visited before. Though I wanted to disregard such thoughts, I couldn't. I clearly remembered the occasion he had complained about the five-hour loss of time on the canoe trip when he was thirty-three.

Even more vivid in my memory was the night when he was twenty-five. Perhaps it's because of my own fears that night that I recall it so well. It was the first night I had ever spent alone in my life. I've never forgotten the fear and worry I felt.

I didn't know Ed when he was seventeen, but that incident had still bothered him enough years later for him to tell me about it after we were married.

Whether Ed or I wanted to admit it, it seemed there might be more to these phenomena than we had previously thought.

FEBRUARY 10, 1988—MUFON FOUR-LENS NIMSLO CAMERA

There had been some past discussions with investigators about my old Polaroid camera. Since many of the pictures I had taken were very dark, I asked them about using a different camera that might give better results. They thought I should continue with the Polaroid and not change anything. Their conclusions had usually been based on the generally accepted idea that it would be very difficult to tamper with a Polaroid camera or its film.

As time passed and many of the sightings were occurring in the darkest night hours, the question again came up about using a 35mm. Bob Reid offered to lend me one of his 35mm cameras, but I had already borrowed one. I had been told the best film to use was a fast one, like ASA 1000, especially designed for night shooting. I had the camera but not the film the night of January 26th, when Frances took photos 22 and 23.

Before I had a chance to try using the 35mm, Bob came by my house about 8:00 the evening of February 10th with his son. He had been given a special "MUFON camera" by Don Ware to bring to me. Their hope was that I could photograph the UFO with this new camera. And what a camera it was. It came with two pages of instructions and rules.

As Bob Reid explained to me from the instructions, "The camera is special in that four frames are exposed at the same time, allowing for more than one almost identical negative. This allows us to preserve at least one negative intact, undisturbed, while the other negatives can be used for reproduction and analysis by different laboratories at the same time. In addition, the details provided by this camera will yield more information than can be gained from normal cameras.

186

"The camera is sealed to reassure the security and integrity of the exposed film. If you do expose the film of this camera to the UFO phenomena, it will be handled by at least two people throughout the process of removing the film, developing the negatives, and secure storage of the negatives. The camera and negatives will remain in two-man control, with signatures for any transfer, until such time as all analysis is complete."

The camera, a Nimslo 3D, was very official and very MUFON controlled. Not only was it sealed, but a picture had already been taken to serve as a control. In the event that somebody tried to remove the film, doctor it, and reload it, the sprockets would not line up.

The camera had four lenses, which I guessed were all set a certain way to better catch the UFO for verification and study of the negatives. The lenses were also fixed, to eliminate the photographer having any control. All that was necessary was to aim and shoot.

I welcomed the camera as Bob Reid explained it to me. If I could catch a shot of the UFO with their camera and have them develop the film, that should resolve the questions and we would have the proof many people had sought for years. At the time I didn't understand the pressure inherent with my willing acceptance of the camera.

The first time I realized the problem was when I read a MUFON statement insinuating that if I did not take a picture with this special camera, it would reflect on the credibility of the case. In other words, I had to hope the UFO would come back so that I could photograph it, thereby supporting the other photos, or I might be criticized for "non-photography."

I faced a dilemma. I had been hoping the UFO would get out of my life. Now I had to pray that it would return for at least one more photograph.

As the days and nights passed with no hum and no sighting, I began to worry. Maybe the UFO had gone, at least for me. There were other sightings being reported around town, but I saw nothing. I carried the MUFON camera with me everywhere and began to hate it. I resented the pressure this camera put on me.

There was pressure coming at me from every corner. A book publisher was trying to get me to agree to a ghostwriter who would come stay with our family. That's all I needed. I finally stopped returning their calls. Other people wanted to have the right to sell the photographs to various magazines. There was no way to know what was best, so I developed the policy of just saying, "No. At this time I'm not interested."

I still had to deal with the agreement Duane Cook had negotiated with the *National Enquirer*. In the beginning Duane had control over the first five photos and he had obligated an option for one-time use in the *Enquirer*. By now we all agreed that publishing them in the *Enquirer* was not desirable. Since the newspaper now seemed to want more than just the first five photos, I stalled, waiting for their option to expire, which it did. That was a spark of good news during that intense time.

Later in the week Charles Flannigan came by the house to arrange an appointment for the well-known physicist Dr. Bruce Maccabee to begin an extensive study of the photos. We also discussed the possibility of a CATscan and a polygraph test.

There was some suspicion that I had an implant in my body, placed there during an abduction. The hum in my right forehead was the cause of this speculation. I knew nothing about how a CATscan worked, but I knew that if it involved shooting dye into my bloodstream, then I was not interested. I left the subject open if the CATscan was something more like an X ray. But I still worried that if there was an implant found in my body, somebody would want to take it out. Sorry, no thanks.

When we discussed the polygraph test, I was insulted. The catch-22 with a polygraph is, if you refuse to take one, then you are assumed to be lying. The reason Charles gave for asking me to take the test was to silence any critics who would be quick to ask, "Well, has Mr. Ed taken a lie detector test?" I knew I was telling the truth, but I wasn't confident that the test would tell the truth. This was a big decision, and I told Charles that I would think about it.

There were more interviews scheduled throughout the week, all of which I allowed as long as my name was withheld. One reporter from the *Orlando Sentinel* occupied many hours of my time over several days, but in doing so managed to get the story almost correct. Again this demonstrated the necessity of my writing the story exactly as it had happened. The newspaper and magazine articles just could not get the facts 100 percent right.

FEBRUARY 18, 1988—POLYGRAPH EXAMINATION

had called Harvey McLaughlin, Jr., a well-known polygraph examiner, the night before to ask for an appointment. I was reluctant to tell him the details over the phone and only requested that we meet. All this must have sounded very mysterious to Mr. McLaughlin, and he hesitantly set up a time to meet at his office.

At 3:00 P.M. Mr. McLaughlin shook my hand and greeted me with an obvious level of suspicion. I sat down in the square, rigid examination chair, which has a certain resemblance to an electric chair, and asked Mr. McLaughlin if he had been reading the newspaper reports on the Gulf Breeze UFO?

He looked at me as if I were wasting his time and answered, "No. I have no interest and haven't read about any UFOs."

My heart sank. This man was certainly going to ask me to leave unless I could quickly assure that I wanted to hire his professional services. I handed my photo album of UFO photos to him while explaining that the implications of not taking a polygraph test could be detrimental to the credibility of the sightings and events I had experienced.

He asked me a few questions, but I wasn't sure he was convinced I was on the level. Maybe that was the attitude required of an examiner in his line of work. While explaining the blue beam and the visitor on the back porch, I imagined I could almost read his thoughts. *Sure, sure, and I'm the man in the moon.*

For two hours I reviewed the UFO incidents. The preinterrogation involved a lot of personal questions about my past. Mr. McLaughlin was persistent, repeating questions over and over again until every drop of information was squeezed from me. I couldn't believe that I was paying somebody to do this to me—payment that had been made in advance, I'm sure, so as to guarantee an unbiased examination. If the examinee didn't like the results, too bad, it was already paid for.

The procedure was intimidating, but I had gone this far and I didn't want to back out. I wanted to eliminate the innuendos in, "Well, has Ed taken a lie detector test?" We proceeded with the interview part of the examination until he was ready to administer a few tests.

Test after test, each test was repeated several times. This was *not* what I had envisioned. How wrong I had been to think I would be in and out of his office in half an hour. Three hours after I arrived, Mr. McLaughlin walked me to the door and told me to call and set up another appointment.

I expected that I would receive the results then. Later I discovered that McLaughlin had wanted to confer with some of my references and had also wanted to ask the MUFON investigators what particular questions they wanted to have answered.

Four days later, on February 23rd, I was notified that Mr. McLaughlin wanted me to come to his office. To my shock we started from the beginning again, with more direct questions. I found myself explaining my life history and reliving the UFO sightings one by one in the most specific detail. Once again strapped to the equipment, the test started. No talking. Simply yes or no. No moving. Look at one place on the wall and answer the emotionless questions put to me by an examiner determined to get to the truth.

Another three hours passed, I was unstrapped and excused. I would be notified of the results in the mail. I was sure I had passed but admit in all candor that the polygraph test was most disturbing. I had no doubt a guilty person would have no chance of lying to Harvey McLaughlin. My consolation was knowing I had told the truth.

Here are the exact results of the polygraph, which I later received:

March 1, 1988

Client: Edward Daniel Walters
Type of Examination: Specific Issue

Examinee: Edward Daniel Walters

Date/Place of Examination

This examination was conducted on February 18 & 23, 1988, in Pensacola, Florida.

Purpose of Examination:
To verify the authenticity of photographs, personal sightings, experiences, and general information supplied by Mr. Walters concerning his experiences with UFOs since November 1987.

Pre-test Interview:
Prior to the examination, an agreement granting permission for the examination was signed by the examinee and an explanation of the polygraph instrument was made by the examiner. Each question to be asked was thoroughly reviewed with the examinee prior to actual testing.

During the pre-test interview the examinee furnished the following information concerning his employment with the above-named organization.

1. On both testing dates the subject is thoroughly interviewed concerning his multiple sightings of unidentified flying objects in and around his residence in the Gulf Breeze community. He claims numerous sightings by himself since November 1987.

2. The subject presents approximately 20–25 photographs of various flying objects in different locations that are of an unknown origin. He claims there may have been humanoid beings that were seen, unusual lights emitted from these structures, and some type of physical contact made with these craft.

3. During the approximately 5–6 hours of pre-test interviewing the subject sincerely presents this information and states that it is his desire only to aid in the verification of this information that he is taking this exam. He claims to desire no personal gain or remuneration from these sightings.

Polygraph Examination:
Following two separate multiple chart specific issue examinations there were no specific physiological reactions of a deceptive nature noted to any of the reviewed test questions. General areas of questioning followed as: "Did you lie or falsify the information you have furnished me concerning the UFOs you have seen?" "Did you in any way falsify or lie about the photographs you have presented concerning these UFOs?" "Did you in any way falsify

or lie about the humanoid beings that you saw or any other physical evidence that you have presented?'' With the information that is present at this time, furnished by the examinee, no consistent deceptive responses are seen.

Opinion(s):
   With the information that is available to this examiner at this time it is felt that Mr. Walters truly believes that the photographs and personal sightings he has described are true and factual to the best of his ability.
   Approved:
   (Signature)
   Harvey W. McLaughlin, Jr.
   Examiner

FEBRUARY 18, 1988—FRANCES'S ACCOUNT

It was more than a week since Bob Reid had brought the special 3D camera to us. What should have been relief that the UFO was leaving us alone, that it had possibly even gone, had turned into anxious nights as we approached the record of twelve days since the blue-beam incident and there was still no sighting. We were haunted by the fear that failure to use the camera would be used by some as proof that the UFO didn't exist.

   It rained off and on all day. The damp chill didn't help my spirits any while I waited for Ed to return from taking the lie detector test. He hadn't known what to expect and was gone much longer than he had thought he would be. I had already fed the children by the time he came home. While I reheated his dinner, Ed told me what he had gone through and that the examiner wanted him to come back again.

   Seeing Ed tired and frustrated made me angry. Angry at the UFO for coming into our lives in the first place, and angry at the investigators for making things even harder on Ed. What right did they have to tell him to take a lie detector test, and have a CATscan, and be hypnotized? On top of that, they expected him to take photos of the UFO with their camera, as if he could command the craft to appear for a photo session.

   Ed calmed me down and, in doing so, calmed himself as well. I brought him up-to-date on what I heard about the UFO reports that

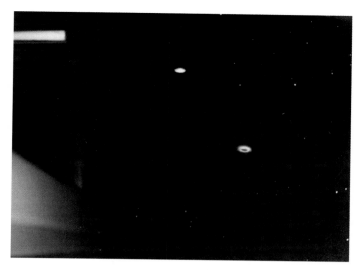

Photo 20

Photo 20, light-blasted and enhanced for detail

At one o'clock on the morning of January 16, 1988, Frances watched from the front door as I stood in the yard, searching for any movement in the sky. I knew the UFO was there somewhere. Suddenly, a red glow that looked about the size of a star grew larger as it dropped from the sky. Hovering about two hundred feet from me, it was very different from the others that I had photographed. A red transparent veil of energy whirled beneath it, and within seconds another UFO appeared.

Photo 21

Photo 21, light-blasted and enhanced for detail

By January 24, 1988, I was desperate for the encounters to end and encouraged investigators to set up a dusk-to-dawn surveillance operation. Through radio communication, I could call for immediate help if needed. I took this photo during a forty-five-minute incident that was video-recorded by Duane Cook, the *Sentinel* newspaper publisher.

Photo 22

Photo 22, light-blasted and enhanced for detail

On January 26, 1988, my hopes for an end were dashed when the smaller UFO with the red veil hovered low across the field behind my house. While I was in the shower, Frances took this photo. Our dog barked and looked back and forth from her to the UFO. A voice from the UFO said, ''Zehaas, sleep and know.''

Photo 23

Photo 23, light-blasted and enhanced for detail

Angry and upset, I ran past Frances and outside to confront the UFO. I wanted it all to stop, just to go away. I yelled at the UFO to "land or get the hell away!"

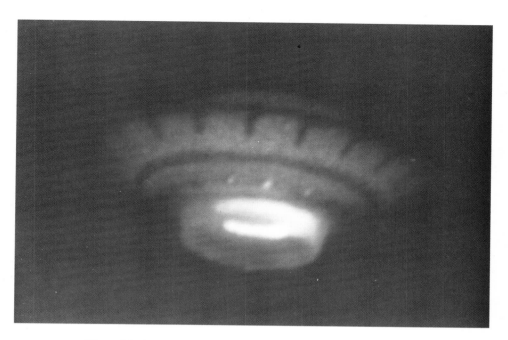

Photo 23, light-blasted and enhanced for detail, enlargement

Photo 24, light-blasted and enhanced for detail

Twelve days later, on February 7, the UFO displayed its blue beam again. Frances was caught outside and just managed to dodge the beam as she ran inside through the kitchen door and fell on the floor. With no time to aim the camera, I snapped the shutter and caught photo 24.

Daytime photograph of possible landing site

This circle of dead grass in the field behind my house is thought to be the location where a UFO may have landed. It is twelve feet in diameter, approximately the same as the UFO. Detailed soil tests could not explain why the grass died.

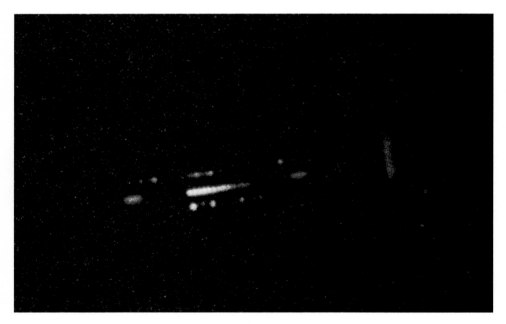

Photos 25–34, light-blasted and enhanced for detail, enlargements

I had been asked to use the four-lens Nimslo camera during a sighting if possible. It was sealed and test shots taken to ensure that it would be impossible to tamper with the film. On February 26, 1988, I shot ten photos of an object that seemed to be huge and far away. Frances disagreed, insisting that the object was close and therefore small. She was right. The object has been called a probe by UFO investigators, and was only approximately three feet long. Photos 25–34 all show the same array of lights.

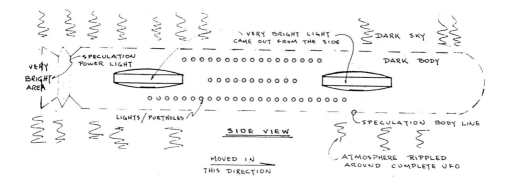

This is my drawing of the February 26 "probe" UFO. It was approximately thirty-six inches long and also appeared in a future sighting.

This is the sealed, four-lens, 3-D camera that I used to take ten photos of the "probe" craft, also known as the Nimslo craft.

Photo 35

Photo 35, light-blasted and enhanced for detail

I had purchased a new Sun 600 Polaroid camera the day before this March 8, 1988, sighting. I sent the original of this photo directly to Dr. Maccabee, who said, "The combination of the well-formed image of the UFO with the faint streaks suggests the object streaked upward just before the shutter closed in one third of a second. The UFO was about 264 feet away and the speed of ascent would have to be between 40 and 150 G's." This was the second photo in which I caught the UFO streaking away.

continued to stream into the offices of MUFON, ABC local news, and our weekly newspaper. Some of the reports were of IFOs (identified flying objects), but many of the reports seemed similar to Ed's sightings.

The *Sentinel* had come in the afternoon mail while he was gone, and I asked if he wanted to read it. The reports in the paper were from people testifying to having truly seen strange objects in the sky. The reports had been made in person, and those who withheld their identities from publication were known to the reporter. This is what the *Sentinel* reported:

On November 24, of 1987, around 7:30 P.M., a Villa Venyce woman was returning from Pensacola with her 11-year-old daughter and 15-year-old son. As they drove down Highway 98 through the Naval Live Oaks area, the woman spotted a lighted craft in the air across from the Santa Rosa State Bank. She teased her teenage son, saying, "Look, it's a UFO!"

As they got closer they were surprised at the strange shape of the craft and the red and white lights that seemed to be spinning around. They drove into the bank parking and rolled down their windows to watch the craft.

The craft seemed to be about 100 yards off the ground, possibly over the bay. (There are woods and a few houses between the highway and the bay.) It appeared that the whole craft was spinning around while at the same time hovering steadily and silently.

At this time they were beginning to believe it was a space craft of some kind. Then they saw a "red ball of light" drop out of the craft straight toward the ground, make an abrupt 90 degree turn, then another 90 degree turn toward the sky, straight up until it disappeared into the stars.

Several minutes had passed when they decided to rush home and get binoculars. By the time they were able to get back outside the craft was gone.

The 15-year-old immediately drew a picture of the craft to show to his father, a retired Air Force officer. The woman described the craft as looking like the Space Needle in Seattle, Washington.

On Friday, February 12, at 6:12 P.M., the same family along with another 13-year-old boy were leaving Villa Venyce for Gulf Breeze when they spotted the same craft moving west along the highway over the bay. Again it was about 100 yards high and they had a "perfect view."

The UFO seemed to move along the highway at about the same rate of speed as the car. There were the same red and white lights. The craft appeared to be spinning.

Twice the UFO lurched forward leaving a "streak of white light."

As they neared Shoreline Drive, the UFO veered off and disappeared over the bay.

Other sightings were also reported during this time, and they are included in Appendix 2.

FEBRUARY 19, 1988—ENCOUNTER WITH COPYCAT

It was about two weeks before the airing of the WEAR-TV 3 documentary, and already the attention was stirring the emotions of those who wanted to see the UFO for themselves. Earlier in the day Dari Holston at the *Sentinel* had received an interesting phone call from a man claiming to have seen his friend beamed aboard a UFO the night before. He was apparently convincing enough to arrange an in-person interview with Duane Cook and Dari at the Sheraton Motel in Fort Walton Beach.

When Dari told Frances and me about his report and asked if we wanted to hear his story also, I agreed. After all, as strange as it sounded, who was I to disbelieve before I heard the details. My own sightings and events certainly sounded equally outrageous until all the facts were told. And who better to listen to his story than Frances and I, armed with our photo album of UFO prints. (The originals were almost always locked away and most of the time were not even in the house.)

Fort Walton is about thirty-five miles east of Gulf Breeze. As we drove along the dark two-lane Highway 87, I noticed an array of lights to the northeast, to my left and slightly behind me. The lights were above the tree line, which hugs close to the road's edge. Frances and I dismissed the lights as an airplane even though Frances seemed sure the lights were smaller and closer than I judged them to be.

We arrived at the motel a little late and were introduced to a man named Carl, who was sitting with Duane and Dari. Carl was telling them his story, and after a brief recap that brought us up-to-date, he continued. Mostly we just listened without interjecting any key facts from our on-going sightings.

195

Now and then Carl would try to question me, and I would tell a select bit of information, something like the beam that I saw was blue. Within a few minutes somehow the red beam that he had been talking about had suddenly turned blue. On and on, Carl's story slowly adjusted to the details I would mention from my events. Those of us from Gulf Breeze began to look at each other like, okay—end of story.

I mentioned the white beam briefly without saying that it was more of a flash. Soon after that Duane asked Carl to go get his wife and two other friends who, he reported, had also seen the UFO. We told him we would wait for him there while he went to get them. Once Carl was gone, we talked about his story and laughed, our suspicions definitely aroused.

When Carl returned by himself, about ten minutes later, the story he told was almost too ridiculous for me to keep a straight face. He said, "Oh, my god. We're in big trouble, eh." (Carl's Canadian, and we heard a lot of *ehs* that night.) He continued, "I called the motel, and my wife said that the UFO was there hovering over the roof and it was asking my buddy for me."

I thought to myself that any normal man would have been running as fast as possible back to where his wife was, not sitting there with us. Then Carl said, "My wife saw the UFO as she went outside to the Coke machine. It shot a white beam at her that hit at her feet and popped her legs open."

I could picture that scene in my imagination. I laughed out loud and said that it sounded like the UFO had a bunch of men on board who had been traveling for too long. Everyone laughed except Carl. He didn't seem even to notice what I had said.

By now those of us who had driven over from Gulf Breeze were ready to bring the meeting to a close and politely excuse ourselves. Carl followed us out to the front of the motel, and I couldn't believe it when he said he wanted to meet again the next day. I told him I couldn't come back to Fort Walton again, and he said he would drive over to Gulf Breeze.

The next day Dari called and told me Carl had shown up at the newspaper office and told them he had a message from the UFO. If they didn't run his story in the *Sentinel,* the UFO would blow up the town. I couldn't believe it. No wonder the reputation of credible witnesses and valid sightings are dismissed when they are lumped in with such stories as Carl's.

This had been a learning experience, and even though we all laughed it off, we fully expected to have to deal with this type of fringe element again. Next time we would be better prepared to spot a suspicious story.

There would be people who would say that I was no better than Carl, people who would charge me with a "hoax." I knew I might later have to learn to deal with the skeptics who, if they couldn't disprove the photographs, would try to discredit me personally. I and my credibility would be the target. I would have to decide how to defend myself without hurting my family in the process.

FEBRUARY 20, 1988—DR. MACCABEE BEGINS

B ruce Maccabee, Ph.D., optical physicist, was due to arrive at the house sometime on Saturday, the 20th. Early that morning the doorbell rang and there they were—Charles Flannigan, Bob Reid, and the long-awaited Dr. Maccabee. I showed them into my office.

As the meeting started, I knew Dr. Maccabee would want a complete set of first-generation slides for his records. I was still working over in my mind whether I was going to release copies to him when we started with what the scientists consider the most important photo, the UFO hovering over the road (photo 19).

Dr. Maccabee took out his measuring equipment, set up his portable computer, and began to calculate the UFO's size compared with known distances and measurements, such as the width of the road and the distance of the UFO from the camera. There was a lot of talk about focal length of the camera, and he soon had that measured to the millimeter.

Using the known factors, Dr. Maccabee worked it out one way and said that the UFO was at least thirteen feet in diameter. He calculated it again, backward this time, and said that thirteen to fourteen feet in diameter and a power ring of seven to eight feet were very close. He told us that he might have to adjust this later, after he had studied all of the photos more. He needed to determine which of the UFOs were the same and what the exact shape of the crafts were.

Dr. Maccabee continued to adjust his measuring scales and peer into his magnifying glass while explaining that he needed a complete set of photographic slides. He said that if the photos checked out, then he must have a complete set to finish his study. He would have to retain the slides so that he could respond to questions and criticism from other reputable scientists.

His point was well taken. I could not ask a photo expert with his credentials to put his reputation on the line and then withhold the principal evidence.

Photograph by photograph, he recorded, scaled, and rephotographed in slide form. As Dr. Maccabee worked on his calculations, he recorded the details of each sighting. With each photograph he found more information and took greater interest.

The first photograph I took on November 11, 1987, shows the UFO moving out from behind the branch of a pine tree in the front yard. This photo was a fortunate mistake, because I had snapped the shutter a moment too early rather than waiting for the UFO to clear the pine tree. I hadn't thought about how catching the UFO behind the branch was important photo evidence.

Dr. Maccabee studied the photo and felt it was very important. Along with the "road shot," it made a strong case that the photographs were not double exposures or models on a string being hung a few feet from the camera. His preliminary calculations showed the UFO in the "road shot" to be about 185 feet from the camera.

It would be eleven o'clock that night before most of the reporting and calculating was complete. There was some discussion between Bob Reid and Bruce about the strange colorings to the overall film appearance. Also, how could the camera get as clear a shot as it had with such low light? I didn't know. All I had done was aim the camera and push the button. Sometimes there was a flashcube and sometimes not. Perhaps they could take the camera and figure out why.

With that in mind, we went outside to reenact my first sighting using the streetlight to simulate the UFO. I took the camera and, without leaning on the wall to steady it, I took a photo of the light. We did it over and over again. Each test shot showed the light clearly with almost no movement on my part.

Bruce figured that the shutter exposure was almost a full second. He and Bob were shocked to see a one-second exposure of a streetlight at least eighty feet away with no blur in most shots and very little in others. Shot after shot also showed irregular color tones on the test shots. For no apparent reason, one shot would be a blue color and the next, taken from the same spot, would be a brown color. Everybody finally agreed that the variation was an official, witnessed unknown.

The "tree shot" also showed the lighted streetlight. Dr. Maccabee used another device to measure the amount of lumins the streetlight gave off and compared that with the light coming from the UFO. All of the results of these tests would be completed by Dr. Maccabee after he returned to his home.

Two days later I received a phone call from Charles Flannigan, who with Dr. Maccabee was measuring and confirming the angles and dimensions at the "road shot" site. I volunteered to reenact the incident for photo 19 so that Dr. Maccabee could measure and ask direct questions at the scene.

After several dozen test photographs Dr. Maccabee established an almost exact location of the truck and my position in it at the time of the photograph. That done, a 4-by-8-foot piece of plywood was held at the calculated location of the UFO approximately 185 feet down the road. Again many test shots were taken until Dr. Maccabee seemed satisfied that he had the data needed for his further evaluations.

Another test, for which I wasn't present, had taken place the same night. Charles and Dr. Maccabee went to Soundside Drive near where I had taken the "road shot" for a nightime reenactment. They wanted to examine the nature of the UFO glow, which shows clearly on the road beneath the craft.

They used a large floodlight to cast a glow on the road and then photographed it from various distances down the road and with the light held at different heights above the road. The preliminary conclusion was that the glow shown in photo 19 was produced by a power source possibly one thousand times brighter than the floodlight used in the test.

That same evening, Dr. Maccabee and Charles Flannigan arrived at my door and excitedly waved a photo before me while pointing to the sky. They had just seen the UFO and photographed it. I dodged between them and looked where they were pointing. The photo showed an orange light, but it somehow looked odd to me. The whole event was a trick, and shortly thereafter Dr. Maccabee explained what he had done. I was disappointed and a bit frustrated, but understood that every angle of this case had to be considered.

FEBRUARY 20, 1988—FRANCES'S ACCOUNT

When the doorbell rang at 9:00 A.M., Ed and I were still in bed. We had been up late the night before in Fort Walton with Carl the Canadian. I grabbed my bathrobe and, pulling it on, hurried to the door. Bob Reid was standing there. I explained to Bob that no one had told us what time everyone would be coming over. He said, "Right now."

Sure enough, Charles drove up with Dr. Maccabee about the same time Ed came into the foyer still tucking in his shirt. Since I didn't really want to meet anyone new looking like I did, I made my escape to our bedroom before the two other men reached the front door.

Twenty minutes later, dressed and made up, I joined the men in Ed's office. Ed immediately put in a request for coffee all around. I supplied each of us with a steaming cup and sat down to watch Dr. Maccabee work.

It wasn't until my stomach protested its lack of food that I realized how much time had passed. The calculations Dr. Maccabee had been making and the things he could tell from the photographs had held my complete interest. We broke for lunch, sort of. Dr. Maccabee, Bob, and Charles went to a nearby fast food restaurant while I fixed sandwiches for Ed, Dan, and myself. Half an hour later we were back at work in Ed's office.

This was the first time I had sat in on any discussions with investigators, and I found that I loved it. By listening to all they had to say I came to understand the whole UFO phenomenon better. Our own experiences seemed less bizarre and unsettling.

I think it was during that marathon session that Ed came to realize that, while we needed to continue to protect our children from unwanted pressure from the investigators, I was quite capable of handling the situation without it upsetting me.

Charles left sometime in the afternoon, but Bob and Dr. Maccabee stayed on. As interested as I was in all the calculations and tests, I still had children to feed, but I made a concession since it was Saturday. I took orders from everyone, including the men in Ed's office, and went out for some hot sandwiches. The work continued unabated.

Finally, around 11:00 P.M., Bob and Dr. Maccabee left. The last thing Bob said was, "This is the twelfth day." As much as I wanted the UFO to come back so that Ed could photograph it with the MUFON camera, I hoped it wouldn't come that night. We were both tired and needed some uninterrupted sleep.

FEBRUARY 26, 1988—SIXTEENTH SIGHTING—MUFON CAMERA

The pressure to photograph the UFO with the special MU-FON camera was building with each passing day. The twelfth day since the last incident had come and gone without a sighting. We had dismissed the "array of lights" we had seen on the way to Fort Walton to meet the Canadian, Carl. Something as uncertain as three rows of lights didn't qualify as a sighting as far as we were concerned. It had to be a definite, identifiable UFO.

Emotionally Frances and I had been forced to hope for a return visit and a chance to photograph the UFO. This radical change from hoping it would leave us in peace was an additional strain. We were torn in two directions at once.

In desperation we had given up on sitting in our backyard each night waiting for a glimpse of the UFO. Instead on Tuesday, February 23rd, we had decided to visit a local park that overlooks Santa Rosa Sound. Maybe the UFO would show itself over such an open expanse of water. At about 9:00 P.M. we took the MUFON camera and drove the mile and a half to the pavilion at the west side of the heavily wooded park. We had a clear view south across the sound toward Pensacola Beach, but our view to the east, north, and west was limited to above the tree line.

On weeknights there is little activity in the park, which is crowded with picnickers and boat trailers on weekends, even during the winter. On this night there were a few parked cars with boat trailers attached, but no sign of other people except for an occasional "drive through" car that would come down the hill, circle the parking lot, and leave.

Frances and I sat under the south edge of the pavilion and waited. We talked about family activities, ball games, and such and kept a nervous eye on the sky. After two hours we were tired, cold, and disappointed. We left.

The next night we tried once more and again sat in the empty park hoping to use the strange four-lens camera. Again, nothing happened, no ship, no hum. It seemed to be over. In one sense we were relieved and in another disappointed and prepared to hear the skeptics cast a suspicious word such as, "I didn't think they could photograph the UFO with the sealed, control camera."

On Thursday night Don Ware was scheduled to give a slide presentation on UFOs to a local adult group. He invited us to attend, and feeling it was useless for us to return to the park again, we accepted.

Without exposing our identities, Frances and I sat and watched Don's presentation, then listened to the question-and-answer session that followed. An impromptu poll was taken on the question, "Do you think UFOs are of extraterrestrial origin?" Of the eighty people in the room, seventy-five raised their hands yes. Frances and I smiled at each other and squeezed hands. That was just the encouragement we needed to keep trying.

About 9:00 the next night I picked up the MUFON camera and walked over to Frances. Without hesitation she said, "I'll get my coat." She knew, as I did, that we had to try again.

When we arrived at the park, the pavilion area was empty, although there were a few boats being pulled up the boat ramp as the fishermen headed home for the night. The sounds of activity behind us continued as we took up our familiar position on one of the pavilion benches.

We quietly sat and listened to the tide pull at the water's edge and to the sound of a distant tugboat pushing its burden along the Intercoastal Waterway. The last fishing boat was loaded on its trailer. As they started up the only road to the park, I knew that if the UFO were going to show, then it would wait for us to be alone. We were alone now. We had no weapon, only each other.

Frances sat close to me, and my left arm across her lap moved as she breathed. I knew she was frightened, but she wouldn't leave me. The quiet of the park was disrupted by several cats jumping into the large garbage container, thumping and banging in their search for food. We said nothing; we waited.

I stared at a cluster of stars and wondered. How could space just go on forever? Was the UFO from a distant star system? Maybe some kind of time travel would be the final answer. The way the UFO winked in and out seemed to make any speculation possible.

Frances nudged me. "There. Look over there."

She was looking off to my right, toward the west-southwest. I followed her line of sight, and there it was. But this was very different from what I had photographed before. All I could see were three rows of lights with a trailing light. The lights were definitely not those of an airplane, and there was no sound. This was not what I had expected to see, but it was a UFO of some kind.

The top of the west tree line obscured the UFO briefly, and I rushed over toward the edge of the woods so that I could see past the closest tree. The craft moved slowly across the sky, which made me assume it was very large and very far away. Looking through the camera viewfinder also enhanced the appearance of greater distance from this strange array of lights. I decided it didn't matter. I had to photograph this UFO even though it was different and seemed far away. This might be my only chance.

I began pressing the shutter release, taking photo after photo as the craft continued to move, at times partly blocked by treetops. Frances had backed up and kept saying that the lights were too clear for the UFO to be over a thousand feet away, as I had said. Still shooting photographs, I insisted that it must be huge and swore that everybody in Gulf Breeze should be able to see this tremendous sight.

It seemed so large to me that when I noticed the peculiar atmospheric disturbance that surrounded the UFO, I was convinced. It had to be the craft's enormity that caused that effect in the air. Nothing Frances could say would make me think otherwise. I shot all ten exposures that were in the camera (photos 25–34). Just like the UFOs I had photographed so many times before, this one suddenly winked out.

With Frances at my side I retreated to the pavilion. We looked across the parking lot to see just what we expected. Nobody was there; the park was empty.

I was excited to have the pressure concerning the MUFON camera relieved, and when we arrived home, I made several sketches so that I could make a better drawing later. The rows of lights were orange, and I thought they were portholes. There were larger orange half-saucers protruding from the side of what I called a cigar-shaped central body. The atmospheric disturbance that rippled from the UFO completely encircled the craft. This rippling resembled the heat waves that rise from an asphalt road on a summer's day.

February 26, 1988—Frances's Account

Ever since Bob had given him the special camera, I knew the pressure to produce Ed had been under. Though I hated to, I hoped for a sighting. We had made a conscious effort to watch for the UFO. By the time we gave up sitting outside each night, we were chilled to the bone.

Our nights watching had yielded us nothing. When Ed shifted our hunting ground to Shoreline Park South, he offered to go alone, knowing how I hate to be cold. There was no way I could let him do that. I simply bundled myself up against the cold and went with him.

At the park we didn't even have the readily available comforts of home to ease the hours of sitting and watching. Cold and discouraged, many times we thought of giving up. Sheer determination kept us coming back, and we were finally rewarded by the appearance of a triple string of lights the night of February 26th.

This was nothing like any UFO we had photographed before, but it bore a striking resemblance to the lights we had identified as an airplane over Eglin AFB the night we went to meet Carl. Now, standing in the open where I could see better, I knew this wasn't a plane. There were no strobe lights, no sound, and no plane I had ever seen had three parallel, horizontal rows of windows and a large round light that seemed to cover the aft section of the craft.

I followed Ed almost to the edge of the woods, where he started taking pictures. He kept saying the craft was huge, but I wasn't so sure. The lights were quite clear and distinct. I could see each individual glow. Since my hard contact lenses make lights "halo" at night, especially those at a distance, I felt that the craft was much closer and therefore much smaller.

While Ed continued to photograph, I backed up, thinking that that would put the craft higher above the tree line. Although I moved almost to the pavilion, the UFO remained just above treetop height. To me that meant it had to be quite close, because a distant object should have appeared higher the farther back I was from the trees.

I tried to tell Ed what I thought, but he was adamant. I didn't push the point, just thankful something had appeared for him to photograph, thus relieving the pressure on him from MUFON.

When we arrived back home, Ed tried to call Charles Flannigan, but there was no answer. Now that the camera had been used, we wanted to turn it back over to someone from MUFON as soon as possible. Maybe then we could forget about UFOs and investigators and get on with living our lives.

MARCH 3, 1988—MORE WITNESSES

There were other sightings of UFOs the night of February 26th, and still other sightings within the next few days. Here are brief accounts as reported in the *Sentinel:*

John Fletcher was returning to Gulf Breeze from the beach last Sunday (Feb. 28th) at 9:45 P.M. As he drove north across the Bob Sikes Bridge, he noticed strange lights off to his right, over the sound.

"I've lived on the water all my life and I've never seen anything like this before," he said of his sighting. He described "weird golden amber lights" that made up a circle and appeared to be about 25 feet over the water about 25 yards off the north shore of the sound.

He slowed down to watch the lights and noticed that the lights seemed to spin in a slow circular motion. He saw about six complete revolutions before the lights went out one at a time. He estimated the diameter of the ring of lights to be about 20 feet.

Last Tuesday (Mar. 1st), around 8:00 P.M., Debra Kneff was on her way home from Pensacola. As she passed the Food World grocery store, she noticed a "yellowish-looking light" in the sky "above the trees but not as high as an airplane. It was bigger and brighter than a star and was moving slowly across the sky," she reported. "I didn't know what it was, but I knew it wasn't an airplane."

As Debra drove east on Hwy. 98, the light moved north across the highway toward the bay. Although she was very startled by what she was seeing, she turned left onto College Parkway and drove to the end of the street, where she watched until the light "vanished" over the bay.

A 15-year-old GBHS student was at the beach on Friday night (Feb. 26th) with several friends. A friend pointed out some strange lights that seemed to be hovering over Gulf Breeze. The group watched the lights for a while until they moved out of sight. The teenagers could not see any particular shape and they were unable to provide more details.

17-year-old Chris Poole, a GBHS student, was at McDonald's at about 8:30 P.M. (Feb. 26th) when some friends pulled into the parking lot and reported seeing a UFO from Hwy. 98. He went outside to look for the UFO with six other GB students. They all watched a large yellow light that appeared to be hovering over the bay "pretty low to the ground."

The light grew brighter, then dimmed and went out completely. When it reappeared moments later, the light was in a slightly different location. The students watched for about 10 to 15 minutes until the light disappeared.

MARCH 4, 1988—PHOTOS FROM MUFON CAMERA

The extraordinary precautions involving the MUFON camera continued. The camera had been scheduled to be opened, and the film developed and printed, all with journalists and TV reporters recording every moment. These precautions were to prevent any later criticism that the film may have been switched.

The camera-opening press conference was scheduled for 10:00 AM., March 4th, at Coast Photo Service, a film-processing laboratory. Walter Andrus, the international director of MUFON, had flown in from Texas and would be in charge. Frances and I wanted to be there, but the thought of all those cameras and reporters made us too nervous. We told the MUFON investigators and Duane and Dari that we would wait down the street at a fast food restaurant.

When I had returned the camera to the MUFON team, I prepared a receipt that acknowledged that the negatives belonged to me. I not only wanted to be sure that I received a set of the photographs but I wanted to have some control over what happened to them. That's why I also requested that a set of prints and negatives to sent to Dr. Bruce Maccabee. Very likely there were other experts who could, and would, study the film, but, in my opinion, Dr. Maccabee had the credentials to make an undisputable analysis.

Upon arrival at the restaurant, Frances and I ordered coffee and waited in a corner booth. I had assumed it would take a half hour or so before the investigators would be able to come and show us the results. Almost an hour and a half later Dari Holston came in with a smile that covered her face.

"It's there. It's little, and they almost didn't see it, but it's there. It must have been far away. They have enlarged it twice. I knew you'd want to know. It's there. You're a father."

Dari was right. We had been sitting around as if we were in a waiting room, but instead of asking if it was a boy or girl we were asking, "Is it there?" and "What is it?"

As more and more of the investigators arrived, the talk grew more excited. I was excited because they were excited. The animated conversation centered on the craft, and the description "mothership" popped up and started bouncing about from one group of us to another. Pretty soon the "mothership" term stuck.

By now it was almost lunchtime. Charles Flannigan asked if he could arrange a meeting between Frances and me and a few of the investigators, including Walter Andrus. We all agreed to meet at Charles's house after lunch.

MARCH 4, 1988—FRANCES'S ACCOUNT

When Ed and I had driven past Coast Photo on our way to wait for the others, the parking lot had been full of cars and reporters. That added to our anxiety as we waited for the photographic results for what seemed like hours, sipping coffee and worrying about why it was taking so long. Dari had finally come to bring us up-to-date, knowing the anxiety we would be experiencing.

About half an hour later Duane and the investigators arrived, and Ed and I got our first look at a picture of the craft he had photographed. It was little more than an array of lights. The outline was indistinguishable, and there was no visible evidence of the atmospheric disturbance we had seen.

I guess I shouldn't have been surprised at the quality of the pictures. It had been so dark and the lights so small. Still I was disappointed. My disappointment didn't last long. Everyone else was so excited, it was infectious. And after all, Ed had managed to photograph something.

Walter Andrus had asked for us to meet with him at Charles's house around 1:30 P.M. It would be my first real meeting with him. When Walter had been at our home before, I had been introduced, answered one or two questions, and then excused myself.

That afternoon there was a crowd at Charles's—Walter, Bob Reid,

Gary Watson, and of course Charles, as well as Charles's wife and what I think were someone's two grown children. They took no part in the meeting, so I didn't really meet them. The first thing we did was examine the photos and, very carefully, the negatives.

The question of the size and distance of the craft was raised. Ed again repeated his belief that the craft was large and far away. Though I didn't do so with much authority, I said I wasn't so sure about that. My comment was given a polite nod, then ignored. Everyone but Walter Andrus seemed to have already decided that this was a "mothership." They had already begun calling it that.

In the face of their certainty, I began to doubt my own theory and didn't pursue it. Maybe I was wrong and they were right. After all, they had much more experience with this sort of thing than I did. Who was I to disagree? My night vision isn't the best; neither is my ability to estimate distances. I *was* sure of one thing: In order for me to have seen the UFO as clearly as I had, if it were not close, then it was indeed huge.

Once we had finished looking at the photos, we sat around Charles's dining room table and talked. Ed told them that he had taken and passed the lie detector test. He asked Charles and Walter, both of whom have reported UFO sightings, if they had been asked to take a polygraph test to verify their experiences as he had been asked to do. As we expected, neither of them had even been asked, nor had they taken such a test. Ed recommended that they never put themselves through it.

We talked for hours, recounting sightings, with me giving my thoughts and feelings about it all. Walter made good use of this opportunity to talk to me in person, and I answered whatever questions he asked. I told Walter and the others that in the future I planned to sit in on any meetings Ed had with any of them. When he met with them alone, they could talk him into agreeing to anything. It was my intention to see that that didn't happen. I wanted to break from all the commotion with which we had been surrounded for months.

Before the meeting was over, Walter told Ed he wanted him seriously to consider hypnotic regression, and the possibility of a CATscan was again mentioned. Then he asked us about a book. I told him if a book were to be done, we wanted it handled in a readable, but scientific manner, with absolutely no sensationalism. We could well imagine how some events could be distorted and wanted none of that. Walter agreed completely.

We stayed so late at Charles's that we barely made it home in time to watch the UFO documentary. WEAR-TV aired *The Sightings* at 8:00 that night. We set up the video recorder even though Ed was to get copies of the program from ABC.

About halfway through the broadcast I wished we had accepted Duane and Dari's invitation to accompany them to the local party that concluded a month-long drive for the Cancer Society. They had planned to have televisions there so that people at the party could watch the documentary. It would have been interesting to see how our fellow citizens reacted to what they saw. At least I would have a report from Duane and Dari later on what people had said. I just hoped it would be favorable.

MARCH 5, 1988—MEDIA REVIEW OF THE MUFON CAMERA FILM

I was up early, anxious to read the *Pensacola News-Journal*. A front-page story by Michael Burke reported the results of the news conference the day before:

The sense of anticipation was keen as a gaggle of reporters, television cameramen, and UFO investigators jammed together to witness the opening of the sealed camera.

The gathering had all the markings of a classic media event: a dramatic buildup, an extended wait as the film developed, and yes, a mystery that was to unfold. The only element missing was Geraldo Rivera.

But when the wax seal on the camera was broken and the photographs developed Friday morning, the results were interesting—but not conclusive.

An anonymous Gulf Breeze businessman who used the sealed, four-lens camera supplied by UFO investigators had indeed photographed SOMETHING. But it was not shaped like the possible spaceship he produced in more than 25 previous photographs, most of them taken with his own Polaroid camera.

This film, developed during the press conference at Coast Photo Service, in Warrington, showed a small, distant object that, when magnified, looked like some kind of lighted vessel, aircraft, or spaceship. The thin, elliptic object was defined primarily by specks of lights, a few that looked like portholes, against a black background of night.

The anonymous businessman, identified as Jim [a psuedonym], had told investigators from the Mutual UFO Network (MUFON), a private group of UFO researchers, that he had used their sealed camera to take 10 photographs on the night of Feb. 26 at Shoreline Park South in Gulf Breeze.

Previously the businessman had showed investigators a series of detailed photographs and a videotape that appeared to depict a spaceship or group of spaceships. Jim said some were shot at an estimated distance of 200–300 feet. Jim claimed he photographed the UFOs on 16 different occasions beginning with his first sighting on Nov. 11, outside his Gulf Breeze home.

In an attempt to verify the credibility of the other photos produced by Jim, MUFON put film in its special three-dimensional camera and had the camera sealed with wax.

Jim was given the camera and told to use it when he witnessed the spaceship.

After Jim shot the photos last week, MUFON retrieved the sealed camera and arranged to have the press witness its opening.

Before the camera was opened, Walter Andrus, Jr., international director of MUFON, acknowledged that a double exposure could have been made with Jim's original Polaroid camera. But he added: "We have found that the original 25 photographs seem to stand up very well as far as their credibility is concerned."

MUFON investigators were not with Jim when he took the photographs. And they have not seen the spaceship themselves, although they staked out Jim's house on nine nights.

But Andrus told reporters that the photographs taken with MUFON's camera were "Taken under scientific, controlled conditions where there is no opportunity whatsoever to hoax, fake it, produce double exposures or anything of this nature. That's what makes this so significant," he said.

After the new photos were enlarged Friday, Andrus said MUFON would need about seven days to analyze them in detail. Andrus' only conclusion for the moment: "He actually photographed something in the sky."

The following Thursday, March 10th, the next weekly issue of the *Sentinel* hit the newsstands. An article by Diana K. Hansen covered the opening of the camera:

The reports of the Gulf Breeze UFO sightings have become big news around town. When a press conference was called to witness the opening of the sealed MUFON camera, a crowd of about 30 photographers, writers, newscasters, MUFON members and "Ufologists" gathered at the Coast Photo shop on Barrancas Ave. to watch.

The camera was a Nimslo 3-D provided to "Ed" by the MU-FON investigators. Just a few days before he had photographed what he believes to be a much larger UFO than the ones previously photographed.

MUFON international director Walt Andrus addressed the press. "This is the first time in recorded history that we've had the opportunity to work so closely with a witness as sightings are still being made. . . . It was a one in a million chance that we could get something on film, but here we are." He added, "We don't know if anything will show up on this film. There are so many things that could go wrong."

With the camera still sealed with wax, the spectators were able to witness the entire process of removal of the Kodak film, then the developing and printing.

As the pictures came through final processing, reporters were able to see small lights on the dark prints.

Enlargements were made to bring out as much detail as possible.

The *Sentinel* printed one of the photographs on which I had outlined, with pen, the ship and the lights. They also reported another sighting, which had taken place the evening the camera was opened. The article was written by Robin Fuchek, who, along with her children—Connie, eleven; Loren, nine; and Allen, eight—had witnessed the UFO.

Inspired by something in the sky over Tiger Point March 4, 1988, 6:45 P.M. Here's what we saw, driving on Ceylon Drive from Sabertooth Circle to Tiger Point Blvd.

Through the treetops appeared to be a large heavenly body of some sort. As we cleared the trees it appeared to be moving. I stopped the car to make sure, and it continued to glide across the sky—an unwavering oval orange light. We watched for several seconds and there were no strobe lights or flashing wing lights such as an airplane or helicopter might have. There were no trees between us and the object, but it winked out and then appeared again. Then suddenly, several lights in different colors on one side of the orange glow began blinking rapidly, and a few seconds later the whole thing winked out again. We had tickets to *Disney on Ice* [a skating show] that night, and I began driving again, saying, "Well, it's gone—let's go." As we turned onto Tiger Point Blvd., the boys in the back seat yelled, "No, it's not—it's following us." Loren said, "Oh, my gosh—it's moving around all over." They described the motion as wobbling, but still seeming to chase after the car. They wanted me to drive faster to get away, but it didn't bother us.

MARCH 7, 1988—PURCHASE NEW POLAROID

Our decision had to be final. This focus of the media on everything that happened to us had to stop. Even if the UFO persisted, we didn't have to make things more difficult by exposing ourselves to public scrutiny.

The only question that still clung to this decision was, Would I take pictures if the chance was there? Just take the picture and not tell anybody, and if I did, should I use the same old Polaroid 108 camera? It had been criticized for its capability to take double exposures.

I considered the possibility of a 35mm, but it had drawbacks too. For one thing, double exposures would still be possible. And although there might be more detail, I would have to have it developed and printed somewhere. I could just see the look in the eyes of a clerk at a film-processing store as he developed a roll of film with UFOs on it. No, that would never do.

The next best thing was to buy a newer-model Polaroid, one of the kind that at the press of the shutter button automatically ejects and develops the film before your eyes. In the event that I should take a picture, it might as well be one in which the skeptics could not claim "tampering."

I had heard several times that "superimposition" had been ruled out by Dr. Robert Nathan. Dr. Nathan had apparently tested the originals, delivered to him by Duane Cook in December 1987, for evidence of superimposition and had told Dr. Maccabee that the original photographs had not been superimposed. But Dr. Nathan hadn't addressed the question of double exposures.

There was no way I could completely satisfy everybody, and I knew

217

it. But having a different camera might help. So Frances and I went to a department store and bought a Polaroid Sun 600 with automatic flash. Given our decision not to show any more pictures should we take them, or make any more reports, I should not even have bothered, but still, if this new camera could settle the double-exposure question, that was best.

The new Sun camera was still in its box on my desk at dinnertime. The conversation was normal, involving school activities and such, and mixed with the sound of the television coming from the living room. Suddenly a swift hum passed through my right forehead. About four or five seconds of hum was all I heard.

I looked up at Frances and said, "I just heard a hum."

She was quick to ask, "You don't hear it now?"

I answered no, then we were silent and continued eating. I had a feeling that if I had gotten up and looked outside, the UFO would have been there.

At first we were a bit nervous, but as the hours passed, we were satisfied that I had ignored it and nothing had happened. Maybe if I continued to resist responding to the UFO, it would go away.

Later Frances and I prepared for bed. I could always understand the subtle motions delivered by her body language, and I smiled, knowing she was at ease.

About 11:30 P.M. I was lying awake when I heard the hum again. Twice the hum passed through my head for five seconds and then a pause of three or four seconds, followed by another five-second hum. Then a quiet, deep voice said, "Zehaas. Zehaas."

I whispered to Frances what I had just heard and started to sit up. Frances caught my arm and pulled me back. I eased over to her, thinking she was going to say something. She said nothing, but quickly wrapped her arms and legs around me. Though it would have taken some force, I could have broken away from her, but I got the message and didn't resist. If she didn't want me going out to confront the UFO, I wouldn't. But again the feeling was powerful that it was out there waiting for me, calling for me to come out.

Frances held me for hours until I finally felt her grip loosen and her breathing deepen in sleep. She was right. We had agreed to ignore the UFO, but I was being torn apart. The UFO's presence made me want to go to it, to see what it wanted and photograph it, but the strength of my family was stronger. With Frances beside me, I knew I could hold out.

MARCH 8, 1988—SEVENTEENTH SIGHTING—HONEYSUCKLE SHOT

Each passing day made me understand that a lot of people, especially people that I did business with, had figured out that I was the "Mr. Ed" so often mentioned in the newspaper. Several mortgage brokers and real estate agents had hinted their suspicions to me, thinking that I might talk about the UFO to them. My standard answer was that the UFO phenomenon was very interesting and that I, too, would like to learn more about it.

My daughter had complained that a few classmates had told her that their parents thought that "Mr. Ed" was her father. She always just walked away and said nothing. She did not understand that I had to withhold my identity in part to protect her from direct confrontation. If it became official and the press published my name, there would be no stopping the media onslaught.

The problems with shielding my family from reporters, investigators, and public exposure were difficult, but the recurring visits of the UFO was a problem that seemed to grip my soul. I sat in my office and considered the past four months and how the UFO had overwhelmed our lives. There was a secret connection that I could not deny or understand, a connection that brought the UFO back time after time.

Quietly, to myself, I said, "Zehaas, Zehaas? What does that mean?" Then suddenly a hum began in my head. I did not move as I listened to the hum slide quietly across my forehead.

The new 600 Sun camera was ready to be loaded for the first time, and that is what I did while slowly walking through the kitchen toward the back door. Frances was busy frying chicken and did not pay any attention as I passed. There was a light, misty rain falling. It was 5:30 P.M.

219

I walked to the end of the swimming pool deck and looked across the open field. The streetlights were on in the parking lot beyond the high school. The overcast rain clouds could have hidden a complete air force, but I wasn't looking for ordinary aircraft. The craft that was calling me was special, and abruptly there it was, off to the left about three hundred feet beyond two pine trees. I could see that it was partly obscured by one of the trees, so I deliberately steadied myself and took a deep breath.

I had to walk down to the back fence near a honeysuckle vine before my view was no longer obstructed. The scene was very clear to my eyes, but when I tried to frame the UFO in the camera viewfinder, I noticed I could not see the trees because the darkness seemed to be deeper when viewed through the camera.

Having never used the camera before, I fumbled with the shutter button but finally took photo 35. When I looked up from the viewfinder, the UFO was not there. The film ejected instantly and I tried to cover it from the rain, not knowing that this new film has a plastic coating that protects it from water.

When I returned to the kitchen and showed Frances, she was both excited and upset. We studied the picture and quickly noticed the reason I had not seen the craft when I looked back up. The UFO had shot straight up leaving light streaks on the film. It had flashed away during the time the shutter had been open.

This photograph was very similar to the shot taken with Duane Cook, photo 21. I recalled that when I shot photo 21 it had also been raining slightly. Was there a connection?

Had the light streaks not been there, I would have put the picture away and not mentioned it to anyone since I had decided not to report any new sightings. Instead I phoned Bruce Maccabee. Even though I was late for a meeting of the city planning board, of which I am a member, I felt it was important that I talk to him first.

When Dr. Maccabee answered the telephone, I explained that I couldn't talk long. It was soon obvious that the few minutes I had free were not going to be sufficient. I told him I would call back as soon as my meeting was over. Less than an hour later I was on the telephone with Dr. Maccabee again.

After explaining what had happened and the resulting photograph, I said that I would only report this sighting to the investigative team if it remained out of the news. Photographs in the newspaper created unending turmoil. Dr. Maccabee recommended that this photograph, and any future ones, not be publicized.

At the end of our conversation he suggested that now that I had two Polaroid cameras, maybe a stereo photograph could be taken of the UFO. He was quick to explain how the cameras could be set up. I listened politely, although I didn't want anything to do with encouraging the sightings. But it was an intriguing idea, and while I was trying to ignore the stereo camera instructions, I knew that I might try to do it.

MARCH 9, 1988—DR. MACCABEE'S "STEREO CAMERA"

The suggestion by Dr. Maccabee that I mount two cameras parallel to each other just in case I might have a chance to catch another shot of the UFO was disturbing. My first impulse was to reject the idea, but I listened to Dr. Maccabee explain that with such a double camera we could possibly obtain much more dimensional information than with a single shot.

I was persuaded to try, but insisted that if I tried, then it was my decision to do, or not to do, with no insinuated pressure. The last time I had agreed to a camera proposition was with the MUFON camera, and the pressure to photograph the UFO had been intense. Plus, by agreeing to construct a double camera (soon to be named a Self-Referencing Stereo Camera or SRS camera), I did not want to open the door to any and every other camera idea that could turn my house and backyard into a camera circus.

With some hesitance I proceeded and managed to mount a two-foot-long board across a camera tripod. I strapped my SUN 600 Polaroid to one end. As luck would have it, Duane Cook had an identical camera, which I borrowed and mounted parallel on the opposite end.

My efforts to construct the SRS camera were time-consuming, but I realized how important an SRS photograph could be. Such a photo would offer proof of distance and size—proof to anybody who challenged my word or the other photographs.

I worked hard and long trying to stabilize the SRS camera so that it could be broken down for transport, then easily reassembled. I made some test shots for Bruce Maccabee to study. The test results of the distance measurements were encouraging, but he suggested some refinements, which I made. Dr. Maccabee has provided further details in the photo analysis chapter.

222

MARCH 11, 1988—IDENTITY EXPOSED IN PARK

The city was in a stir, and talk of the UFO sightings could be overheard from conversations everywhere in town. Frances and I had been told it was not unusual to see UFO watchers sitting in their lawn chairs on the side of the road on County Road 191-B. Also, due to the sightings in South Shoreline Park, we had heard about groups of people on watch there too.

Frances and I were curious, so we drove to the park and inconspicuously walked along the beach. There were a number of cameras set up and several groups of people watching and talking among themselves. As we approached the pavilion, I heard someone call my name.

"Hey, Ed. Hey, Ed! Hey, everybody, that's Ed."

I was stunned. I could feel everybody in the park looking at me, and I swung around to see who had called. Nearly a dozen people stood fifty feet away, between me and a bonfire that backlit the group. With no light on their faces, I had no idea who any of them were.

The voice continued, "Hey, Ed. Come on over. Hey, everybody, that's Ed Walters."

By now I wanted to turn and run, but I answered, "Hi, who's that?" as Frances and I kept on walking.

"It's me, Dick Smith. Come on and join us."

All the UFO watchers who had been talking among themselves were silent. I knew that everybody within shouting distance had heard Dick say "Ed Walters." The camera around my neck suddenly felt huge as I tried to hide it beneath my coat.

I made a feeble answer of "Hi, Dick. Good to see you, but we have to leave."

223

All these exchanges were yelled back and forth across the park, but it was Dick's "Hey, everybody, that's Ed Walters" that echoed through my head. It didn't take a genius to interpret the inflection in his voice: "Hey, everybody, that's 'Mr. Ed,' the UFO photographer."

We left for home, disturbed by what had happened. We found out later that the UFO had been out that night also. The *Sentinel* reported,

This week's UFO update contains the stories of two recent sightings as seen by eight different witnesses. The first sighting was of a small round craft between 6:30 and 7:00 P.M. Friday evening March 11th. The second sighting was of the large elongated craft about 8:00 to 8:10 P.M. Monday evening March 14th.

The following report was related to us by a witness I can only describe as "above reproach." He is a minister of one of our local churches, and understandably asked that he not print his name. His sighting took place in the Tiger Point/Bay Ridge area.

"I was going to a meeting at a quarter to seven Friday night, and I just saw some lights up in the sky over the trees just across from my house over here in Bay Ridge. When I walk out my front door looking straight out in front of my house the bay is over in that direction about a mile from my house. I just saw the lights and didn't really think much about it. I just looked up to see what it was and kept looking and it was just sitting there and instead of blinking, it was like lights going around in a circle. I saw it very distinctly, a round object with lights going around the bottom and it was very much like the picture that I've seen in the newspaper. I stood there and looked at it just in awe and kept thinking I was going to figure it out in a minute and then I hollered inside and said come out and look. I didn't know where a camera was at the time and didn't really think about a camera. My wife was at a meeting but Stephanie (the baby-sitter) came outside and she saw it too. I watched it a total of about a minute and then we started walking out toward the street and it kept just going farther and farther back until it disappeared out of sight.

"I never heard any sound, that's what is bizarre. It was totally quiet. I got in my car and drove over to the bay to see if I could see. I stayed there about 10 minutes but I didn't see anything else."

(The other sightings from the night of March 11th, as well as those from March 14th can be found in Appendix 2.)

MARCH 12, 1988—1986 WITNESS CALLS

The phone rang about 10:00 P.M. A late call like that would normally have been from a subcontractor, and that's how I answered the phone, with just a "Hello, this is Ed." The soft voice of the woman who answered me caught me by surprise.

As soon as the caller identified herself, I switched on the speaker phone and signaled Frances to take down what was said, word for word. The first few sentences are reconstructed from memory. The rest of the conversation is from Frances's notes.

ED: "Hello, this is Ed."

CALLER: "Ed, my name is . . . Jane."

ED: "Hi, Jane. How can I help you?"

JANE: "I'm the one who took the pictures of the UFO in Shoreline Park in '86." (She said this very fast, as if she were afraid she might change her mind and hang up.)

ED: "Jane, let me interrupt. Do you mind if I turn on my recorder?"

JANE: "No! Don't. I'll hang up. Someone might recognize my voice." (There was genuine panic in her voice.)

ED: "Okay, Jane. I won't." (Calm and soothing.) "Thanks for calling. How did you find out my name?"

JANE: "I can't tell you that, somebody could figure out who I am. I can't have that." (Again the fear.)

ED: "Okay, I understand." (Calm and reassuring.) "I'm just happy you called. Tell me everything about the photos."

JANE: "I hid them from my family and everybody. Nobody

225

knows. They'd laugh. My church wouldn't approve."
(Still nervous, sounding unsure.)

ED: "I understand." (Tone meant to reassure her, keep her
          from hanging up.) "You don't have to tell me who you
          are, but some things would help. How late was it when
          you took the photos?"

JANE: "Not so dark as the pictures appear. Maybe seven-thirty.
          The sun was just going down. I had walked to the end of the
          pier to shoot the sunset. The night before it was beautiful and
          I thought it would be the same, but it wasn't. I had just started
          back home, and I was just at the bottom of the hill going up
          the road. I stopped and focused one more time on the sunset.
          A flash of light shot over the trees." (Her voice had calmed,
          but at the end the tension began to come back.)

ED: "How high above the trees?"

JANE: "I can't really say—maybe fifty feet."

ED: "What did you think it was?"

JANE: "I knew what it was." (Very sure.) "No way was it a jet
          plane. It went like a . . . uh . . . it was fast, like a flash-
          light beam flashing across the sky. Then it stopped dead
          still. That's when I took the second picture. I was scared,
          so I started running up the road. I looked back as I ran. It
          had moved lower—almost in the trees." (There was some-
          thing else in Jane's voice, maybe some embarrassment in
          admitting she had run.)

ED: "Was it landing?"

JANE: "No. It was still above the trees. It just sat there. I kept
          running and looking back. I ran off the road and almost
          fell, then flash, it went back the way it had come." (Voice
          less quiet, more animated.)

ED: "How long could you see it leaving?"

JANE: "It was gone by the time you could snap your fingers. It was
          fast!" (A hint of awe or disbelief at the speed of the craft.)

ED: "What color was it?"

JANE: "Well . . . ah . . . the pictures look kinda orange, but I
          remember it looked white on top, dark in the middle,
          really gold—fire gold—on the bottom."

ED: "Was fire coming out of the bottom?"

JANE: "No. No fire that I could see. Just a really bright bottom."
          (Calm. Sureness in her voice.)

ED: "Jane, I'm trying to put everything down on paper that happened to me. Do you mind if I write what you told me?"

JANE: "Well . . ." (A long pause.) "No . . ." (Another pause, a little shorter.) "If no one can tell who I am." (Obvious concern for being revealed in her voice.)

ED: "Don't worry, they won't. Jane, one more thing. Could I have the negatives? It would help the UFO investigators."

JANE: "No. I don't have them anymore. I threw them away. I was afraid someone would find them. All this UFO talk made me nervous."

ED: "It's okay, I understand. Anything else you want to tell me?"

JANE: "No, just thanks for talking to me. I feel better. I won't tell who you are. I understand your worry." (A kinship in the way she speaks. She knows the same fear and understands.)

ED: "Thanks, Jane. Listen, call again if you need to. Okay?"

JANE: "Okay, thanks. 'Bye."

ED: " 'Bye."

No sooner had "Jane" hung up than I wondered if there were other things I should have asked her, things that would have helped the MU-FON investigators. At least I had gotten some information from her that no one had known before. The most disturbing was her revelation that the negatives were gone. But there was nothing I could do about that, so I let myself concentrate on the fact that she had called.

That "Jane"—and I never once believed that was her real name—had happened to call the day after my name had been exposed to several dozen people in South Shoreline Park seemed like a strange coincidence. It was only speculation that she was in the park that night, but it was a definite possibility as far as I was concerned.

Frances and I talked about "Jane." With the things she had told us, we might be able to ask around and figure out who she really was, but we didn't want to do that. If she wanted to remain unknown, we would let her, but we did wonder if she would ever come forward. We doubted it, and with what I know now about the debunkers, I cannot blame her. In fact, had she asked me, that's the advice I would have given her: Don't ever let anyone know who you really are.

MARCH 13, 1988—ON WATCH WITH STEREO (SRS) CAMERA— FRANCES'S ACCOUNT

My hope that the photos Ed had taken with the MUFON camera would end our involvement with the UFO had been dashed. It seemed it wasn't destined to be. The UFO continued to come back, and his plan not to take any more photographs for investigators had already failed.

Many of Ed's free hours were spent trying to figure out how to put together the dual-camera contraption suggested by Dr. Maccabee, but there were times when I insisted he take a break from that and do the things we would have done had the UFO never entered our lives. We took the time to enjoy being with our children and each other. Laura had softball practices, Dan band concerts, and there were nights when I just wanted to get away from the house and the telephone.

Even when we were not home, the problems of the SRS camera were with us in our conversation. The camera was finally ready, but it was quite a conspicuous setup. We wondered how on earth Ed could ever take photos with the SRS without everyone who saw him figuring out who he was. It was one other inconvenience we would have to cope with, another thing that would chip away at Ed's anonymity.

Late Sunday afternoon, March 13th, we went to see Duane and Dari. Ed wanted to tell them about ''Jane's'' call and show them the SRS. They asked when Ed planned to try to use the camera and suggested we meet them in Shoreline Park around six o'clock that evening in the hope that the UFO would show. Ed agreed and said he had promised to call Peter Neumann if we went out again so that Peter could bring his camera and cover anything that happened for the TV news.

Later, when we all met in the park, there was an undercurrent of excitement that helped us ward off the early-evening chill. Peter's wife, Phyllis, had come with him, and the six of us congregated around one picnic table in an open area of the park. Ed took some test shots with the SRS, and we waited. Not long after we arrived, we saw two satellites go over, one west-to-east very fast, the other north-to-south more slowly. Then across the sound we saw fireworks set off by spring-breakers at the beach.

We had been there about an hour when a man and his son out UFO watching came by and asked if they could sit with us. Duane knew the father and guided them away from where the rest of us still sat watching the sky. The man told Duane he felt sure that either Ed or Peter was "Mr. Ed." Who else would be out there with that strange camera setup? He just didn't know which one of the men was the photographer. Duane explained that that was how we wanted to keep it and asked the man not to try to join our group or we would all leave and a photo opportunity might be lost.

The man agreed, but it made no difference. We stayed in the park for more than two and a half hours with no sign of the UFO. Finally, the wind now blowing off the water and freezing us, we decided to call it a night. We should have stayed a few hours longer, as the following report from the *Sentinel* indicates:

On Sunday night, March 13, around 10–10:30, Dennis Warren received a call from his mother advising him that a friend of theirs was watching a UFO. Dennis, who lives on the sound side of Pensacola Beach, south of Shoreline Park, took his binoculars out onto the deck and saw two very bright lights moving toward him down the Gulf Breeze peninsula.

The lights went below the tree line near Shoreline Park, but popped back up, first moving westward past Deer Point, then eastward toward Shoreline Park, finally vanishing below the tree line once again. Dennis continued to watch as the lights popped up once again over the trees and moved off to the northeast and out of sight.

"I watched the whole thing through my 7 × 50 binoculars,"he said. "No helicopter or airplane light configuration matched what I saw.

"I'm not going to jump on the band wagon and tell you I've seen a UFO," he added quickly, "But I did see something I've never seen before. The intensity of the lights kept me from seeing what was behind them."

MARCH 14, 1988—MORE WITNESSES

Laura came home from school at about three o'clock complaining that her left wrist was hurting badly as a result of an earlier fall. I took her to the hospital to have it X-rayed. Frances had to accompany Dan to the orthodontist to see if he would need to have four wisdom teeth pulled, so she didn't go with me.

Later Frances helped Laura, her wrist wrapped to protect three torn ligaments, finish her homework while I tried to catch up on work in my office. We had decided not to go out UFO hunting that night, but the UFO was active. The *Sentinel* reported that on Monday night, March 14th, several people saw what was thought to be a larger and slower UFO moving up and down the Gulf Breeze peninsula.

One of these accounts was given by a family—father, mother, and adolescent son. At about 8:00 P.M. they saw a large UFO approaching Gulf Breeze from the southwest, which they watched for several minutes while attempting to follow it.

At one point the son screamed that he heard an adult male voice in his head command, "Stop!" The boy said it wasn't as if he were being spoken to, but more like he was overhearing the voice speaking to someone else.

The mother explained that her son, who isn't easily frightened, was very upset and physically ill that night after the incident.

I have included this highly condensed report here because of the apparent telepathy with the boy. The complete account of this, and other sightings, from this date are included in Appendix 2.

MARCH 15, 1988—MORE STRANGE RADAR

Across the sound, to the south of Gulf Breeze, is Pensacola Beach on Santa Rosa Island, a tourist area complete with all the trappings. A landmark sign proclaims the "World's Finest Beaches," and that's probably closer to the truth than most advertising.

On the west end of the island are the remains of historic Fort Pickens, a part of the National Park Service. Tourists abound in this park area, which leads me to the unexplainable selection by the military of the fort's parking lot as the site to set up a portable radar unit. A large color photo of the unit was published by the *Pensacola News-Journal* (see photo following page 256) accompanied by what sounded like a spontaneous answer to the reporter's question "What's this doing here?" The caption under the photo read,

> Visitors to Fort Pickens for the next month will see an Army Mobile Hot Bench, which serves as a radar test station. It's an all-terrain vehicle with an arm that can lift a globe-enclosed-radar 150 feet. The truck was developed by Westinghouse Corp., in conjunction with the Army, to monitor weather and for air traffic control. Fort Pickens was selected because it is a federal installation close to the Naval Air Station, said Army Lt. Col. Nelson Johnson. The station had to be close to NAS because the Army is also testing other devices at the base. But, Johnson said he could not say what other devices are being tested.

There must be a dozen active federal installations near the Naval Air Station, but the tourist parking lot at Fort Pickens is certainly the closest to Gulf Breeze. If the military was trying to triangulate the area with radar, then all they needed was another unit to the east in order to tie in with the NAS and Fort Pickens units. Later in the week reports came in that the first ''mysterious radar blimp'' that had been anchored in Pensacola Bay was now anchored to the east, near Navarre. The triangle was complete.

MARCH 17, 1988—EIGHTEENTH SIGHTING—SHORELINE PARK WITH SRS CAMERA

The number of radar units in the area didn't seem to bother the occupants of the UFOs. There were rumors of several sightings from the previous night that were being covered by the local ABC television station. I went to the *Sentinel* office in the afternoon to discover what they knew about these reports.

While I was there, a flurry of investigators arrived asking questions; others were on the telephone with Duane wanting names and addresses. I sat quietly on a sofa and listened to the excitement. Suddenly a hum shot through my head. It was 4:30 in the afternoon, with people coming and going in such a rush of confusion that I said nothing.

Ten minutes later I heard the hum again but still said nothing. After a few more minutes I got up to leave. Walking down the hall toward the lobby, Dari passed me, and I whispered to her about the hum. Her eyes widened and she said, "Oh no, what should we do?"

We went out the back exit to check the horizon, but there was nothing there. I really didn't expect to see the UFO, since I had never had a daytime sighting. The closest I had came was dusk and dawn. Some of the others noticed what we were doing and suspected our reason. A lot of cameras were quickly loaded and held at the ready.

After half an hour of heightened anticipation I was sure that nothing was going to happen. The UFO had simply hummed for reasons unknown. I excused myself and left to go back to work at a job site that needed my attention.

Trying to learn about other people's sightings distracted me from my everyday work and made it necessary for me to put in some long hours at night. After dinner that evening, while trying to keep my mind on a set of house plans I was drawing, the phone rang. I answered to find Duane and Dari calling on their car phone from South Shoreline Park. They were UFO watching and wanted to know if Frances and I wanted to join them. I answered with an indifferent "maybe" and qualified it with "only if Frances wants to go with me."

Shortly after talking to Duane, before I could ask Frances if she wanted to go to the park, I heard the hum—just a brief buzz. I called Frances into my office and we talked it over. The arguments against going were winning when the hum returned, a very short burst of heavy humming. I would have left for the park right then, but Frances was still against it.

During the next hour, between 7:00 and 8:00 P.M., as we continued to discuss going to the park, there were five of these occurrences. Finally, convinced that these hums were some kind of signal, we loaded the SRS camera into the truck to drive to the park. I had promised to call Mayor Ed Gray, Councilwoman Brenda Pollak, and News Director Peter Neumann in such an event, so before leaving I called. The only one home was Ed Gray, who felt he should pass on this opportunity and wait for another day.

When Frances and I arrived at the park, only five minutes from our house, there was no sign of Duane and Dari. We stepped out of the truck to be buffeted by the icy wind blasting across the rough sound water. Frances promptly complained about the cold and got back in the truck.

As chance would have it, there were several sheets of four-by-eight plywood in the back of my truck. I told her to wait in the truck while I used one of the pieces to form a windbreak at the most sheltered waterfront picnic table. I returned to get Frances and the SRS just as a car pulled up beside my truck and a couple named Clayton stepped out with a smile and knowing attitude.

I was talking with the Claytons when Duane and Dari returned with refreshments for what they planned to be a long night. After a bit more conversation the Claytons left, and the rest of us proceeded to the picnic table.

The tripod was stationed in front of the windbreak with the cameras pointed south. While I continued to set up the SRS camera, Duane went back to try to contact the Pollaks and the Neumanns on his car phone. About the time I finished adjusting the camera by connecting the center rod per Dr. Maccabee's instructions, the Neumanns arrived. We were still expecting Buddy and Brenda Pollak.

The SRS hadn't been loaded yet, and I handed two new, unopened boxes of film to Peter Neumann. Peter opened the boxes, and the camera was loaded before the eyes of everyone. I was very cautious to make sure this loading process was duly witnessed and handled in a controlled, scientific manner, the way the investigators would want it to be.

Within a few minutes Buddy Pollak drove up saying he had left a message for Brenda, who would be along later. I had learned what the debunkers would claim, so I took a control shot with the SRS that showed Buddy in the foreground. The bushes that helped protect us from the wind, and curious outsiders, were clearly visible in the background.

This control shot would establish the location and the fact that it was the shot taken in the presence of those witnesses, plus there were serial numbers on the back of each photograph. These serial numbers corresponded with the numbers on the film boxes. It was easy to tell which photo was from which camera. The left camera serial number was different than the right camera's.

With the cameras ready, we all settled in for some interesting conversation and waited. The minutes passed slowly and the cold wind blew in our faces. The plywood windbreak was the only thing that allowed us to stick it out. We took turns sitting behind it.

The SRS camera was very imposing and very noticeable. The few people remaining in the park, besides ourselves, were persistent UFO watchers, some with cameras in hand. They put two and two together and quickly realized that somebody in our group was probably "Mr. Ed."

Some of these "watchers" edged closer and closer to our picnic table. Buddy Pollak walked over to guide them away. He returned saying he knew the people and had simply asked them to respect our privacy. I learned later that these "watchers" were Carlos Hill and his son, and two other young men still unknown to me.

We continued our vigil, watching every bright spot in the sky undisturbed. Across the sound we could see the skyline of Pensacola Beach, and the question arose as to whether or not the SRS camera could pick up the building lights at that distance, about two miles. Peter suggested that we shoot another test shot, which we did. Only the brightest lights showed in the photograph.

The cold was settling deeper into our bones, and by 10:00 P.M. a motion was made that everybody should leave except Frances and me in the hope that the UFO might show if there was no crowd. The others agreed to go after hot chocolate and coffee and return in half an hour or so. Peter and Phyllis Neumann said they had an early schedule in the morning and left for home.

Frances and I believed that we were alone, secluded by the surrounding trees that obscured our picnic table from the parking lot. Unknown to us, our fellow watchers had agreed to pretend to leave, going so far as to drive out of the parking lot, then had stealthily returned without their headlights on to give them away.

Their presumption was that if the UFO was reading my thoughts, and I thought that they were gone and that Frances and I were alone, then the UFO might show up. They may have been right. Only a minute after everybody left, I heard a hum—the first in over an hour. We watched the sky with nobody, we thought, to call to. About four minutes later I glanced southwest and saw the UFO wink in.

I jumped for the camera and turned the tripod control handle. My heart was pounding and my legs felt suddenly weak. I kept saying, "There it is! There it is!" I fumbled for the shutter buttons and shot the photographs (photos 36L and 36R). The double flashes lit up the trees in front of the camera. When I looked up, the UFO was still there for a few more seconds, then it winked out. The time was 10:10 P.M. The whole sighting had lasted only about ten seconds.

Frances had leaned over the plywood to watch the entire event, and now she told me to get the pictures. The pictures had automatically ejected from the front of the cameras and were hanging there, flopping in the wind. I pulled them out and carried them to the table.

We tried to use our flashlight to watch them develop but couldn't get it to work. A rechargeable Black & Decker, the light was working when we arrived at the park, but it hasn't worked since. Anxious to see if anything would show on the film, I dashed down the path between the trees to the parking lot to use my truck headlights to view the photographs. As I emerged from the trees, I saw Duane and Dari in their car and waved at them to come over. Buddy drove up from the other end of the parking lot as I turned on the headlights.

I hurried to the front of the truck to hold the pictures in the beam from the headlights. The UFO was still developing on the film as we all huddled around in silence. Then, in a burst of exhilaration, there were people I didn't know running around us saying, "Oh no, I can't believe I missed it."

"I was just out on the pier; if I had only stayed there!"

"It must have been behind those trees."

"Let's do it again. Let's hide and see if it will come back."

Brenda Pollak drove up in the middle of the excitement with an equally exciting story of her sighting, which had occurred on her way to find us in the park. Duane asked if she would let him put her story in the next issue of the *Sentinel* and she agreed. Her story told, Brenda wanted to be brought up-to-date on what had happened with all of us.

Duane told about the little trick they had played on me, pretending to leave. They had all seen the flash up in the trees but, as with the others in the park, had been prevented from seeing the UFO by the thick growth of trees to the southwest. (We later realized that was the only location in the park the UFO could have used that allowed Frances and me a view while denying all others in the parking lot any opportunity to see it.)

Then everyone asked me exactly what had happened during the sighting. We trooped back out to the picnic table, where Frances and I reenacted the sighting several times, and then I took two more sets of control shots using Carlos Hill and his son as foreground reference. (One of these sets we gave to Carlos as a souvenir after verifying the numbers on the back.) That made a total of five shots taken with the new pack of film, which had ten exposures.

Before moving the SRS camera I asked Carlos to note and say aloud the numbers on the film counters on the back of the cameras. Both read five remaining shots. Every shot was accounted for and the film pack numbers were correct, but more important were the witnesses seeing the film develop before their eyes in the truck's headlights. The only thing that would have been better was if the whole group had seen the UFO with us.

The following week Duane printed the photographs in the *Sentinel* along with his corroborating account and Brenda's story, which can be found in Appendix 2.

March 17, 1988—Frances's Account

As soon as I stepped out of the truck, I knew it was going to be the coldest night I had ever spent in South Shoreline Park. I had thought I could never be colder than I was the night of March 13th, when we sat in the park with the Neumanns and Duane and Dari in our unsuccessful stakeout for the UFO, but even though I was wearing thermal underwear this time, the cold cut right through me.

By the time ten o'clock rolled around and the others said they were going for hot chocolate, I was ready to go with them. Instead I stayed with Ed, praying the UFO would come so that we could leave. My prayer was answered, and I had the excitement of the moment to warm me.

After the photos had been taken, Brenda had told us of her sighting, and we had re-created ours, we lingered in the park only a few more minutes before everyone decided there was no reason to stay out in the cold any longer. The Pollaks and Duane and Dari planned to drive out to Soundside Drive to see what, if anything, was happening out that way.

Ed and I declined their invitation to go along. We waved good-bye to them, anxious to get home. Before we could finish loading the SRS camera back in the truck, another car pulled up beside us, and a friend of ours, Reggie White, got out.

Reggie told us she had been parked at the east end of the park the whole night and had seen the flash and the commotion. For weeks Reggie had been telling Ed she was sure he was "Mr. Ed"; now she had her proof. Ed asked her why she hadn't come down and joined everyone else to look at the photos. Her answer that she hadn't wanted to intrude touched me. Ed showed her the two pictures, we talked for a few minutes, then we all said good night and left.

Ed and I were at the turn to go home when he remembered that he had promised Peter and Phyllis Neumann that we would come by and tell them if something happened after they left. We detoured to their house and got out and rang the bell. After a few minutes Peter came to the door, followed by a very sleepy Phyllis. We related the story to them while they looked at the photos through a magnifier.

They told us that after leaving the park they had stopped by their house to check on their son, then gone down to Deer Point. From that vantage point on the water, they had looked back to the east and seen a flash go off. We decided there hadn't been time for them to get to the point before the UFO had appeared, so what they had seen had to have been the flash from one of the control shots taken afterward.

We thanked them again for having endured the cold with us, especially since it had been such a disappointing ending for them personally. Then we went home.

I fixed hot chocolate for us, and while we sipped it, we looked at the double photographs Ed had taken. Maybe this was what Dr. Maccabee wanted and needed. I hope so, because what I wanted and needed more than anything was never to have to go out looking for the UFO again. Never to have to feel the obligation to take its picture. To be able to tell Ed, "Let it hum. Maybe if you ignore it enough times, it will just go away."

MARCH 18, 1988—CRITICS FROM AFAR

The day after the successful trip to the park with the SRS camera, Peter Neumann stopped by my house and explained that he had been asked to try to get me to call and talk with one of their network correspondents. Just talk to them, that was all. He assured me they were very professional and would respect my desire to withhold my identity.

I called while Peter was still sitting in my office. The correspondent promptly set up a conference connection with a co-worker. We talked for two hours, during which time I recounted most of the sightings and events. One voice at the other end of the phone was familiar to my ear, having heard it in various reports of news events. The face that went with the voice eluded me, but the man sounded receptive and excited as I answered his questions. Little did I know that he was trying to bait me into a trap.

This correspondent had from afar, with only a copy of the half-hour documentary with its TV-enhanced photos to guide him, concluded that the UFO photos were double exposures. He never indicated this to me during our long conversation, nor even hinted that he had doubts. But later I would discover that he had taken it on himself to telephone Mayor Ed Gray and, by using his position with ABC (but withholding his name), managed to convince the mayor that "anybody can take a double exposure using two pieces of glass and a black curtain."

When this anonymous ABC critic was challenged to send us an example of the "road shot" or even photo 1, partly obscured by the tree, he could not. When asked to explain the SRS camera shots, he merely brushed them aside saying, "There must be an explanation."

239

On that point he was right. There was an explanation, one that was obvious to most of the researchers and investigators, and more and more obvious to the general public. There was an unidentified flying object in the skies over Gulf Breeze.

Had I known of the "armchair" critics who wouldn't wait for the facts but would prematurely give their opinions in order to get their names in the paper, I might have been even more reluctant to share the photos and events with the media. I would learn that media coverage is the adrenaline that pumps the hearts of the debunkers, whereas patient research scientists work steadily to prove or disprove the UFO phenomena uninfluenced by the media hype. Later I would also learn that some of the controversy, generated by people who had never even been to Gulf Breeze to investigate, was political—UFO politics between different investigation groups.

One UFO group found the Gulf Breeze case a perfect means to excite a controversy. It quickly published a *Bulletin* that bordered on slander. No evidence was given to support its charge of a hoax. It did get the attention it wanted, but most of it backfired, and several months later the group would jump on the fence by releasing a position statement saying, "The Gulf Breeze case is a significant case yet to be proven." Given the earlier outrageous *Bulletin,* this new position was a complete turnaround.

MARCH 20, 1988—NINETEENTH SIGHTING—BEHIND TREE SRS

I now understood that the most credible camera was the SRS. This camera, along with Dr. Maccabee's abilities to analyze the results, was hard to dispute. A single camera gave the analyst much less to work with, especially if the photograph was a night shot with little foreground and no background. A 35mm was an easy camera to discredit because of its built-in ability to double-expose. My old 108 Polaroid was also easy to double-expose, but the new 600 Sun cameras didn't have that drawback. With auto flash and immediate ejection of the film, they were by far the best to mount on the SRS camera tripod.

Having taken one double shot with the camera and realizing the scientific importance of the new photos, I was convinced to try again if the UFO would give me the chance. For two days the SRS camera remained set up on my back porch in the hope that I would hear something. Then, at 10:50 P.M. on the 20th, I was brushing my teeth when I heard, "Zehaas. Zehaas, sleep and know."

I quickly grabbed my bathrobe and stepped out onto my back porch. The covered, screened porch offers a restricted view, so I took the SRS camera and set it up on the east side of the swimming pool near the gate in the back fence. I sat quietly, and within a few minutes the UFO appeared to the north of me. I leaned over to aim the tripod and look through the right viewfinder.

The UFO was the same shape and color as the one photographed on the 17th in the park. I flashed the right-hand camera then fumbled for a few seconds with the left shutter button before it fired. As before, the

241

UFO remained for only a few seconds after I shot the photographs. This seemed to be intentional on the UFO's part, as if it were calling me to come out and photograph it. But why? I could only conclude that the beings aboard the craft knew the importance of the photos and wanted the investigators to have the best photographic proof they could.

I carried the SRS back to the porch and took the photos (37L and 37R) into the house to look at them. They were disappointing to me because the left image of the UFO was obscured by a tree branch and only partly showed through the pine needles. A day or so later I mailed the originals to Dr. Maccabee for him to analyze.

Later I learned that on that same night, earlier than my sighting with the SRS, there were two other sightings, one involving a report of the blue beam. Here is that report, as published in the *Sentinel:*

Roger McCann and his 13-year-old daughter, Jennifer, and 8-year-old son, Trey, had a very exciting experience on Sunday night, March 20.

At about 8:10 P.M., the McCanns and three adult friends spotted three UFOs hovering in a triangular position above the beach. "We were about one half way between the second water tower and the National Seashore," Roger reported. "One of the ships was larger than the other two."

The owner of McCann Insurance Agency and the Jolly Roger charter boat, Roger had been very skeptical about the reported UFO sightings in the area. "I have never seen any of the pictures or articles that have been published," said Roger, "so I don't know what everyone else has seen. I just know that these were not experimental aircraft . . . this was for real."

The group had been watching the crafts for about ten minutes when another small ship whizzed by about 1000 yards offshore. They were able to get a good enough view to give this description:

"It was kind of oblong—almost like you'd see in a space movie. There were four strobe lights on the top of the craft. The lights were pulsating. Toward the lower middle of the craft there was a row of yellow lights that were fixed . . . these were portholes we think. Along the bottom of the craft there was a row of rotating lights. They were a yellowish color."

The group of six were all trying to share two pairs of binoculars so things were confusing at times. But two of the group reported seeing blue beams shooting out from the largest ship. One observation was that the largest ship seemed to be pulsating—changing shape.

The ships moved out of sight once an aircraft appeared in pursuit. But not before the group enjoyed about 15 minutes of entertainment by the UFO.

"Now I'm anxious to see the pictures and articles that have been in the *Sentinel*," said Roger. "This was the most exciting thing I've ever seen in my life."

Several other sightings reported during this time are included in Appendix 2.

As a curious aside, Duane Cook received a phone call from Ada Vasquez, who lives in Orlando, Florida. She suggested that the name given to me by the aliens was actually Spanish and spelled *cejas*, meaning eyebrows. She had read an article about the Gulf Breeze UFO reports that mentioned my curly eyebrows and she concluded that the aliens would likely be impressed by such eyebrows. She went on to explain that *cejas* is pronounced, "See-hass."

Whether her speculation was correct or not, I didn't know. But it was possible that since the beings had no eyebrows, my rather prominent ones would be something they would easily remember. The idea that the beings might be doing what our researchers do when studying a wild creature, finding some distinguishing mark to help identify their subject, was not at all pleasant. Maybe that is why I continued to write "Zehaas" in my journal entries.

APRIL 18, 1988—DEBUNKER CONTROVERSY

Almost a month had passed in a blur of confusion mixed with excitement and disappointment. Reporters and interviews were the daily norm. I so much wanted to say no. No especially to the reporters, who seemed never to get the story exactly right. Some were worse than others, and even talking with them for hours didn't seem to stop them from turning times, places, and events around.

The Sunday magazine insert in the Orlando *Sentinel* managed most of the facts, but still played hide-and-seek with a lot of the minor details. Although the mistakes were not major, they were still mistakes, like claiming that our dog appeared in a certain photograph when it was a different one she was in. It wouldn't have been all that important except that the reporter used the reaction of the dog to come to a negative, and incorrect, conclusion.

The errors in the media were frustrating, but not as disturbing as other news. I learned of a local juvenile who was being quoted by a critic as having claimed that I was a dangerous person. The critic, eager to uncover something negative, believed everything he was told and made no attempt to discover if there was any validity to what the boy said.

Had this critic bothered to do a little investigating, he would have learned that this boy had been banished from our home and parties because of undesirable behavior, which he refused to change. Instead of doing the responsible thing, this critic made as big a fuss as possible. The man wrote a rash, sixteen-page letter, bordering on the libelous, trying to cast doubt on my character, then circulated this letter to all of the investigators. My wife and I heard of it and demanded a copy. Frances was so outraged she responded with a fact-by-fact, detailed rebuttal.

In the midst of the written and verbal thunder that fell on my family daily, we tried to continue with as normal a routine as possible. My regular work load was sprinkled with various community service projects. From speaking to a class at the high school about architecture and building techniques to helping the high school band boosters organize a bingo parlor as a weekly fundraiser, I was very occupied.

Each day that passed I considered a victory as long as the UFO stayed away and my wife and children were not ridiculed. This was not to continue to be the case. As these overwhelming events gained more and more public credibility, the critics, who seemed to have trouble accepting the obvious, appeared infuriated.

There were very few of these critics, but they were vocal. One afternoon I received a hate letter in the mail, which was also directed toward Duane Cook. We later discovered that many, many copies had been circulated around town by someone who had a history of trying to discredit UFO sightings.

The debunkers were trying to turn my friends and neighbors against me. The letter contained my phone number and challenged people to call and harass me. Nobody called. My community rejected the attempt to discredit me, and I felt proud of my neighbors and grateful to those who knew the truth about me. Gulf Breeze residents were far too open-minded to believe that all the sightings I had witnessed and the hundreds that others had witnessed could be anything other than real. The people of Gulf Breeze are the best, and I thank them.

The sightings continued in every area of town. If you spoke to somebody about the UFO, either they had seen it themselves or they knew somebody who had. The sightings were so numerous that many never made the newspaper or any official report; others didn't get published for days or weeks after they had been called in to the *Sentinel*. Here's a brief account of a sighting made by a local minister. This was the second minister to report seeing the UFO.

A prominent Gulf Breeze citizen reported a sighting he witnessed back on March 3. He and his wife were on College Parkway in Polynesian Isles. They both noticed two oblong-shaped crafts with very bright lights hovering over Whisper Bay. After a few minutes the UFOs moved out over the bay and disappeared.

See Appendix 2 for a listing of sightings during this same time period.

While other people continued to have sightings, I, blessedly, had none. Although the attacks by debunkers had to be answered, Frances and I vowed not to let that become the focal point of our lives. In an effort to return to normal we decided to have a spring-break party for the local teenagers. I almost felt guilty for having gone so long without the get-togethers the teens were so accustomed to.

The games we played were inspiring, and I managed to completely wrap myself in laughter. During one game I laughed so hard my cheeks ached. The game was "people stack." We took two sets of twenty balloons and began stacking people on top of each other, lying down on the balloons, until the balloons began to pop. Each team tried to get the most people on their balloons before the stack toppled or the balloons popped. It sounds silly, but seeing the stacks of people . . . it was funny.

APRIL 18, 1988—FRANCES'S ACCOUNT

The spring-break party with the kids had been just what our family needed. For those hours we had totally forgotten the UFO, the debunkers, the reporters, everything. When the next issue of the *Sentinel* came out, we learned that while we hadn't given the UFO our full attention, it had still been busy.

The *Sentinel* recently received a roll of film and a hand-drawn picture along with a note written on a brown paper bag that was left in the night drop.

The note read: "This was in the sky over the beach last Saturday, April 2. Maybe a jet. I think it was the UFO. Other people saw. Five minutes and disappeared."

And along with the drawing, another note: 11 P.M.—Later that night we were on the beach. It came overhead, maybe 100 feet. A white light hit us. I think we were out."

When the roll of film was developed by the *Sentinel*, the prints showed large balls of orange light.

Along with the article, the paper ran one of the photos with the caption: "This picture of a large round orange object was photographed on the beach. If anyone saw this or can identify this object, please call the *Sentinel*." In a later edition of the newspaper they asked if anyone knew the photographer, who had signed his name, for them to call the *Sentinel*. They never received any calls.

There were other sightings reported in that same time period. One was of particular interest to us, although we already knew the details. The sighter lived in our neighborhood and had called Ed the morning after her experience to see if he had heard or seen anything the night before. Though surprised that she knew his identity, Ed had gone to see her and had done his best to reassure her and her daughter. Here is her story as it appeared in the *Sentinel*:

A Gulf Breeze woman and her young daughter were left very frightened by an experience they had with a UFO last Sunday morning (April 3).

"Ann" (she has requested that we not use her real name) was awakened at about 2:45 A.M. by a "thumping sound." She got out of bed to take a look around the house. After checking the other rooms and looking in the backyard, she did not find anything. As she was re-entering her bedroom she noticed a bright glow coming through her bedroom window.

At about that time, Ann's daughter woke up and came into her room. She had been awakened by the commotion and was coming to find out what was going on. They looked out the window and were shocked to see a UFO hovering beside their house at about the same level as a street light.

According to Ann, the "saucer-shaped" craft emitted an orange blinking light and made a sound similar to a loud heartbeat. The craft appeared to be round and moving in a circular motion. (Although Ann heard the thumping sound during her entire ordeal, her daughter heard no sound.)

The two were extremely frightened and did not know what to do. Ann said she felt as though the ship was watching her. She thought about calling the police, but felt they could not really be of any help. She and her daughter laid down on the bed and waited in fear. They listened for about an hour as the craft continued to hover outside until finally the UFO moved off and disappeared.

"My daughter was scared to death . . . I felt total fear and panic," Ann said of her close encounter. "Before this happened, I didn't believe . . . period. I had refused to read your (*Sentinel*) articles." She says this experience has definitely changed her opinion.

The debunkers were also still busy. They had failed to discredit Ed locally, so one of them had written a sixteen-page letter entitled, "The Other Side of the Coin," which he sent to all investigators involved in the case and many not directly involved. When rumors about this letter reached Ed and me, I demanded and received a copy. I wrote a twenty-seven page response, refuting this debunker's "facts," which I hoped would make the critics at least stop and think, and take the time to check things out, before they printed anything else.

Unfortunately that was not to be the case. A condensed version of "The Other Side of the Coin" was used as the basis for a *Special Bulletin* which was mailed nationwide. Told of the libelous nature of the *Bulletin*, Ed and I made a concerted effort to get a copy. On reading it, we were shocked that the writers, representing a reputedly legitimate UFO investigative group, were so obvious in their bias. I hoped that surely no one would believe such slanted, fabricated foolishness.

As the debunkers swung into high gear, so did the radio and TV news coverage. Local stations, as well as the *News-Journal*, had received copies of the *Bulletin*. To counter its distortions and outright lies, Ed had to agree to more live interviews so that the public could hear the real story and hear him respond to questions. He felt that given both sides, the public would reject the false charges of the *Bulletin*.

I agreed with him, primarily because the debunkers had not confined their attacks to the validity of the UFO sightings. If they had, I might have been inclined to let the experts resolve it, but many of their charges were leveled at Ed personally. We felt we had to do something, although neither of us liked waging a battle over Ed's character in the media.

The media calls were no longer just local, or even just from Florida. Ed did several live radio call-in shows for stations as far away as Maryland. Then KNBC-TV in Los Angeles, California, requested a copy of the one-minute thirty-eight-second video tape to accompany a miniseries they were doing on UFOs. Ed sent them a copy. He said he couldn't roll over and let the debunkers discredit the Gulf Breeze sightings. Instead he did all he could to get the facts out.

I guess that's why I could not really understand the debunkers. If Ed had been the only person to have seen the UFO, or even if our family had been the only ones, then maybe the debunkers' attacks would have made some sense. But it was difficult for me to understand why the debunkers chose to ignore all the other sightings, many made by highly respectable witnesses. Almost every day something new was being reported to the

Sentinel or the investigators. Here is one of those reported sightings, which the debunkers seemingly chose to ignore:

On Wednesday, April 6, at approximately 9 P.M., 16-year-old Brandon Wheeler spotted something unusual over the Gulf Breeze area.

"We were going into Gulf Breeze on Hwy. 98 (from the east) and we had just passed the Naval Live Oaks sign when we noticed a big white ring over the trees," Brandon reported.

Brandon was with two friends, 16-year-old Tabitha Rodenberry and 17-year-old Chuck Jordan.

"The lights started glowing brighter and brighter. My friends were freaking out and screaming." Brandon watched as the lights "moved from the left to the right and crossed over Highway 98."

It appeared to be over Gulf Breeze. After the lights moved back across the highway to the left, they "totally disappeared."

APRIL 19, 1988—SKEPTICS

Certainly in an event of this magnitude there is bound to be controversy. That controversy takes many forms, some of them not very pleasant.

SKEPTICS

I, too, was a skeptic before November 11, 1987. My brief exposure to news accounts of UFOs had not caused me any concern, nor created any definite opinion in my mind as to their existence. I fell into the open-minded category that considered other life in the universe possible, but I also retained the attitude of "show me." I can find no argument with the open-minded skeptics.

CRITICS

One type of critic will not allow for the existence of any UFOs not conforming to their own personal theories. Another kind of critic may be selective and choose what event has merit depending on the evidence. The first type is a selective debunker just using another label; the latter is frequently a skeptic who has decided to take an active role in the investigation of the UFO phenomenon.

A UFO critic should study the sighting and, on the basis of the facts, make a personal decision in each case. I can find little argument with this procedure. Unfortunately many critics will read a report written by a debunker and be unduly influenced.

DEBUNKERS

The debunker is the person who unequivocally denies the possibility that UFOs exist and who, in trying to discredit a UFO sighting, will stoop to any level of distortion to convince others that all cases have no merit. They do not have to see any firsthand evidence of a sighting, nor do they have to talk to any of the witnesses before they claim "weather balloon, Venus, airplane, witnesses are liars, and witnesses are perpetrating a hoax."

Debunkers come in many disguises. Sometimes they have scientific backgrounds and make a living writing anti-UFO books. They are sometimes members of UFO investigative groups. Whatever form they take, their method of operation is the same: get the most negative information possible in print.

Two or three debunkers have been hard at work trying to disprove the sightings I have reported. They began by trying to discredit the evidence, compromising the facts if that suited their purpose.

It is very important to the debunker that the public believe them so a standard trick is to circulate a "news release"—the more official-looking the better. I saw one such "news release," which began,

GULF BREEZE, FLORIDA, UFO REPORT ESTABLISHED TO BE OF NO SCIENTIFIC VALUE

This headline was no doubt impressive to the media, but the "release" never mentioned who had "established" this bold statement. We did find out later that the person who had circulated the misinformation had no scientific background that would qualify him to make such a claim.

One researcher from central Florida reported that he had concluded after extensive study that the UFOs in photo 18 "if real, were much closer than indicated by the witness." He calculated the tree line to be 440 feet from the camera, and that was the figure he used in his computations. But when the tree line was measured, it was 175 feet away, quite a difference. Later, when confronted with the numerous errors in his report, the central Florida debunker said he had "filed the corrections under miscellaneous for future reference."

The same man, after many calculations, concluded that the November 11, 1987 sighting had not taken place in about five minutes as I had said. Based on the advancing darkness shown in photos 1 through 5, he claimed that the elapsed time between the first and last photos was more like thirty minutes. Therefore, he claimed, "It is evident that "Mr. Ed" has lied."

However, the truth of my statement was easy to prove. On several different evenings, at Dr. Maccabee's suggestion, I took a series of photos with my old Polaroid camera over a period of five or so minutes after the streetlights went on. I found that the increase in darkness evident in photo 4 relative to number 1 occurred within about five minutes. Dr. Maccabee told me that he, too, had done photographic brightness tests in the evening using a Polaroid Model 600 camera and found that pictures of the sky got very dark over a period of five minutes or so, starting several minutes after the streetlights came on.

Thus, again the evidence was verified and I was exonerated. But it didn't seem to matter. The debunker's accusations were made public and the corrections were ignored. The difficulty the debunkers had encountered in refuting the evidence was directly reflected in how low they reached in their efforts to attack me personally, for that is the trump card of the debunkers—assault on the witnesses' credibility. At any cost the witness must be discredited and made out to be a liar. Ridicule of the witnesses in the public media, which seemed to be the most satisfying to the debunkers, continued.

The *Special Bulletin,* which Frances mentioned earlier, was mailed out by a group claiming unbiased reporting. They proceeded to quote a *Miama Herald* photographer who said, "It [the UFO] just doesn't look right." There were no details given as to the credentials of this photographer and no mention of the ongoing analysis by Dr. Maccabee.

When I was asked to take a lie detector test, I was insulted, but within a week I took the test. This *Bulletin*, which claimed unbias, reported it this way:

> After some prodding, Mr. Ed took a lie detector test, which he passed. However, it is well known that sociopathic personalities can pass lie detector tests even when telling falsehoods. We don't put much stock in lie detector tests.

That quote didn't sound unbiased to me, and I could not help wondering what they would have said had I failed the test. Would they suddenly have professed a belief in polygraph tests?

The debunker's chief line of attack here is to get whatever it is into print and hope that it catches on and is quoted as fact by others. If a debunker says something loud enough and long enough, somebody will believe him.

While considering the attempts by the debunkers to discredit the Gulf Breeze sightings, and in the process slander my family, I realized I should verify the examination of the liquid I had seen fall from the UFO. A sample of this liquid, which I had retrieved from the field behind my house on December 17, 1987, had been given to a man who at the time portrayed himself as a serious investigator.

A month or so later, this man had pronounced the liquid to be ''of no significance,'' claiming it was nothing but rainwater. I had always been reluctant to agree.

Several of the investigators had seen the bubbling action of the liquid, but no one was ever given a copy of the lab analysis that was supposed to have been done. Later we discovered that no lab test was ever requested and that this person had taken it solely upon himself to proclaim the liquid to be of no importance. This should have been an early warning that he was a debunker, for he was making quick judgments without facts.

I had saved a portion of the liquid and, four months later, carried it to Pioneer Laboratory in Pensacola to have it analyzed. Their report was startling. The rainwater claim was completely wrong, and I couldn't help wondering whether it was an intentional deception. The liquid had a seawater base in addition to other elements (see report in Appendix 2), a very strange mixture to find in my backyard. I felt the analysis vindicated my report of seeing the liquid fall to the ground from the UFO.

APRIL 20, 1988—BUDD HOPKINS RETURNS

Mark Curtis, WEAR-TV 3 reporter, called before noon and gave me some startling news. They, and every other TV station, radio station, and newspaper in the area had received a ten-page report written by a debunker who had taken it upon himself to "check out" the Gulf Breeze UFO from the standpoint of weather conditions. His premise was that the November 11th first sighting could not have happened on November 11th because the clouds in the photos were moving from left to right. He calculated that the clouds should have been moving from right to left.

The report he issued was very impressive and to the average reader sounded correct. The letterhead it was written on boldly proclaimed "Project Starlight International," with a copyright notice that insinuated that the information was worth copyrighting.

Unfortunately he approached his research from afar without knowing the two most critical points to determine the validity of the conditions of the cloud formations shown in photos 1, 2, and 3. I need not go into the reasons his report was incorrect. Suffice it to say that the camera angle and wind direction that he used were wrong, so his conclusions were wrong. The media, however, didn't take the time to check the validity of his report. His conclusions were broadcast that night on the local news and printed in the *News-Journal* the next morning.

The very next day, after the report had all the media in an uproar, the critic had to retract the report verbally to the local TV station and newspaper and also issue a written retraction to all of the parties who had received the incorrect report. His retraction read:

254

I am now convinced that the pictures were in fact taken on that Wednesday. I don't mind admitting that I am wrong. Do not judge this case on the basis of this [my report].

Unfortunately a retraction never gets the attention of the initial media coverage, especially with a front-page headline of RESEARCHER SUSPECTS GULF BREEZE UFO PHOTOS FAKE. Even a friend of mine, the mayor of Gulf Breeze, was influenced, and the critic asked if I thought it appropriate for him to call the mayor and retract personally. I told him that, yes, I thought that was the least he could do. I didn't remind him of the promise the newspaper had quoted in its original article. The critic had said, "If I am wrong, I will completely resign from this field." He never mentioned that quote again either.

Two hours before the critic's false accusations were to be aired on the April 20th nightly newscast, Budd Hopkins, Charles Flannigan, Don Ware, and Bob Reid arrived for our 4:00 P.M. appointment. I had expected to spend many hours of serious study with Budd Hopkins, but that was not to be. The meeting was interrupted many times by the turmoil of the upcoming evening news. It was hard to keep my mind on the discussion at hand knowing I was due to be falsely accused of faking the photos.

I tried to tell Budd Hopkins and the other investigators about something I had been doing for the past few weeks. On March 31st, I had begun a serious attempt to discover the meaning behind the message, "In sleep you know." Each night I had concentrated quietly before going to sleep, repeating a thought or question over and over again, hoping to recall from my subconscious an answer that in my sleep I might know.

My flashes of insight were truly bizarre and so cryptic as to be extremely difficult to understand. I had written down each of these insights for later analysis, and that was just one of the things I had planned to discuss with Budd Hopkins during his visit. But with this latest news media activity, most of my attention was concentrated on maintaining my credibility. I couldn't ignore the attempts of the debunkers to discredit me and tarnish the photographic evidence.

The subject of hypnotism was uppermost in the minds of several investigators at this point. Also WEAR-TV 3 reporter Mark Curtis wanted to select a well-known professional psychologist who would hypnotize me. I had completely agreed to the procedure; it was just a matter of when. At the time I would ask Budd Hopkins to participate should he choose to advise. But the bigger questions and possible answers that could be gained from hypnotism were being sidetracked because of the need not to allow the debunkers to get away with their false accusations.

In my present state of aggravation I didn't even want to discuss hypnotism, so we pursued another line of thought. Once again the conversation touched on the times in my life when I could consciously remember missing time or other unusual events, I had always rationalized these incidents, but the chances that they had been earlier abductions seemed more and more likely. These three possible abductions had occurred at eight-year intervals.

When I was seventeen years old, my older brother, Bert, and I lived in a small "mother-in-law" apartment connected to our house. It was about 3:00 P.M., and my mother asked me to go to the local grocery store for a loaf of bread. I raced off on my bicycle with little notice of the large, black dog sitting at the corner of our yard near the road.

As I pedaled along the flat pavement, I felt uneasy and looked back. The black dog was behind me. I mean right behind me. I jerked to the left when I saw it and ran off the road into the ditch.

I looked up from my uncontrolled stop. The dog was nowhere in sight. It was gone. Chills raced down my spine. I righted my bike and took off as fast as I could, trying to get to the store and people.

There were another five blocks to go when I felt that same eerie feeling again. I knew if I looked around, the dog would be there. I didn't look. Instead I pedaled faster and leaned forward to get all my weight into my speed. When I hit the curb at the grocery, I glanced back. I saw only the vacant road.

I walked slowly through the aisles to the bread section and took my time getting to the checkout counter. I wanted to give that strange black dog a lot of time to get someplace else. Finally I left the store and rounded the corner to get my bike. There sat the black dog, with its head next to, and taller than, my handlebars.

Frozen in my tracks, I stared at the dog. It didn't flinch. It just looked at me. I eased over to the opposite side of the bicycle and slowly wheeled away. As soon as I dared, I jumped on the bike and took off.

I had never pushed a bike so hard—must have been a speed record—but the black dog followed. It should have been impossible for it to keep up with me. But calm and unwavering, it just looked straight at me, keeping up that steady gait.

I rode into the yard, jumped off the bike, and let it fall as I ran for the front door to our apartment. I slammed the door behind me and yanked the shade down over the window. My heart was pounding. I doubled over, pulling air into my lungs in a mad rush.

Photo 36R, light-blasted and enhanced for detail, enlargement

Daytime photograph at the location of photos 36L and 36R

After the sighting, there was a great deal of excitement in the park. We took several area-documentation photos, taking special care to record the film numbers. The stereo camera confirmed that the UFO had been a distant object in the sky.

Photo 37L

Photo 37R

At first, the results of this second set of SRS photos, taken on March 20, 1988, were disappointing to me. The left camera had photographed only an odd, broken line of light. The investigators discovered later that the left camera angle had been blocked by a tree branch sixty feet away. Reenactment photos proved that the UFO had been a large, solid object hundreds of feet away. I had pressed the shutters on the stereo cameras about a second apart, which caused some difficulty in the calculations.

RADAR ABOVE THE BEACH

Radar screening

Charlie Steed/News Journal

That mysterious blimp attached to the commercial ship "Jan Tide" in Pensacola Bay is part of an Army research project on radar reflection, said George Roberts, an Eglin Air Force Base public affairs specialist. The ship will remain in the area until late January or early February.

These newspaper clippings demonstrate the sudden interest in low-level surveillance shown by the military only a few weeks after my first sighting. Radar equipment such as this had never been seen before in Gulf Breeze. These pieces were removed a week after my May 1, 1988, sighting.

Bruce Graner/News Journal

Visitors to Fort Pickens for the next month will see an Army Mobile Hot Bench, which serves as a radar test station. It's an all-terrain vehicle with an arm that can lift a globe-enclosed-radar 150 feet. The truck was developed by Westinghouse Corp., in conjunction with the Army, to monitor weather and for air traffic control. Fort Pickens was selected because it is a federal installation close to the Naval Air Station, said Army Lt. Col. Nelson Johnson. The station had to be close to NAS because the Army is also testing other devices at the base. But, Johnson said he could not say what other devices are being tested.

Photo 36L

Photo 36R

On March 17, 1988, Frances and I and six other townspeople were on a UFO watch with the SRS (Self-Referencing Stereo) camera designed by Dr. Maccabee to measure distance and size. After several hours of waiting in the cold Santa Rosa Sound–side wind, I shot these SRS photos. We all stood in the headlights of my truck and watched the Polaroid film develop.

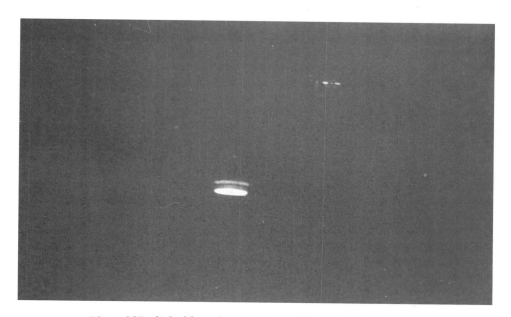

Photo 38R, light-blasted and enhanced for detail, enlargement

Daytime photograph at the location of photos 38L and 38R

After I took the photos with the stereo camera, the UFO suddenly was almost directly overhead, perhaps thirty feet above the nearby oak tree. The second object in the photo was the same size as the ''probe'' craft that I had photographed with the 3-D Nimslo camera. A study of the stereo photos verified that the larger UFO had been over 470 feet away and the ''probe'' just over 130 feet away.

Photo 39

On December 3, 1987, ''Jane'' delivered the above photo and one other to the *Sentinel* newspaper, along with a statement that she had taken the photographs during the summer of 1986.

Photo 40

On December 22, 1987, ''Believer Bill'' photographed the same UFOs that I saw the following morning, when I took photo 18.

Photo 37R, light-blasted and enhanced for detail, enlargement

Daytime photograph at the location of photos 37L and 37R

The enlargement, *above,* of photo 37R shows the same type of UFO that I had photographed so often. The daytime photo, *below,* shows the tree branches that blocked the left camera.

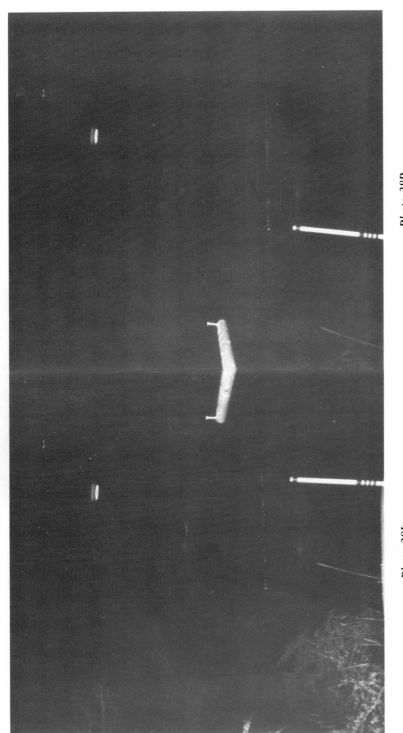

Photo 38L

Photo 38R

On May 1, 1988, with the SRS camera set up overlooking Santa Rosa Sound, I waited for the chance to photograph a UFO. The camera was now improved with a heavy tripod and additional measuring rods. The park was empty at about 1:10 A.M. when I saw a UFO hovering over the sound. I hit the shutter buttons, then looked up at the UFO. There was another object off to the right of the first UFO.

Something was very wrong with that dog. It was much too deliberate. I leaned against the doorframe and peeked out the window. The dog slowly turned its head and met my eyes with a vacant glare. I let the shade drop back in place. After a few minutes I took another peek.

The dog sat there, on the small entry porch, as if it were in a trance. Unmoving, barely five feet away, it was as if it were a guardian. Had there been another one on the opposite side of the porch, they would have resembled a pair of sinister statues. I waited and kept checking for about a half an hour before the dog was gone.

Later that night, as my brother and I prepared for bed, things were normal. Mom had turned on the yard sprinkler, as she did every night during the summer. Around ten-thirty I put the cat out, locked the door, and turned off the light on my way to bed.

Sometime later I felt a force press down on the outside edge of my bed close to my feet. My mind registered that it was the cat jumping on the bed. Again the bed pressed down, and my knees dipped and raised as the mattress absorbed the pressure.

Suddenly my mind whirled and adrenaline rushed through me. I had put the cat out! What the hell was creeping along the edge of my bed? I wanted to jump up and scream, but I was too afraid. I lay there and listened.

The silence was thick, and I could only hear the sound of my breathing. Then the sprinkler splashed water against the front windows. My head was aching, and I felt a knot in my stomach that had turned to nausea. Fear paralyzed me, but I had to do something.

I was lying on my side, my left eye covered by the pillow. Ever so slowly I cracked my right eyelid to peek through my lashes. The room was dark, my vision fuzzy. I could see shadowy gray forms move back and forth as I tried to focus my eyes.

At that moment, straining to see, it happened again. The bed pushed down, this time harder. My chest moved sharply with the direction of the mattress. I was just short of panic. The thing was moving closer and closer to my head.

I closed my eye tightly and pretended to toss in my sleep so that I could curl up into a ball. *There must be a madman in the house,* was all I could think of.

Again the bed went down, this time within inches of my head. The pillow tugged downward and my head bobbed down, then up. A sour scent wafted across my nostrils. I wanted to jump up and scream. But what if the ''madman'' had a knife?

Once more I edged my eyelid open just enough to see. My muscles locked in rigid fear. A slight gleam of light from a crack in the curtains reflected off a bald head just six inches from my face. Large blackened sockets, with no outline of brows or normal features, filled my view.

Eye-to-eye with this thing, terror seized me. I squeezed my eyes closed and screamed in my head: *I'm asleep. . . . I'm asleep. . . . Please go away!* I lay ever so still for a few minutes, conscious of every sound, every feeling. I noticed how wet the pillow was beneath my head. I was sweating, but not enough to have soaked it. The sprinkler pattered against the window, the sound muffled by the blood pounding in my ears.

Panicky, I couldn't stand it anymore. In one motion I grabbed my pillow to the front of my chest—hoping for some protection—and leaped for the bedside lamp. At the same time I started yelling, "Bert! Bert! Wake up! There's somebody in the house!"

Bert answered with a grumpy "What do you want?" as I turned on the light.

Nothing! I could see nothing in my room. I squatted on the floor next to my bed with my back against the bedside table. I called to Bert that there was something on my bed. He reacted in a sleepy voice.

"Yeah, it was the cat. It was on my bed too."

I quickly said, "Turn on your light. Somebody's in here. I put the cat out."

His light snapped on and I saw Bert coming toward me. I jumped up and ran toward him. We met in the small hallway and whispered a plan to check the closets and bathroom.

We whipped open each closet door, ready to run, only to see nothing but hanging clothes. When we started to check the bathroom, Bert noticed that the hallway and bedroom floors were wet.

Strange, wet footprints led from the locked front door, down the side of my bed, and to Bert's bedside. The small tracks showed the paths of several comings and goings. Most of them turned into my room. Shaped like flat-bottomed slippers, the tracks covered much of the floor with wet prints.

Then Bert noticed that I was wet, as if I'd been outside. I told him that I hadn't been anywhere. But I couldn't explain why I was wet or what I had seen.

When I was twenty-five years old, I had been married for two years, and Frances and I had a one-year-old son, Dannie. As with most young couples trying to get ahead, we worked hard.

I worked as an architectural draftsman and welcomed all the overtime

I could get. We had recently invested all of our savings into an older apartment building near the beach. The renovations were taking every extra penny we could earn.

One day the chief architect asked me to go with him after work to meet a client and take notes on a proposed building design. Not knowing how late I would be, I called to Frances to tell her I wouldn't be home for dinner.

The meeting went on and on, finally breaking up about eleven o'clock. I was anxious to get home. Since it was only a thirty-minute drive, I left quickly, without calling Frances again.

Halfway home I noticed something strange about the darkness behind me. As I passed a streetlight, or a roadside building, I could see it go by, but it didn't show in the rearview mirror. Both the inside and the outside mirrors were black.

I turned my head and glanced back. Again, all I could see was blackness. It was just as if a huge black blanket was blocking out the sight of everything behind me. I shook my head, rubbed my eyes, and stepped on the gas. The engine revved, but the car gradually slowed down. I steered to the right, coasting to a stop on the side of the road.

What the hell!? I looked down at the gearshift. It was in neutral. How had I done that? I decided I was more tired than I had realized. What I needed was to stretch my legs for a minute, make sure I was awake, then drive home. I stepped out of the car, confident that everything would look normal.

I looked to the front first. Everything was as it should have been. Then I looked behind me. The darkness was gone. I shook my head. Some trick of the light had to have made my mirrors seem dark.

Way down the road I could see a single light, like the headlight of a motorcycle, only brighter. Faster and closer it came, then rose above the road. I jumped into the car, locking the doors as I started the engine. I fishtailed back onto the pavement and looked in the rearview mirror. The light was gone. The darkness was back.

Racing down the road in panic, I could see the blackness obscure everything I passed. Maybe it *was* a trick of the light. I rolled down the window and stuck my head out for an unobstructed look.

Less than ten feet behind me was a black, rippling wave that blocked all vision. It seemed just to hang there, shimmering, veiling everything. The hair on my left arm stood straight up. The air was heavy with a burning smell.

I turned back around. As I rolled the window up, the car's right front tire went off the road. I slowed and struggled to maintain control. When I glanced back again, the darkness was gone.

Once more a single light approached from the rear. It raced toward me, and I feared it would run me down. I pressed harder on the gas pedal and jerked the car back onto the road. I was trying to outrun it. In seconds it grew to the size of an airport spotlight, flooding the interior of the car with light.

Six hours later, sitting behind the wheel of the car on the roadside, I awoke with no memory of those lost hours.

When I was thirty-three years old, we had only recently returned from living in Costa Rica and set up housekeeping in Corpus Christi. I went out on a solo fishing/canoeing trip, expecting to spend the day relaxing. If I managed to catch a fish or two, fine.

The wildlife along the coastal barrier islands was spectacular. I should have taken a camera instead of a fishing pole. The water cut cleanly beneath the bow of the canoe as I slowly passed hundreds of brown pelicans nesting in and around the trees of the protected islands. The waterway I was in was deep, about fifty feet, and quite often I could see porpoises breaking the surface of the water.

At about noon I was drifting with the current and decided to see what Frances had fixed me for lunch. As I reached into the bag, the bottom of the canoe hit something, then was suddenly still, as if I had run aground. But the sound was like metal on metal. Before I could lift my paddle, the canoe drifted free and continued on.

I looked back, but saw nothing in the clear water that could have snagged me. Turning around, I saw a stream of bubbles stretched out in front of the canoe, racing ahead of me. My attention was no longer on the banana nut bread in my hand, but was glued to the strange bubbles. This was no porpoise.

As the bubbles burst, I could smell the scent of chlorine. The current continued to push me forward, but the bubbles had stopped in my path. I paddled to the left to avoid them. The bubbles moved left. I veered to the right. The bubbles moved right.

Only thirty feet away I could make out a green glow beneath the water. Very big and getting bigger. I tried to backpaddle. The current carried me forward, closer to whatever was rising ahead of me.

What seemed like moments later I found myself sprawled in the bottom of the motionless canoe. I looked up to find I was beached near the mouth of the channel, miles from where I had last been. A barge passed by into the Gulf. My food had flies on it, and my watch read five o'clock.

MAY 1, 1988—TWENTIETH SIGHTING—
THE FINAL ENCOUNTER

When I was forty-one years old, I photographed a UFO and was abducted.

Frances and I continued to disagree about the distance and size of the object we had seen and photographed with the MUFON camera in South Shoreline Park. This debate prompted us to return to the park briefly many times until we decided to take the SRS camera and patiently wait each night for at least two hours in the hope the same craft would reappear.

We started this on Tuesday, April 26th. Dr. Maccabee knew of our attempts and had advised us to take along the video camera and a radio, which would validate the time. He also asked that additional measuring posts be placed in a circle around the SRS camera. Each post was white and placed ten feet from the camera lens.

Our routine usually began at 11 P.M., after the children were in bed asleep. On the 27th the mosquitoes were so bad we stayed only an hour or so. I would have stayed longer had Frances been able to fight off the mosquitoes; they seemed to prefer her over me for their meals. I was always disappointed when nothing happened. A halfhearted promise I had made to Frances made it even harder to call it quits that night and go home.

She was leaving Friday morning to chaperon the high school band on its trip to Nashville. She would be gone four days, and she didn't want want me to go to the park again until she was back home. Since she had to leave so early on Friday, the chances were we would only go to the park on Thursday night for a short time, if at all.

At four o'clock Friday morning Frances left on the Friday-through-Monday trip, and all day I had the feeling that I was not going to be able to resist setting up the SRS camera in the park while she was gone. I wanted to get that photo. After Laura had gone to bed, the temptation was too great. I loaded into the van the rigid frame and tripod that held the SRS camera. Moments later I arrived at the park, followed my equipment-mounting routine, and sat quietly examining the night sky for any movement. Hours later I was disappointed, with only a lack of sleep to show for my trouble.

Saturday night Laura was a bit later going to bed, so I arrived at the park at 11:30 P.M. There were several late-night couples parked overlooking the sound, plus a few boat trailers awaiting the return of the fishermen to haul out their boats after their fishing trips.

The area where I set up the SRS camera was the same picnic table, secluded by trees and bushes on three sides and overlooking the water to the south, that we had used so many times before. The SRS tripod was capable of swinging 360 degrees and elevating in the event the UFO showed above the tree line in any direction.

There was a very slight sprinkle of rain, but I continued setting up the perimeter of measuring poles at a ten-foot radius from the lenses. I used a flashlight and tape measure to make sure the poles were located that exact distance from the camera. Finished, I sat down to wait. The concrete picnic bench got harder the longer I waited.

At 12:30 A.M. I took a break and went to the van to relax in the adjustable captain's chairs. I was less than fifty feet from the setup and there was nobody walking around, so I was not worried about the cameras. Some time later, while I relaxed, I tried to picture the UFO in my head, and at that moment I heard the hum. Very distant, and for only a few seconds, the hum passed across my forehead.

I sat up and looked over the park into the darkness that surrounded me. My heart began to race as I got out of the van. The other cars I had seen earlier were no longer there. Only a single boat trailer, sitting at the other end of the park near one of the few streetlights, was visible to me.

A shiver came over me, and I suddenly thought about Laura, alone in the house. I had to resist the urge to grab the cameras and quickly get out, get away from this presence that was someplace in the darkness. The breeze off the sound felt cool on my face. I noticed that I was flushed, and beads of sweat touched by the breeze caused a chill to shudder through me.

I whispered encouragement to myself, "Calm down, they haven't hurt you lately." Then I said aloud, "Hey, here I am. You call me Zehaas. Here I am."

I looked at my watch; it was 1:10 A.M. I started along the path back to the SRS camera. The tree branches were close by, and my imagination heard sounds in the bushes. I said again, this time louder, ''You call me Zehaas. I want this to be over. I want you out of my life.''

When I reached the picnic table, I sat at the edge of the bench with my hand on the tripod handle. I heard faint sounds coming from the bushes that surrounded my small clearing. My veins throbbed as my heart beat with rapid-fire pounding. I yelled, ''I know you are here. Just do whatever you have to do to get this over!''

My attention was mostly toward the right, to the area in the southwest where the UFO had winked in on March 17th, but as I turned my head to the left, there it was. The glow from the bottom was intense, and the small top light was again clear. The midsection was much darker, but I could still see several small lights around the middle. This familiar, yet incredible, sight caused a tingle down my neck and across my temples.

I took a quick breath to steady myself and swung the tripod around to aim the SRS camera toward the UFO. Through the right-camera viewfinder I could clearly see it rocking gently back and forth. The bottom glow would almost disappear and then return. I fired the shutter buttons and took photos 38L and 38R.

When I looked back up, the craft was still there, but off to the right and a little bit higher was another array of lights. It looked very similar to the object I had photographed with the MUFON camera. This second UFO was moving to the right, so I lowered my eye to the viewfinder again but I saw nothing, not even the bright glow of the first UFO.

My instinct was to quickly adjust the tripod, so I looked up to see where to aim the camera. In a fraction of a second my eyes caught the glow of the UFO about thirty-five feet above me. I flinched, and my right hand squeezed the shutter button, resulting in photo 39. Then, with the UFO just above a small oak tree, my eyes went completely white, just as if a flashcube had gone off in my brain. I could not tell if the whiteness was also around me, like a floodlight, or just within my head. Instantly I felt nothing, no sensations from my body, only a vague sense of falling.

The next instant I was lifting my face and chest up off the sand at the edge of the water. My head pounded, and as I tried to stand, I stumbled in dizziness. Disoriented, I crawled up the beach twenty feet to the bench and sat there with my head in my hands.

A smell from my hands was making me nauseated. Then it dawned on me. How could I fall to the ground while standing at the SRS and get up a second later twenty feet away? I checked my watch and couldn't believe the time. It was 2:25 A.M. What had happened to the hour and fifteen minutes between taking the photographs and finding myself on the beach?

I shivered and sat and shook my head. I had a massive headache, but finally managed to stand. I yelled obscenities into the night sky, then started to cry. I wasn't crying from pain, nor was I emotionally out of control, but as I collapsed the SRS camera, tears ran down my face. I needed to see Frances, but she was far away.

Laura! Laura was alone. I had to get home and check on Laura. I loaded the equipment back into the van, leaving some of the measuring posts in my rush to get home. When I arrived at the house, I saw that Laura was resting peacefully. Still I sat up outside her door the rest of the night, harboring a fear that "they" might return.

At daybreak I was exhausted and collapsed into bed. My right hand smelled so bad, even after washing it, that I had to wrap it in several towels to block the odor. At noon I awoke suddenly and cried out for Frances. She could help me talk about what had happened, but at the moment she was where I couldn't reach her. I got up, but made no mention of the incident to Laura.

In the bathroom I ran a comb through my hair and felt a bump at the back of my head very close to the center of my neck. It felt bruised, and I went to the mirror to try to see what I could feel. When I looked into the mirror I couldn't see the lump, but as I turned around, I immediately saw more than I expected to.

A large bruise, with a red dot in the center, was prominent between my eyes right at the bridge of my nose. Two more similar red marks were centered on my temples, each surrounded by a bruise. I was shocked. What the hell had they done to me?

Later I decided to call Dr. Maccabee just to give the facts to someone, but as I detailed the event, I was swept away and began reliving the moment-by-moment feelings. Dr. Maccabee was a concerned and patient gentleman, who listened and recorded the details.

I complained several times about the stench from my hand and during the course of that phone conversation discovered that the odor was coming from tiny bits of black material beneath my fingernails. Dr. Maccabee asked me to save the black material and put it in the freezer. (This material is to be analyzed as soon as the sophisticated equipment necessary is located.)

Very obviously something strange happened to me during that missing hour and fifteen minutes. One day before too long I will try to discover the secrets locked in my subconscious. There are even now fleeting memories in the morning when I awake, and strange "in sleep you know" messages compel me to undergo regressive hypnosis.

EPILOGUE

The encounters and events from November 11, 1987, to May 1, 1988, have changed my family's and my life forever. No longer can I look at the night sky and disregard the possibilities of intelligent life somewhere in the heavens.

The sightings have stopped, taking with them the strange uneasiness that pierced my every waking hour. But other feelings remain. The aliens tormented me, and I resent them. My character has been assaulted, and that I cannot fully forgive or forget.

The battery of photographs have been studied and restudied. The videotape has been examined closely. The more than one hundred other witnesses have been steadfast in proclaiming what they saw. We have experienced an encounter of spectacular proportions in which several other Gulf Breeze residents have also reported periods of missing time.

The "why me" question is being uncovered through regressive hypnosis under the supervision of Dr. Dan Overlade, clinical and forensic psychologist. The "in sleep you know" memories fit into the emerging picture as does each piece in a puzzle. As the picture develops, the missing-time events indicate repeated contact and abduction spanning most of my life.

The personal stigma I carry in revealing the true story of these emotional events becomes less and less important when compared with the reality of the UFO—proof positive.

INVESTIGATION AND PHOTO ANALYSIS BY DR. BRUCE S. MACCABEE

"I live every day as if this weren't real."
Dr. J. Allen Hynek

Introduction

I'm sure that the story you have just read has boggled your mind as it did mine. Even though I lived through the latter part of the story of these sightings, I still find it incredible to read about them. You may be thinking that all of these sighting events could not possibly have happened as Ed and Frances have recounted them. Certainly, if I had no information other than what is in the preceding chapters of this book, I would assume that the whole unbelievable story was an extremely clever hoax concocted by Ed and his family.

Yet, in my opinion this is not a hoax. After an extensive investigation I have concluded that everything described here actually happened more or less as they have described it.

Accepting this conclusion was not easy for me. I am a scientist with many years of experience in experimental physics. The actions of these UFOs appear to contradict known physics. Therefore to admit that they could be real requires going against what I have learned about the "known" world.

Even though I realized many years ago, after studying numerous UFO sightings that go back as far as 1947, that at least *some* UFO reports absolutely could not be explained by conventional means, I do not automatically assume that each new sighting must therefore be real. Instead, I require that each sighting prove itself to be true independent of previous sightings. For this reason each sighting investigation has to be thorough, with the hoax hypothesis being considered as a possible explanation. Ed's multiple sightings, photos, and contact with creatures made these reports even more difficult to accept as real than the more usual "night light" UFOs or the so-called "daylight disks."

How I concluded that Ed and Frances's sightings were real events is a story that runs along in parallel with the latter part of the sightings. I am

267

recounting it here so that you can see how certain important facts about the sightings affected my thinking and led to my conclusion.

For the local investigators (Don Ware, Charles Flannigan, Bob Reid, and Gary Watson) the work began in late November 1988. I was a relative latecomer. I didn't hear of these sightings until after Ed and Frances had already had some of their most frightening experiences.

Early January 1988

I first heard of the Gulf Breeze sightings while I was at a meeting of the Fund for UFO Research in Washington, D.C., in early January. I was told that several interesting photos had been taken in Florida and that the local investigators thought the sightings could be important even though they didn't know who the photographer was. I paid little attention to this verbal thirdhand report.

About the middle of January, I received halftone copies (pictures made up of tiny dots so that they can be printed in a newspaper) of the first five photos but no other information. There was the suggestion that I might want to travel to Florida to see the originals and to investigate the sightings. The pictures were not very impressive. They showed a strange-looking object silhouetted against the background of the sky. So what? I can make a picture that shows a strange object in the sky, even though the object might not have actually been in the sky. I suspected a hoax.

The only one of the five pictures that was interesting was the first one. "Creating a picture of an object partially blocked by the tree would be a tough double exposure," I said to myself. Since I had no information about who had taken the pictures, or when or where or how, I couldn't rule out the possibility that whoever had taken them actually had the capability to do such an exposure.

There is a lesson to be learned in my immediate response to the pictures, namely, "Photos do not a UFO make." Many people think that the existence of photographic evidence is tantamount to proof. However, this is not true in general, and it may not ever be true, because photos can be hoaxed in many ways (and numerous UFO photographic hoaxes are known). What is needed is photographic evidence combined with a complete story of when, how, under what conditions, and by whom the photos were taken. The photos can then be considered as an accurate aid to the witness's memory, but they are not, by themselves, proof that the witness is telling the truth. For this proof one must look to the story, the "circumstantial evidence." A lawyer once told me that very often a case in a criminal court is not made by the physical evidence (the "hard facts"), because "facts" can always be disputed by the "experts." Instead, a case is made based on the circumstantial evidence that supports the "facts."

One thing the photos can do independently of any circumstantial evidence is to suggest *how difficult* the photographic part of the hoax might be. It is very simple to create a picture of a light in the sky and claim it is a UFO flying by. It is more difficult to produce a convincing picture showing an apparently solid craft in the sky, because this requires the building of a model, the painting of a picture (to photograph), or whatever, depending upon the hoax technique used. It would be even more difficult to create a picture in which a UFO is partially blocked by an object that is at a distance from the camera. It would be still more difficult to create a convincing movie or videotape of a moving UFO.

When I first looked at the pictures, I could see immediately that they required some time and patience on the part of the photographer, assuming they were hoax photos. The first photo in particular indicated some skill in matching the edge of the UFO to the edge of the tree. But without any circumstantial evidence to go on, I had no way of knowing whether or not such photographic capabilities would be consistent with the capabilities of the photographer.

My interest in the Gulf Breeze sightings probably would have ended with a cursory study of these photos if Ed had not revealed who he was to the investigators on January 7, 1988.

January 26, 1988

I was in Los Angeles on business and decided to visit Dr. Robert Nathan at his office at the Jet Propulsion Laboratory in Pasadena. I had been there many times before to discuss UFO photo cases. I walked into his office and before I could bring up the subject we were going to discuss (some other UFO photos), he pointed to some eight-by-ten black-and-white glossy blowups lying near his desk. He asked if I had seen these and I recalled the halftone copies I had received in the mail several weeks before. His copies were much, much better. He went on to tell me that the original Polaroid pictures had been brought to him in early December by a *National Enquirer* reporter and another newspaperman (Duane Cook) for an immediate evaluation. The photo lab had made black-and-white blowups while the newsmen were there. He showed these to me and said that the reporters didn't know who the photographer was. He was not impressed and told them that he thought they were a hoax. Subsequently someone had sent him a copy of a page from the *Gulf Breeze Sentinel* that had a letter from "Believer Bill" and a photo of three objects in the sky. It appeared to us that "Bill" had taken the photo at the top of the page, which showed three objects. (Only later did I find out that Ed had taken it.) Bob and I joked about the gullibility of the press, publishing photos from anonymous photographers. We did, however, agree that at the very least the first photo would be a tough double exposure. Bob had several copies of the pictures and gave me a set.

February 12–14, 1988

On the night of February 12th I received a call from Budd Hopkins. To my great surprise he began to talk about the Florida sightings. He said that he had been to Gulf Breeze and interviewed several people there. From what he said it was clear that there was a lot more to the sightings than what little I had heard. Many sightings had occurred in the previous months and many photos had been taken, the most recent only a few days before Budd's visit. The local newspaper had reported numerous sightings in the area. Budd said that he had interviewed the photographer. Based on his interview and other information he had learned from the local investigators, he felt that there was some validity to the case but that the photos would have to be evaluated before any conclusion could be drawn. He pointed out that the local investigators had neither the equipment nor the technical ability to thoroughly study the photos. He knew that I had studied several well-known UFO photographic sightings in the past, so he suggested that I go there and evaluate these sightings.

I was completely surprised. Here was a man I respect telling me that he was seriously considering that the Florida sightings were real, sightings that I had glibly written off as a hoax. Was he being a bit "soft-headed" in thinking that the sightings could be real or was I premature in my conclusion?

Budd also said that the local newspaper and TV station were planning, independently, to publicize the sightings. In particular, the TV station, WEAR, was working on a documentary about the sightings. This worried me. From my point of view these sightings had not been sufficiently investigated. It seemed quite probable that several weeks or months after the airing of the documentary someone would prove that the sightings were a hoax. Then the media and skeptics would have fun laughing at gullible ufologists. Clearly a good investigation should be carried out *before* the documentary, with its attendant publicity, was presented on TV. (I did not know that the sightings had already received a lot of publicity in the *Gulf Breeze Sentinel.*)

The impending publicity added a feeling of urgency to Budd's request for me to investigate. I told him I would think about it and hung up.

I did think about it for two days. I could afford neither the time nor the money to fly off to Florida on a wild-goose chase. Like most UFO investigators I am not independently wealthy, so my UFO efforts are carried out during my spare time. Nevertheless I decided that if it were that important, I might be able to travel there over a weekend if I could get my trip paid for by the Fund for UFO Research, which has (limited) funding for immediate investigations of sightings. In order to determine just how valuable such a trip would be, I contacted Donald Ware. He gave me further details, said that he thought the sightings were real, and suggested I call Charles Flannigan, who lives in Pensacola. I called Charles and he gave me even more details of the local investigation. He said that he could arrange an interview with the photographer. This was of prime importance to me and I wouldn't have considered going to Florida if I couldn't speak to the photographer. I then talked to Dr. Willy Smith, who told me that an investigation was necessary because he strongly suspected a hoax. I called Robert Nathan, who said that he would help with the photo analysis if I could get the original photos.

After all these calls it seemed to me that this was, indeed, a "hot case" and that, if it were a hoax, it should be laid to rest very quickly. I discussed taking the trip with the members of the executive committee of the Fund and they agreed it would be worthwhile. I made my travel arrangements and, on Friday evening, February 19th, I landed in Pensacola. I estimated that three days at the most would be necessary to resolve the hoax question. I never suspected that I was stepping into the center of a UFO investigation that would become so controversial that within months it would almost tear apart the small community of UFO investigators.

February 19, 1988

Charles met me at the airport, and began to fill me in on what had happened up to that date. He told me things I hadn't heard before, things I could scarcely imagine. A creature in the bedroom window? A blue beam lifting the photographer? A blue beam in a photo? Voices in the head? A dozen photos? A videotape? I had only been there a few minutes and already I was approaching credibility overload.

When we reached his house, he showed me some copies of the photos and one of the reports he had done on the sightings. I was astounded. There it was in black and white, a history of events that I would never have imagined outside a science fiction book. The preliminary field-investigators' report looked like a solid investigation. So why hadn't they concluded already that it was a hoax? Charlie told me that the biggest argument against a hoax was Ed himself. Everything came down to two major points against a hoax: first, aside from the photos, which were my job to evaluate, they had found no clear evidence of a hoax; and second, they couldn't believe that Ed would do this. Charles explained that Ed was reasonably wealthy, well known in the community of Gulf Breeze, and, in the opinion of the local investigators, would have neither the time nor the motive to fabricate all these photos and the story that went along with them.

Coming at this from the outside, I didn't know Ed from Adam, so I was not particularly impressed by Charles's argument. I was impressed, though, by the quantity of information. Clearly, if this was a hoax, it was a hoax on a massive scale.

I prepared to meet Ed the next day, wondering what he would be like. Would he be helpful or standoffish? Would he regale me with one sighting after another and all the fine details of each, or would he be reticent and unwilling to talk very much? And, most important, would he let me copy his pictures for later anaylsis?

My preconception was that these sightings and photos constituted an elaborate hoax. This is not surprising, since the hoax assumption would be my starting point for *any* UFO investigation that involved multiple photos, and doubly or triply so for this one because the sighting events and photos were so different from previous ones. But I had to give the guy *some* benefit of the doubt until I could conclusively prove a hoax. Otherwise I might just latch on to some *seeming* evidence of a hoax and immediately end the investigation, thereby overlooking some important information that contradicted the hoax hypothesis. (In the following months some investigators did just that.) If I were going to call this a hoax, I had to have good, solid evidence that could withstand critical analysis, almost as in a court of law. It is neither scientifically nor morally justifiable to call a case a hoax for the *wrong* reasons, as debunkers sometimes do.

February 20, 1988

When we arrived at Ed's house, I gave the place a quick once-over and was impressed. It seemed that we might have arrived a bit earlier than he expected, but we were welcomed into his office, where we began an interview that was to last all day.

When interviewing a UFO witness for the first time I prefer to talk as little as possible and not be too friendly. I just sit back and let the witness tell his story. Most people are ready and willing to talk to someone who indicates a strong interest in what they are saying. After I know some key details, I can then go back and probe further. Since I was presented as the "photo expert," we began with a review of the photos. I let Ed talk about his experiences while I examined, measured, and copied the photos. Bob Reid arrived and he and Charles kept Ed talking while I was working on the photos. The conversation was taped for later review.

I had been told about the "road shot" (photo 19) and had seen a poor copy. Now I was looking at the original. It was amazing. The composition seemed so real. Yet there were many immediate questions such as, if this object was so bright, why didn't it light up more of the road or surroundings? "Truth is stranger that fiction," I thought, if this were the truth.

I spent the first hour or so trying to determine the size of the UFO, assuming that it was at the distance that had been estimated by Charles Flannigan and Ed. This was done by using the image dimension and the focal length in combination with the measured distance to obtain the UFO dimension (width, height, etc.) from the camera formula (image size/focal length) × distance = object size. The diameter turned out to be about 7.5 feet at the bottom ring and 13 feet across the midsection, which was very indistinct and difficult to measure. The height from the bottom right to the top of the top light was estimated at 9 feet. Thus the object, if real, was considerably smaller than Ed had estimated but certainly of a substantial size.

After I made these calculations I asked Ed to make a scale drawing of the road scene with the UFO placed appropriately for further analysis. As I relayed dimensions to him, Ed became enthusiastic. I knew I had his attention now. We then went on to other photos, beginning with the first ones. For each photo I had him describe the conditions under which it was taken while I measured and copied it.

Ed was reluctant at first to let me copy his pictures, but I told him that I needed copies because if I got into an argument with someone over one of the photos I wouldn't have a chance of winning the argument without a copy of my own. (I didn't tell him that this would be true whether I was arguing for or against the hoax hypothesis.) Ed was convinced, but he said he wanted the copies returned after the analysis was finished. He was worried about the photos getting out of his control. He didn't want them appearing in newspapers, tabloids, etc. without his knowledge. I agreed to his stipulation, but I didn't specify when I would be finished with them. (In some previous photographic cases I have held on to originals for years.)

The clock ticked and the day wore on. There were more and more photos. My brain was approaching saturation. There were so many things to learn, and so many questions to ask. Ed's wife joined the conversation. Then I saw his videotape and the circle of dead grass in the field behind Ed's house. Patrick Hanks (pseudonym), a friend of Ed's family, dropped in to be interviewed (by Charles) about his sighting. We made tests of Ed's ability to hold the camera steady as he took photos. With only about a 30-minute break for late lunch my mind was approaching a condition of terminal information overload.

"Staying power," that's what an investigator needs. Get the witness to tell you all the details of his sightings, and then ask him again. As time goes on perhaps his story will start to break down. Frances brought supper into Ed's office and we continued into the night.

Finally, after about fourteen hours of continual discussion we called it quits. Ed had been totally cooperative for fourteen hours! He hadn't complained when he was asked the same questions over and over again. He must have answered some of the questions a dozen times in the previous weeks, yet he didn't rebel at answering yet again. Obviously this was a serious guy. His diligence in attempting to supply me with necessary information was totally consistent with what he had told me about his decision to publicize his first photos: He told me that it was his civic duty to let people know what was flying around. He said, "What if some child was picked up by the beam and disappeared? No one would know where the child had gone. I just had to alert the community to this possibility."

I was impressed by Ed's staying power. He hadn't complained about the length and intensity of my interrogation of him. I was also impressed by the fact that Ed wasn't afraid to say "I don't know" to some questions I asked. Of more interest was the fact that he turned down the opportunity to use the circle of dead grass as direct evidence for his sightings over the field. He could easily have said that there was a UFO hovering over that particular area and that the circle proved the UFOs were real. Instead he said, "I would like to say that I have seen a UFO over that area, but I can't say that because I haven't seen one over that area." The diameter of the circle was about thirteen feet. This is essentially the other diameter of the UFO photographed in the "road shot." If the sightings were a hoax, then the circle was probably also a hoax. Would a hoaxer reject evidence that he had created to support his sighting reports? I doubted it. I left feeling that if this guy was a hoaxer, he was a most unusual one.

When I finally got to bed Saturday night, I was "zonked." Nevertheless, I awoke early and immediately my brain began to work double time. While at Ed's I had used a portable computer rather than writing notes by hand. This seemed to impress Ed. That was fine with me. I wanted him to know I was serious. I also wanted him to realize that he was under pressure. I was aware that Charles, Bob, Gary Watson, and Don Ware had had Ed "under a microscope" for over a month already. I hoped that a little more pressure would be the last straw. I wanted to see if he would become fed up with questioning and admit to the hoax or else throw us out. He did neither.

On Sunday afternoon Charles took me to the local TV station, WEAR, which has special videotape equipment. There I viewed a slowed-down version of the December 28th videotape. On the TV monitor the image was small and not very impressive. Moreover, the motion was too complicated for an instantaneous analysis. The UFO did appear to go on the far side of some nearby structure, but I couldn't be sure what it was. The videotape would require many hours of patient study with complex equipment before I could understand it completely. Then Charles and I went to Route 191-B, the site of the "road shot." I realized that I could reposition the camera almost exactly by matching up the tree line in photo 19 with the actual tree line. I told Charles I wanted to try that the next day. Finally we visited a friend of Charles's for dinner and then I saw the videotape made by Duane Cook on January 24th.

After viewing Duane's videotape I knew that if this case was a hoax, then Ed was not only a great photographer, he was also a great actor. If it weren't a hoax, then here was a recorded interaction between "them" and a human being of some considerable bravery and fortitude.

The man on the videotape did not seem to be the man I had spent fourteen hours with the day before. The Ed on the first part of the tape was hypertense, screaming epithets at the air, swearing a blue streak, screaming in pain, and talking to . . . what? whom? Was this another personality of Ed's, one that I had not seen in unstressed conditions, or was he really being tormented?

Compared with Ed, Duane was "Mr. Cool." As he rode along in Ed's truck, he just kept the videocamera pointed at Ed most of the time and spoke calmly, while Ed's voice was continually tense.

Ed said he was hearing the "hum" in his head and he said several times, "It's here, Duane, it's here." Then he groaned and swore and put his hand to his head. "It just said something. It just said, 'In sleep . . . in sleep you know.' " Hearing voices in his head? I wondered. "Get out of my life," he yelled. Then he complained that something was pulling at his face. "Your face looks okay to me," Duane responded when Ed asked if he could see anything wrong with his (Ed's) face. Ed complained of pains going down to his stomach and of feeling as if he were going to vomit. He suggested that perhaps he shouldn't be driving, but this didn't seem to bother Duane, even though Ed was driving at 50 or 60 miles per hour along a major highway in the rain. "Am I driving too fast?" asked Ed. "You're okay," said "Mr. Cool." Not once did Duane indicate that he wanted to get out of the truck, even though later on Ed suggested that Duane was in danger (which should have seemed obvious to any person riding with a man who was hearing voices in his head). Clearly Duane was a man of some bravery—or he was part of the hoax.

As I watched, I could feel the tension growing. Ed was imploring "it" to let Duane film while it did what it wanted to Ed. I didn't know for certain what Ed expected it to do, but it seemed that Ed wanted it to remove his ability to hear the hum.

Ed had been driving for about nine minutes and he still hadn't seen the UFO. "We've got to get off this road," he said. He seemed to think that if they went to a deserted area, the UFO would show up. Ed stopped the truck not far from the main highway and got out carrying his Polaroid camera. The rain had stopped and there was only a slow drizzle. Ed walked to the front of the truck while Duane got out to film whatever would happen. Ed implored "them" to do whatever they were going to do to remove the "hum" from his head.

Ed yelled at them to get it over with, to take back the hum and get out of his life. Then he complained loudly about a pain in his left hand, the hand that was holding the camera. Suddenly he screamed in pain. He was nearly crying. I could see his silhouette in the reflection of a streetlight in the wet road. He was bent way over as he screamed in agony. Then the pain suddenly ceased and the hum began to diminish. "If you're going to do it, do it. I ain't going to do this again." He implored them to get it over with. Then he said, "It's gone. The SOB is gone. I don't hear the hum anymore." Ed sounded disappointed that it had departed.

The first time I saw this tape, I thought it odd that Ed did not seem to be happy about the UFO's departure. It seemed to me that he should be overjoyed. It wasn't until much later that I understood the full import of Ed's disappointment.

It started to rain more heavily. With the pain and the hum gone, Ed walked back to the truck. Duane, who had been standing next to the truck, got back into the cab. Ed stood outside next to the driver's side door. Again he implored them to "do it" because "I ain't going to do this again."

"I think it's gone, Duane." Duane's response was "Perhaps I shouldn't have gotten out of the truck." Then Duane asked how to turn the camera off, evidently figuring that everything was over. "Leave it on," said Ed. "It will help me to remember what happens." And then, only three minutes after Ed stopped the truck and got out, the climax came.

"Oh, f—— Oh, s—— There it *was*!" he yelled. At the same instant the videocamera picked up the flash from his Polaroid camera. The images on the TV screen moved wildly as Duane tried to get out of the truck to see the UFO, but he was too late. The craft had been visible for only a couple of seconds, according to Ed. Ed had tried to get its picture. "I don't know if I got it, Duane. I aimed too quick."

Ed was very angry that Duane had not seen the UFO. "That SOB is just f——with me," he yelled angrily. "It's trying to torment me." Duane tried to calm him down by pointing out that he had, in fact, seen the camera go off. After several minutes of Ed's protestations voiced at "it," Duane reminded him to pull the film from the camera so that it could develop. After another minute Duane pulled the paper off the back of the picture and there it was. The picture showed a UFO above the truck with streaks of light going upward to the top of the picture (photo 21). Duane was elated, but Ed was not. "But you didn't *see* it," he protested. Duane agreed but pointed out that he saw Ed take the picture (or so it seemed) and that he did indeed peel the picture backing off. As far as Duane was concerned, this was almost as good as seeing the craft itself. Ed suggested that he should take another picture from the same position for comparison and he did that. Of course the second picture showed only the top of the truck.

Ed and Duane discussed the events over the next ten minutes or so as they drove back to Duane's office. They tried to recall what the voice had told Ed about half an hour earlier during the early part of the trip, but they couldn't recall that. Ed explained that he had screamed at one time because they were causing extreme pain in his left arm, the arm that was holding the camera. He said he felt that they were torturing him because Duane was there.

Ed gradually calmed down. There was no more swearing and he

began chuckling and laughing again over some of the ironies of the events he had just lived through. This was more like the man I had met the day before. During the first part of the videotape there had been no laughter. Now he was back to what seemed to me to be normal.

The video ended. I was stunned. It was only about forty minutes long, but it seemed a lifetime. I would never have expected anything like this. A long conversation with an enthusiastic person and the discovery of some photographic artifacts of a hoax technique, perhaps, but not a real-time recording of an exceedingly emotional sighting event. Having a sighting recorded in real time is not unique. (I have investigated sightings in New Zealand in 1978 in which two tape recordings were made while the events were happening.) However, having a recording of an apparent personal interaction with *them* in real time is unprecedented.

Was the portrayed anger and frustration real? It certainly *seemed* so. Was Ed truly a man possessed, did he have some severe mental problem, or was this all an act? Ed didn't seem crazy, and certainly mental illness could not explain the UFO pictures. There seemed to be only these two choices, the real thing or an act.

Part of me hoped that it was an act because I hated to think of the implications if the events I had just witnessed had been real. It was curious that the UFO appeared when Duane was looking out the wrong side of the truck to see it. (Duane had been looking to his left toward Ed. The location of the UFO image places the object in the sky to the right of the truck. In the dark Duane could not see through the videocamera viewfinder which direction Ed was looking, so he did not know where to look when Ed yelled.) When it was all over, Ed had gotten a picture of something that Duane had not seen. This certainly sounds suspicious.

Furthermore, I knew how it could have been done using a double-exposure technique. I knew from my experiments the previous day that it was possible to make multiple exposures with his Polaroid camera, that is, to click the camera shutter more than once before pulling his film out to let it develop. He would first take a picture of a small model or paper cutout, appropriately designed to represent a UFO, that was silhouetted against a black background. He would leave the film in the camera, not pulling it out to develop. Then, during the excitement of the moment, while Duane filmed him, he would then make the second exposure using the flash to illuminate the nearby truck. Now when the film was pulled from the camera, the picture would show a superimposition of the second exposure (the truck) on the first exposure (the UFO).

Did Ed really have the knowledge to do that? I didn't think so based on my conversation the previous day, but I couldn't be sure. I decided to test his knowledge.

The next day Charles and I went to the *Sentinel* office, where I met Duane Cook and viewed the photos sent it by two other anonymous witnesses. Here were the original "Believer Bill" photos and the two other photos. They all clearly showed the same objects, although the photographic equipment was different. Bill had used a 110-type camera (he provided the camera along with the photos). The other photographer evidently used a 35mm camera. I copied these photos for later study and then discussed Duane's trip to the Jet Propulsion Laboratory. Duane impressed me as a straightforward newspaper type, not likely to be involved with a UFO hoax.

In the afternoon Charles and I returned to the site of the "road shot." Ed came along to provide the truck. We wanted to determine the exact location of the truck. After we made numerous measurements, Ed reconstructed the events for me. He recounted how he had stopped the truck abruptly on the left shoulder on the wet dirt. One might expect that such an abrupt stop would create tire marks. In fact, there *were* clear tire marks on the shoulder near the location where Ed claimed he had stopped the truck. Yet he denied that these were the marks made by his truck. This struck me as surprising because, assuming the sighting was a hoax, here was Ed once again passing up perfectly good "hard evidence" to support his claim. In the end it turned out that Ed was right: The position of his truck was ten or fifteen feet from the tracks, according to an accurate reconstruction based on the tree line visible in photo 19. Thus, if it had been a hoax and he had used the tire marks as evidence, he would have been contradicted by the photographic evidence.

That night Charles and I once again returned to the road site, this time to measure the reflective properties of the road using a spotlight. Charles shone the 100,000-candlepower light down onto the road while I photographed the spot from various distances using Ed's Polaroid camera. Only when I was within several feet of the spot did the image become bright like the "reflection" under the UFO in photo 19. The results of this experiment indicated that if the glow under the UFO were a reflection in the road, then the amount of light coming down from the UFO and hitting the road was tremendous.

After that, Charles and I went to Ed's house, where I did further experiments with his camera in front of the house before we knocked on the door. I created two "NFO" (nonflying object) photos right before Charles's very eyes, and only after the second one did he realize what I had done. These photos show the streetlight that appears in Ed's first UFO photos and, above and to the left, in the area of the sky just to the right of the tree in front of Ed's house, there appears a bright yellowish blob. I created these photos by first photographing a yellow bulb on a nearby driveway lamppost. I memorized the approximate location within the field of view where the image of the bulb would appear. I then photographed the streetlight while placing its image in the lower right portion of the field of view so that the yellow-bulb image would appear to be to the left and above the streetlight. After the second exposure I pulled the picture from the camera and let it develop. I carried out this procedure twice and explained it to Charles. Then I knocked on the door. Ed was surprised to see us. I told him that we had seen something in the sky in front of his house and that we had photos. He glanced at the photos I had just made and began walking around excitedly, looking into the sky. He said he was glad that someone else had seen the UFO, but he was unhappy that it had returned. He also said that he couldn't understand why the image looked so yellow. (Note: I did not realize at this time that he was more or less expecting the UFO to return because, according to the story he had told the other investigators, it had never stayed away more than twelve days during the previous three months and this date was the fourteenth day after the previous sighting.)

My impression of his reaction to the NFO photos was that he thought I had actually photographed a UFO in front of his house. He gave no indication that he suspected what I had done was a hoax. Then I explained what I had done. He didn't appear to understand until I made one more NFO photo using the same method. After this demonstration it seemed he began to understand the implications of the double-exposure capability of his camera. He took this trick in good humor and we went into his house to discuss other aspects of the investigation.

It certainly appeared to me, as a result of this hoax experiment, that he knew nothing about double exposures and that the idea of taking two pictures before pulling the film from the camera was foreign to him.

On Tuesday morning, February 22nd, I left Gulf Breeze with a collection of notes, papers, tape recordings, pictures, and thoughts. My hopes for a short and sweet investigation had been dashed. I knew that either this was one of the most important UFO cases in the last forty years or else it was an extremely sophisticated hoax. Either way, I had to find out, and this would take a lot more time and effort than I had expected. I began a review of my investigation while I flew home.

Early March 1988

A week or so after my trip to Florida, Walter Andrus asked me to write a paper on my investigation for the June MUFON symposium. This gave me an incentive to begin writing the history of the sightings while I was analyzing the photos. Although this would be a time-consuming task, I knew that I had to become thoroughly familiar with them and the other sightings in the area so that I could properly evaluate the truth or falsity of the photographic data.

On February 27th I learned that Ed had taken pictures with the Nimslo stereo camera. This excited me because I could use the photographs to estimate the distance to the object that Ed filmed and also to calculate its size. The film was developed a week later and sent to Tom Deuley for initial analysis. He had supplied the camera, loaded with film and sealed with wax, to the MUFON investigators to give to Ed. Tom had taken the first photo on the film, one that no one would be able to duplicate, so that he could determine whether or not Ed had switched the film in the camera for an appropriately "doctored" film.

Several weeks later he sent me a set of contact prints of the filmstrip. I then asked him to make a set of test photos of known objects at known distances so that I could check the accuracy of distance measurements made with the camera. I few weeks later I received some test photos, but they were not sufficiently accurate. I asked for a second set and placed the Nimslo film analysis on hold until they arrived in early May. In the meantime I figured that with twenty-three Polaroid pictures and a video-tape I had enough photographic data to keep me busy.

During the evening of March 8th Ed called me to say that he had taken another photo, this time with a new camera. Ed said, "I hadn't planned to tell anybody if I took another photo, but this seemed important. First, it was taken with this new camera. Second, it was taken during a drizzly rain and the photo shows streaks above the craft, just as in the photo I took with Duane."

I was surprised to learn that he had bought, just the day before, a Polaroid Model 600 LMS. This type of camera has a built-in flash and it ejects the photo immediately after it is taken. "I got this because my old camera was discredited." As he said this, I realized that my demonstration of how to fake a UFO photo by doing a double exposure with his old Polaroid had made an impression on him. He said that the UFO was the first thing he had photographed with his new camera.

I found out much later from Robert Oechsler, who had contacted a

Polaroid-company technician, that it is possible, but difficult, to do a double exposure with a Model 600. To do so requires some unconventional manipulations of the camera and film. I never would have thought of it by myself. Would Ed have discovered this possibility after having the camera for only one day? I doubt it.

Our conversation that night covered a number of topics unrelated to the March 8th photo. Ed told me that he was trying to decide what was the right thing to do regarding the release of information about his sightings, about the lie detector tests, and so on. He said that he hated the fact that after "all this stuff my word has to be questioned. . . . I understand it, but I got a right to hate it even though I understand it." Ed went on to say that from this time on, in order to avoid the impact of more sightings and photos on his life, he planned to hold on to any photos he might take. He said, "If the opportunity arises, and my wife doesn't complain, I'll take a picture and stick it in my drawer."

While we were talking, it occurred to me that he could make a large stereo camera because he now had two Polaroid cameras. Half jokingly I suggested that he place his two Polaroid cameras on a board a foot apart with a pole halfway between them, protruding far enough to be visible in the field of view of each camera. A nail at the end of the pole could provide a reference distance, making this a Self-Referencing Stereo (SRS) camera. I pointed out that if he used such a camera to photograph a UFO, I could calculate the distance to it and this would allow me to calculate the size of the UFO. As I explained how to build this SRS camera, I wondered what his response would be: if this were all a giant hoax, I was making a suggestion that could expose the hoax.

A stereo camera capable of distinguishing between a distance of a hundred feet (or more) and a distance of thirty feet (or less) might provide the proof I sought. If the camera showed that the UFO were less than thirty feet away and if the size of the image were also small, then the UFO could be a model. On the other hand, if the camera showed that the UFO were over a hundred feet away and the size of the image was relatively large, then the UFO would be large and probably real. The accuracy of the distance measurement would be of secondary importance. That is, it wouldn't matter if the camera couldn't tell the difference between 15 feet and 25 feet, nor would it matter if the camera couldn't distinguish between 150 feet and 250 feet, just as long as there was no doubt that it could distinguish between, say, 25 feet and 100 feet. I was certain that this level of accuracy would be obtained with a stereo camera made up of two cameras separated by one foot.

Ed sounded interested at the idea of being able to measure the size of the UFO, but he seemed only lukewarm to the idea of building the SRS camera. After all, I was suggesting that he do a little extra work, something beyond his "call of duty" to take the photos. Nevertheless, he didn't laugh it off. I got the impression that this might be something he'd do . . . someday.

Several days later the new photo arrived in the mail (#35). It was, indeed, like the January 24th photo (#21), but the image was smaller and a bit more blurred. The streaks were easy to see and quite straight.

I decided that it would be valuable to have an idea of what the acceleration might have been for the object. To do this, I assumed that the object was 12 feet wide, that it took about one-third of the shutter time, that is, about 0.1 second to reach the top of the picture, and that the acceleration was constant (like gravity). I found the distance to the object (about 246 feet) and the distance that it traveled upward (about 25 feet) by using the assumed size in combination with measurements I made on the photograph and with the effective camera focal length (110 millimeters). I was surprised at the result: to travel 25 feet on 0.1 second starting from zero velocity would require 156 times the acceleration of gravity (156 "g's"). This meant that by the time the UFO was at the top of the picture, it was already traveling about 500 feet per second, or the speed of a jet. If the constant acceleration continued for another 0.1 second, then it exceeded the speed of sound (about 1,100 feet per second). Under ordinary circumstances such a speed would create a shock wave that might be heard at the ground. Yet Ed had reported hearing no sound. What did the lack of noise signify?

Late March 1988

On March 12th, to my great surprise, Ed told me that he had built an SRS camera according to my suggestion but with a two-foot distance between the cameras. Furthermore, he had borrowed another Model 600 (from Duane Cook) so that he had two identical cameras. I was delighted to hear this and immediately asked him to take some test photos so I could determine whether or not the camera could measure distances accurately. I received his test pictures on March 15th. I spent quite a bit of time working out the mathematical equations that allow me to calculate the distance of an object from measurements of image positions on the SRS camera photos. With a two-foot separation between the individual cameras it was easy to determine whether an object was about ten or twenty feet away (hoax distance!) or over a hundred feet away. Ed's test photos proved that the camera worked, although it did have problems.

The first problem was that the pole that held the calibrating nail was not rigidly mounted, so I could not use it to calibrate the camera. Ed told me of another problem (he apparently wasn't sure that this was a problem): He didn't operate the cameras simultaneously. Instead, he took the right camera photo first and then the left. Several weeks later I realized that there was a third problem: Because of the way he fired the cameras he twisted the camera support slightly in opposite directions when he pushed the shutter buttons. This third problem was of lesser importance than the first two in determining the distance to an object.

The second problem was important for two reasons. First, it meant that the camera could give an incorrect distance if the object were moving. Second, and of much greater importance for the establishment of the validity of the stereo photos, as I discovered several weeks later, it could provide a sufficiently astute hoaxer with a means of defeating the purpose of the SRS camera.

On March 17th he took the first SRS camera UFO photos. Would these be the final proof one way or the other? I anxiously awaited their arrival. On March 21st I learned, to my great surprise, that Ed had taken a second set of SRS photos on Sunday night, March 20th. All of these photos arrived at my house on March 25th and I began an intense study of them.

The photos from these two nights have similar images of the UFO: they both show the bottom ring light of the type of UFO that Ed had photographed previously with his old Polaroid camera. In the March 17th photos (36L and 36R) there are also very faint images of the central structure and of the top light. They also show a bush in the foreground. The March 20th photos (37L and 37R) only show the bottom bright ring of the UFO. They also show a nearby fence and bushes in the foreground.

Ed mentioned a peculiar aspect of the March 20th photos when I talked to him on March 21st. The image of the bottom ring in the right-hand photo is clear and bright. However, the image of the bottom ring in the left-hand photo is much dimmer and has vertical dark lines across it. Ed said he was disappointed when he saw the picture.

When I first saw photo 37L, I couldn't understand why the image of the bottom ring looked so different from the image in 37R. It wasn't until several weeks later, after comparing these nighttime UFO photos with daylight photos taken from the same spot and after performing a crucial experiment that I understood why the UFO image in the left-hand photo looks as it does.

Early April 1988

I was not happy with the SRS camera as Ed had built it. It wasn't sufficiently rigid. I asked Ed to rebuild it with a triangular brace to make the pole with the nail more rigid and to fasten the cameras so they couldn't rotate. I also suggested that he practice operating both cameras simultaneously rather than firing them one after the other. He did both of these things, and by the second week of April he was ready to take UFO pictures with the more precise SRS camera. However, he didn't hear any hums and so did not get any photos until the last night of April, even though many other people reported seeing UFOs during the first two weeks of April.

The Middle of April 1988

During the middle of April, Ed was confronted directly with the effects of skepticism. I was, too. The skeptics were calling the investigation inadequate. Naturally this bothered me because my investigative skills and those of several other MUFON investigators were being called into question. I received several letters in which the authors claimed that they had discovered how the photos had been created. They then scolded me for not accepting their various "proofs" that the photos were hoaxed.

The arguments against the photos ranged from the purely subjective (the pictures are hokey; the UFOs have "serious flaws," which a "high-technology flying object wouldn't have") to substantive ("There is a supporting structure holding the UFO" or "The pictures are double exposures"). I could not refute the subjective arguments. I could only point out that they were, after all, opinions and not hard facts. However, I was able to refute the substantive arguments about the photos by carefully studying my copies and (later on) the originals.

Basing their analyses on copies of the originals, the skeptics claimed that there was evidence of a hoax in photo 5. In that picture there is a vertical line that appears, in the copies, to be only above and below the image of the UFO. The skeptics claimed that this was the image of a supporting wire or thread holding a model UFO. Using the original photo, I determined that the vertical line was not perfectly straight (as a suspending wire would be) but wiggly and that it crossed the picture from the top to the bottom. Of crucial importance is the fact that it *crosses over* the UFO image. Upon further analysis this line turned out to be a type of film flaw characteristic of type-108 Polaroid film. It occurred on a number of Ed's pictures, including non-UFO pictures. Ordinarily this type of flaw would not be noticed. However, one can sometimes see these flaws in photos that are taken in the dark or near dark, as were Ed's, if the photo is then illuminated by a strong light in order to see the picture.

I carefully inspected all of Ed's photos, looking for any evidence of supporting structures, and found none.

Some skeptics claimed that the photos were double exposures. This claim was consistent with the capability of the camera to make two or more exposures of a photo, as I demonstrated to Ed and Charles when I was at Ed's house on February 22nd. Nevertheless, I was skeptical about the suggestion that Ed's UFO pictures were double exposures. Ed told me that he knew nothing of double exposures or any other photographic tricks, although he has taken some amusing pictures at parties for children by defocusing the camera. His reaction to my February 22nd demonstration gave me no indication that he knew what I had done. Some skeptics claimed that a party photo he had taken several years before proved that Ed knew how to make double exposures. Some unexpected blobs of light turned up on this picture of a girl. Ed denied that he had intentionally created the light blobs, but that didn't satisfy the skeptics who claimed that these blobs could only have been made by a double exposure. However, this claim was refuted by experiments that showed that similar blobby images could have been created by accidental reflections from a glass partition in the room where Ed took the picture. Furthermore, two of Ed's UFO photos provide photographic evidence that contradicts the suggestion that they were created by double-exposure methods.

The double exposure technique requires two steps: the photographer would first take a picture of a model UFO silhouetted against a black background. The photographer would have to be sure that he didn't create a "ridiculous" picture, such as, for example, a UFO that appeared to be between him and the ground or a nearby tree. It would be most reasonable to have the UFO appear to be silhouetted against the clear sky. To be sure that the UFO image would appear at a reasonable place in the picture, the photographer would have to have some way of knowing where, within the field of view of the camera, the latent (that is, undeveloped) UFO image would be. If the photographer didn't care where in the sky the UFO would appear in the picture, he would need only a crude ability to align the image of the UFO model with the image of the background. (This is how I created the double-exposure "UFO" pictures on February 22nd and temporarily fooled Charles and Ed.)

A double exposure of the type just described can create a moderately convincing UFO photo if it is done correctly. However, this method can create a problem (for a hoaxer) because film exposures add together (the "summation of exposures" problem). Within the outline or boundary of the UFO image the total exposure will be the sum of the exposure due to the UFO model and the exposure due to the background. As an example of this problem, suppose that the photographer put black "windows" on his UFO model, photographed it (against a black background), and then photographed a blue-sky background. Then, in the completed double exposure the blue sky would appear to show through these windows. When reporter Mark Curtis of WEAR, working with several photographers, tried to duplicate Ed's photos this way, the summation of exposures made the windows of the "UFO" image appear blue. (A much more complicated double-exposure technique, the "matted" double exposure, which requires perfect alignment between an opaque black material, the "matte," and the edges of the image of the UFO model, is required to eliminate the exposure-summation problem.) If the sky background were very dark, or black, however, the windows would still look dark. Since Ed's first pictures do, in fact, have the UFO silhouetted against a dark-sky background, it is not unreasonable to suggest that if the photos were a hoax, then they might be double exposures.

There are two pictures, however, that provide clear evidence that the simple double-exposure method was not used. These are photos 1 and 7. A careful inspection (using conventional and computer-aided photo-analysis methods) of the left side of the UFO image in photo 1 shows that the image of the UFO, although brighter than the very dark image of the tree, did not overlap the image of the tree branches. If this were a simple double exposure of a UFO model and the background, the image of the UFO *would* overlap the image of the tree. Similarly, in photo 7 the image of the nearby cedar tree cuts off the image of the right side of the UFO: the UFO does not overlap the darker image of the tree.

It would be possible to create the impression that the UFO was behind the tree in photo 1 (or 7) using a double-exposure technique if two very difficult additional things were done: (a) the left side of the UFO model would have to be cut to fit the outline (shape) of the tree branches where the UFO would appear in the final picture; and (b) the latent image of the UFO model (after the first exposure) would have to be carefully positioned so that the left side of the UFO image would match, or "fit into," the image of the right side of the tree branches.

This sort of thing could be done in a film studio in Hollywood, but not by Ed with a simple camera while standing on his front doorstep in Gulf Breeze. Realizing this, the skeptics suggested that Ed had an accomplice who was able to create sophisticated photo hoaxes, but there is no evidence of that.

Other sophisticated photographic techniques have been suggested by myself and by skeptics. These include "reflection-on-glass" and the "photo montage," but it would be rather difficult to create Ed's UFO photos using these methods. If Ed had been a shutterbug, with lots of expensive cameras around, books on photography, and lots of photo equipment, my evaluation of his potential capabilities for sophisticated photo hoaxing would be different. However, his photographic equipment consisted of only the old Polaroid and a simple, fixed-focus video camera (Sony camcorder). Furthermore, it appeared to me that Ed had only a minimal interest in photography and very little knowledge of photographic techniques. It seemed to me that he would never think of something as complicated as creating a double exposure with accurate position alignment between the latent UFO image and the image of the background. Nor would he think of any of the other techniques, which also require alignment. But even if he did think of these techniques, his simple camera equipment imposed severe limitations on his ability to create hoax pictures.

The most straightforward method of creating a UFO photo hoax without using complicated techniques is to photograph UFO models at various distances. Even though no investigator has found any evidence of UFO models being used, I investigated the model hypothesis. The most difficult picture to imagine being a photo of a model is the "road shot" (photo 19). Besides the difficulty of creating a large, complicated model with all the appropriate lighting, there was also the problem of having to set up the model on a road that leads to a number of houses without some motorist seeing what he was doing. While Charles and I were at the site on Route 191-B to photograph the reflection of a spotlight on the road, several cars went by.

Aside from the road shot, which would require a very large model, the other photos would also require rather large models. Yet no one had ever reported seeing Ed with UFO models. Nor had anyone ever seen such models or evidence of such models at Ed's house. And certainly he didn't photograph a large model during the incident with Duane Cook (photo 21).

Besides analyzing the photos Ed took with his old Polaroid camera, I also analyzed the photos taken with the SRS camera on March 17th and 20th (photos 36L and 36R). These proved to be even more difficult to explain as mere trickery. The March 17th photos were particularly interesting because they were almost taken in the presence of witnesses. Ed has recounted how his friends watched him load the SRS camera with two packs of fresh film. His friends saw him record the two different film-pack serial numbers. They saw him take two test shots and note down the number of each shot on the picture counter on each camera. Then they waited with him and Frances to see if the UFO would show up. They stayed with him for several hours before he told them that he hadn't heard a hum for a while. Duane, Buddy, and the others then decided to pretend to leave. They told Ed they were leaving, and within a minute after their departure Ed heard a hum. A minute or so later he and Frances saw a UFO west-southwest of them. He turned the SRS camera toward it and fired off the cameras. He turned on his flashlight to watch the pictures develop but it wasn't working, so he ran to his truck to look at them in the headlights. He then saw that Duane was sitting nearby in his car with Dari.

They had not left; they had merely driven to the other side of the parking lot, turned around, and returned with the headlights off. They had been gone for only a couple of minutes. As they returned, they saw the flashes go off. They thought that Ed was taking another test shot because they hadn't seen any UFO. (The bushes around the picnic table where Ed had set up the camera probably blocked their view.) Buddy and Carlos had gone eastward in the parking lot (opposite to the direction where Ed saw the UFO). They also saw the flash go off but not the UFO. When they saw Ed turn on his headlights, they, too, walked over to see what had happened.

When Ed saw Duane and Dari, he motioned for them to come over to his truck. Then Buddy and Carlos arrived. They all watched as the photos slowly developed. They became very excited as the image of the UFO became more and more distinct in the pictures. They searched the area for any evidence of the UFO but found nothing.

When I received these pictures from Ed, the first thing I did was attempt to calculate the distance to the UFO by measuring the parallax angle between the sighting lines of the two cameras. (The "parallax angle" is the angle between lines of sight from two separated locations to the same object.) I was able to calculate this angle from the positions of the UFO image in the two photographs. Unfortunately, the calibrating rod and nail, which gave the camera its name (Self-Referencing Stereo Camera), did not provide an accurate reference parallax angle. (These pictures were taken before he rebuilt the camera to make the rod and nail more rigid.) However, my analysis of test photos that Ed had taken soon after completing the SRS camera showed that distances calculated from the parallax angle were underestimates of the actual distances. For example, assuming that the lens axes were parallel, I found that a board with a calculated (from the parallax) distance of about 15.3 feet was actually about 16.7 feet away, a tree calculated at 34 feet away was actually about 46 feet away, and another tree calculated at about 120 feet was actually over 400 feet away. The fact that the camera underestimated distances, with the error growing as the distance increased, indicated that the axes of the camera lenses actually diverged slightly. I estimated the divergence at about six-tenths of a degree, whereas for a "perfect" stereo camera the divergence would be zero (lens axes parallel).

Using the same calculational method that I used on the test photos and assuming that the divergence of the lens axes was still about six-tenths of a degree on March 17th, I found that the distance to the object was over 3,000 feet. Unfortunately the cameras were not rigidly mounted to the supporting board, so they could have twisted slightly when Ed carried the camera to Shoreline Park, and this would have changed the divergence slightly. A calculation based on the unlikely assumption that the lens axes were exactly parallel yielded a distance of 180 feet. Assuming that handling made only slight changes in the camera orientations, the divergence was probably between 0 and 0.6 degrees on March 17th, and therefore the distance would have been between 180 and 3,000 feet. I could not be sure exactly how far away the object was, but the distance was sizable.

My initial reaction to this discovery was that the SRS camera had proven that Ed's sightings were of real objects. But I still had to consider the possibility that Ed had, in some way, defeated the SRS camera. In other words, given that Ed was alone (with his wife) for two to three minutes at the most, could he have faked the stereo photos? I managed to think of several possible methods and then, after further thought, rejected them.

The first method I thought of was to take fake stereo UFO photos from the same location on a previous night and to substitute these for actual non-UFO photos taken at the time of the "sighting." However, Ed was invited, by Duane, to go to Shoreline Park that night; he did not know that he was going out until about 7:00 P.M., nor did he pick the location. How would he know where to take his fake photos in preparation for an invitation to "come out with us and see if you can get some photos?" (Note: a bush appears in the UFO photos, a bush that is at the picnic table location in Shoreline Park.) This fact by itself makes it unlikely that the stereo photos are fakes taken on a previous night. However, a conclusive reason to reject the previous photo hypothesis is that Duane and Dari and the others saw the UFO photos developing before their very eyes. That meant that the photos did not come out of the cameras and start developing until a minute or so before they saw them.

Another way to hoax the photos would be to use a full-size model. Since the distance to the UFO was probably much greater than 180 feet, as I pointed out previously, the model would have to be large. The width of the image on the film (0.024 radians) corresponds to an object width of about 4.8 feet at a distance of 200 feet and to a proportionally greater width at a greater distance (e.g., 7.2 feet at 300 feet). Also, the altitude of the object was about 80 feet if it were about 200 feet away and proportionally higher if it were farther away. How Ed could have pulled off a full-size-model hoax, essentially on the spur of the moment, is difficult to imagine. The object would have been over the water. What could he use to suspend it? A lighted model supported by a tethered balloon would require considerable time to set up, and Ed would have to arrange to have the lights on the object turned on just after the others left him and then turned off immediately after he took his photographs so that no one would see it. But, if he went to all this trouble, why not let the others see it briefly?

Another potential method for hoaxing is to use a small model with which to "defeat" the parallax-angle-measuring ability of the SRS camera. This could be done because the two cameras were operated one after another, rather than simultaneously. It is unlikely that Ed would have known how to defeat the SRS camera (I didn't figure it out until a week or so after he took the photos), but assuming that he did know, he could have proceeded in the following way. First he would take a small (say, six-inch-diameter) model with him in his truck to the park. As soon as the others had left, he would (a) get the model from the truck (without being seen) and (b) suspend or support it about twenty feet away from the SRS camera. He would (c) take the right-hand picture and then (d) either carefully rotate the camera mount clockwise very precisely a few degrees (actually about 5.3 degrees) or move the model to the left a number of inches (actually about 22.4 inches). Then he would take the left-hand picture. If he suspected that the others would return, he would have to hide the model. In the above sequence, step (d) is the step that would defeat the distance-measuring ability of the SRS camera. This is because either of the operations in step (d) would synthesize the parallax angle of a distant UFO. However, note that either of the methods in step (d) would take time, many seconds at least. Since each camera was operated with a flash, the other witnesses would have noted a considerable time lag between the first flash and the second. In other words Duane and Dari and the others would have seen "flash . . . (many seconds) . . . flash."

However, what they actually reported was that there was no perceptible time between the two flashes. Thus there was no time for Ed to carry out step (d). This means that the parallax was not synthesized and the SRS camera was not defeated.

I thought of yet another hypothetical method for creating a photo hoax under the conditions of the March 17th photos. This requires a mind-boggling combination of double exposures made with the Polaroid Model 600, defeat of the parallax using a small model, and careful reloading of two especially prepared Polaroid film packs. All of these things would be done before the sighting. After the people left the area, Ed would have to substitute his prepared film packs for the fresh packs, with the same two serial numbers, without changing the photo number on the picture counter on each camera (each time a pack is inserted, the picture counter is reset to zero). He would then take the second exposure and let the pictures develop before the eyes of the witnesses.

After analyzing the difficulties with all of the possible methods for hoaxing the March 17th photos I decided that it was very unlikely that they were a hoax. But did they constitute positive proof that Ed photographed a true UFO? As of the middle of April I wasn't sure.

On March 19th, at my suggestion, Ed attempted to align the two Polaroid cameras better by pressing a straight metal bar against the front faces of the cameras. In doing so he changed the alignment from what it had been when he took the March 17th photos. On the very next day he took the second set of SRS photos. This time he was alone.

These photos were more difficult to understand. The UFO image in each photo is basically a short horizontal white line (the image of the bottom ring light) with a dimmer image of the structure of the UFO just above (see photos 37L and 37R). The image in the right photo is quite bright and is similar to the images in the March 17th photos. The line in the left photo is very dim and is cut by nearly vertical dark lines. Each photo also shows a nearby fence that was lit by the camera flashes. Ed measured the distance from the camera to the fence at my request. (To make this measurement, Ed repositioned the camera in the tripod holes that were made when he took the March 20th photos.) This measured distance provided a reference that allowed me to calibrate the camera. I found that his attempt to make the lens axes parallel had not been completely successful because the lens axes now converged by about 0.7 degrees (previously they had diverged).

I attempted to calculate the distance to the UFO. The calculation yielded a result I hadn't expected: the sighting lines from the cameras to the UFO diverge very slightly (the divergence angle is about 0.01 degrees). This meant that the UFO moved slowly, or *was* moved, sideways during the time between Ed's taking of the right and left pictures. The very small divergence means that the distance moved was almost exactly equal to the separation of the cameras, that is, about two feet (for any assumed UFO distance less than 1,000 feet).

When I realized that the sighting lines diverged slightly, I knew that I had a problem: I could not calculate the distance to the UFO. It could be at any distance, including short distances such as ten or twenty feet. Unlike the March 17th photos, there were no other witnesses who could state that the time between the flashes was very short (a second or less), so I had to allow for the possibility that the time between flashes was long enough for Ed to move a nearby model two feet to the left after he took the right photo and before he took the left-hand photo. The angular width of the UFO image is only about 0.022 radians, corresponding to about 3 inches at 10 feet, about 6 inches at 20 feet, about 9 inches at 30 feet, 7.5 feet at 300 feet, and so on. Therefore I had to consider the possibility that these photos were of a model.

Upon close inspection I found two puzzling features about the left-hand image that did not seem consistent with the idea that Ed had used a small nearby model. First, the left-hand image was very dim, although I would have expected it to be as bright as the right-hand image. In fact, if the photos were a hoax, Ed could have taken the time to make the images look identical by taking several photos with the left camera, if necessary, until he found one that matched the right-camera image.

The second unusual feature was the dark vertical lines through the left-hand image. These were an enigma until I examined daylight photos, which Ed took, at my request, on March 21st. He placed the camera-tripod legs in the depressions in the dirt that had been created by the tripod the night before. The daylight photos show that the camera on March 21st was in the same position as it was the previous night but that the pointing direction was rotated about half a degree to the left. When I (effectively) superimposed the right-hand UFO picture over the right-hand daylight picture, allowing for the slight difference in the sighting direction, I found that the sighting line to the UFO passed just to the right of a bushy branch of a Florida pine tree that was about sixty feet away.

When I did the same thing for the left-hand photo I found that the sighting line to the UFO passed *through* the bare branches of a leafless bush that was about twenty-two feet away. When I discovered this, the dark vertical lines across the left-hand image were immediately explained: A few nearly vertical bare branches of the bush had blocked small portions of the light from the UFO.

I still wondered why the image was so dim. By comparing the UFO and daylight pictures I could see that the sighting line to the UFO, after passing through bare branches of the leafless bush, also passed through the bushy branch of a Florida pine tree at sixty feet. I wondered, could pine needles within that bushy branch have reduced the intensity of the light from the UFO without blocking it entirely?

To answer this question I needed to carry out a crucial experiment. If no light came through, then the UFO could not have been beyond the tree, in which case it could have been a small model less than sixty feet away. I called Ed and asked him to have someone hold a fluorescent light behind that bushy branch of the tree so that he could photograph it from the location where he took his March 20th photos. For comparison I asked him to also photograph the light when it was not behind the tree branch, but just to the right of it. Ed mounted a fluorescent light on a pole in such a way that it would be horizontal when the pole was vertical. Frances held the pole steady while Ed took photos of the light. He took photos just before dark as well as after dark.

When I saw these photos, I knew the answer to my question. Ed did exactly what I asked him to do and his photos show that light *does* pass through the foliage on the branch. The light that penetrated the branch was considerably dimmer than the light that came directly from the fluorescent light when it was to the right of the branch. This showed that the UFO could have been behind the tree branch. In other words, the UFO could have been hundreds of feet beyond the tree and therefore quite large.

Assuming that the small divergence of the sighting lines was a result of sideways motion of the UFO, I estimated the speed. I assumed the distance was 300 feet (in which case the image size corresponded to a width of about 7 feet). Because the divergence angle is very small, the UFO must have moved about 2 feet at that distance. A careful comparison of the UFO photos with the daylight photos showed that the UFO also moved downward a short distance corresponding to an angle of 0.44 degrees. At 300 feet this small angle corresponds to a distance downward of about 2.3 feet. The actual total distance moved (2 feet to the left and

2.3 feet downward, using the right-triangle rule of Pythagoras) would therefore be about 3 feet. I estimated that the time between the UFO photos could have been about 1 second. To move this distance during 1 second would require a speed of 3 feet per second, or about 2 miles per hour.

This is not very fast. Consider that Ed was looking through the viewfinder trying to point the rather cumbersome SRS camera. The UFO was silhouetted against a black background, so there were no nearby fixed reference points that would make a slow motion obvious. Under these conditions it seems reasonable that he might not have noticed if the UFO were drifting slowly to the left.

The SRS camera photos, especially those taken March 17th, seemed to provide strong evidence against a hoax. When combined with all the previous photos the evidence seemed almost overwhelming that Ed had not perpetrated a hoax.

Late April 1988

Near the end of April I decided it was time to review the situation. By this time I had studied all of Ed's Polaroid pictures. I had found no clear evidence of a hoax in any picture. On the contrary, the sheer number of photos with their numerous variations in the UFOs and backgrounds shown, when compared with Ed's seeming lack of photographic capability, argued against a hoax. I had also studied the Nimslo photos and the videotape, but I had arrived at no definite conclusion regarding them.

Actually the most convincing aspect of Ed's reports were not the photos by themselves. The most convincing aspect was the *combination* of the photos with the stories behind the photos. There was a richness of detail in the stories that seemed to go beyond what any typical hoaxer would bother to invent. But the stories themselves would be less convincing without the photos to provide specific illustrations of what Ed was talking about.

And then there was the videotape taken by Duane Cook. This would not be impossible to fake with a sufficiently good actor (or pair of actors), but was Ed skilled enough to pull it off? I doubted it.

Important support for Ed's claims came from Ed's wife and the numerous other witnesses in the Gulf Breeze area, who reported sightings of similar or identical objects. It was particularly interesting to me to find that on several of the days when Ed had a sighting, other independent witnesses also reported sightings (e.g., November 11th, March 17th, and March 20th).

Of course the fact that he passed two lie detector tests given by a skeptical examiner was important. He also passed a Psychological Stress Evaluation (PSE) test. And then there was the circle in the grass, which has defied explanation.

After reviewing the situation I realized that I was far from proving that Ed's sightings were a hoax, but I just wasn't convinced. I had to allow for the possibility that some new evidence might come along that would prove the sightings to be fakes, but I couldn't imagine what.

The Last Day of April 1988

On Saturday, April 30th, Ed and I talked about the recent sightings including one of his own (with Frances) on April 21st. They were out for an evening stroll when they saw a UFO nearly overhead. He told me that it was similar to what they had seen on February 26th. Ed told me that this sighting convinced him that the UFO was still in the area and so he decided to try to use the SRS camera once again. Although I was skeptical as to his success because of the lack of sightings, I was pleased that he would try because he now had an improved camera.

His rebuilt camera was much more rigid than the first version. He had remounted the cameras on the supporting board in such a way that they could not rotate or move. He then placed the camera structure on a heavier tripod and practiced so that he could fire both cameras at the same time. I suggested that, whenever he set up the camera at some location, he place white pipes or rods around the camera at a distance of about 10 feet. These would provide yet another parallax reference and also a direction reference in the event that there were no nearby background features that could be seen in the photographs. These white pipes were coded with stripes of black tape so that they would also provide a reference for which direction he was looking, for example, pipe 1 might be east of the camera, pipe 2 might be south of the camera, and so on. I had furthermore suggested that Ed have Frances film him with the video-camera while he photographed a UFO with the SRS camera. If she could get both him and the UFO in the field of view at the same time, together they would obtain evidence that would be virtually impossible to refute.

Throughout April I was hoping that Ed would have some chance to use his new SRS camera. However, when the sightings seemed to end, I gave up hope and began to wonder again if this might in some way be a monumental hoax. From the skeptical point of view one could say that he didn't produce any pictures according to these requirements because they would be too difficult for even him to hoax. On the other hand, the sudden dropoff in sightings after the middle of April suggested that perhaps the UFOs had actually gone away, in which case Ed wouldn't have been able to use the camera.

Considering the sharp dropoff in UFO sightings, I was surprised when Ed told me that he and Frances had already spent several late evenings at Shoreline Park. Ed told me that each previous evening except the last night (Friday night) he had set up the pipes around the camera according to my suggestion and that Frances had been prepared to use the camera. Unfortunately, nothing had happened. He then said that Frances had left town with the high school band on Friday. Before she went, he had promised her he wouldn't go looking for UFOs alone, but he had gone out alone last night anyway and was planning to go out again tonight. I didn't think that was such a good idea, since he would be alone if something were to happen, but I didn't voice this opinion. (Many weeks later he told me that he had felt a sort of compulsion to go in spite of the promise to his wife.)

May Day 1988

I was writing the last chapter of the MUFON paper when the phone rang about 1 P.M. I picked up the phone and heard nothing at first. Then I heard a sort of groan.

"Uhhh . . . uhhh . . . this is Ed."

"Hi, Ed. What's happening?"

"Uhhh . . . uhhh . . ."

All I could hear was a weak groan. I was puzzled and then I suddenly became alert. I recalled yesterday's conversation and how he said he had intended to go out to Shoreline Park again . . . alone. Had something happened?

"Uhhh . . . uhhh . . . they did something to me, Bruce."

"Who did something?" Mentally I answered my own question and then hoped I was wrong.

"Uhhh . . . I think they got me last night . . . I think I was abducted."

I nearly jumped up from my chair. My mind began to race. My first thought was that I had better record the conversation. "Ed, can I record this?"

"Yeah . . . uhhh . . ."

I ran to get my recorder. I connected it up to the telephone recording attachment.

"OK. Tell me what happened."

"Uhhh . . . uhhh . . . uhhh . . ."

I verbally recorded the date and time. Ed still wasn't saying anything. I could only hear the faint groans.

"When did you get back to your house?" I didn't even know at what time he had been out, but I was sure that he had been out late the night before.

"About 2:30, 2:40 (A.M.). I've been lying in bed trying to figure out what to do."

Ed went on to say that he hadn't told his daughter, who was the only other person in the house. He was afraid he would scare her. He said he hadn't called any of the local investigators because, although he wanted to talk to someone who wouldn't consider him a complete nut, he didn't want a bunch of people trying to interview him right away. He just wasn't up to it.

"Just start from the beginning and recall what you can," I said.

Over the next half hour, in a halting voice and with many false starts and repetitions until he got the story straight, Ed very laboriously recited the events of the previous night.

He described how he had set up the camera along with the marker poles and then sat in the truck listening to music while he waited to see if anything would happen. Then, about 1:10 A.M., he heard a faint hum. He got out of the truck and stood by the camera and looked around. He saw the UFO southeast of him over Santa Rosa Sound and rotated the camera toward it. He took the first double photo and looked out over the water again. Now he saw two UFOs. The first one that appeared was the type he had photographed many times in the past and the second one was the February 26nd type. He put his eye to the right-hand camera viewfinder once again and prepared to take a second photo, but he could see neither UFO through the viewfinder. He assumed that they had moved. He looked up while placing his left hand on the tripod control lever in preparation for turning the camera. He still couldn't see the UFO out over the water. Then he realized that the first one that appeared was now over his head. It had moved from out over the water to over his head in only a couple of seconds. At that instant everything went white and he fell downward.

The next he knew he was facedown on the beach next to the water, about twenty feet from the camera. He didn't know how he had gotten to the water's edge. He picked himself up and walked to the park bench to sit down and think over what had happened. He could see no UFO anywhere, but his hands had a horrible odor and his head hurt.

He sat there several minutes and then thought to look at his watch. It read 2:25 A.M. There was more than an hour of time that he couldn't account for.

His head started to hurt even more and he suddenly felt a great fear that something was going to happen to his daughter. He walked over to the camera to pack it up. He found a picture hanging from the ejection port of each camera. He also found another picture on the ground below the right-hand camera. He picked up the camera and pictures. He left the marker pipes on the beach, and drove home quickly. He looked into his daughter's room and could see that she was sleeping soundly. Then he sat, awake, outside her room until about 6 A.M.

After daybreak he went to bed until late in the morning. When he got up, he was feeling very sore. He went to the bathroom to wash the foul odor from his hands and to shave. He found that he couldn't completely remove the odor. He then noticed a red mark on his forehead above the bridge of his nose. Subsequently he discovered reddish patches on his temples and a bump on the back of his head.

As he talked to me, he said that he still had some foul-smelling material under his fingernails. I suggested that he scrape it into a sealable container for analysis. I also suggested that he try to contact the local investigators for further documentation. He was reluctant to contact anyone that day.

By the end of the conversation Ed was more or less back to normal in terms of the way he spoke. Initially he spoke laboriously. Later he sounded quite emotional, even crying as he pointed out that he didn't have the videocamera with him because Frances had taken it with her. He became quite emotional as he complained to me that while he was undergoing all these horrible experiences some people were calling him a hoaxer. Talking over the details of the events seemed to bring him out of his depressed emotional state. By the time our conversation ended he was more at ease.

During the conversation Ed described to me the photos he took. Two of the photos showed the UFOs and one showed only a whitish blob. He had concluded that the photo that was still protruding from the right-hand camera after he awakened on the beach was the one showing the blob. (The first photo had fallen onto the ground as the second was ejected by the camera.) He had further concluded that he must have taken the second photo by accident since he had his right hand on the shutter button, whereas his left hand was on the tripod lever, just before he fell. Before hanging up he said he would ship these to me right away for analysis.

Several days later the May 1st photos arrived and I looked at them under a magnifying glass (photos 38L, 38R, and 39R). I was stunned when I first looked at the image of the February 26th type of object because it looked so geometrical. The other object was the type he had photographed many times before with his old Polaroid camera. I did not know what made the white-blob image in photo 39R. I just knew that it wasn't a film defect.

Early May 1988

I immediately began making the measurements on the pictures in order to calculate the distances to the UFOs. Using a traveling micrometer, a device for accurately measuring small distances (thousandths of an inch), I measured the locations of the UFO images and the images of distant lights on a bridge. The bridge lights were at a known distance from where Ed took the pictures. These images allowed me to calibrate the SRS camera for accurate distance measurement. I calculated that the object with the bottom ring was about 475 feet away and about 150 feet above the water of Santa Rosa Sound. The height of the UFO from the bottom ring to the top light was about 15 feet. The diameter of the bottom ring was also about 15 feet. However, I could not calculate the maximum width through the center section because I could see no image of the center section. If it were shaped like the UFO in the road shot, however, it would have been about 25 feet wide. The other, "Nimslo type" UFO was only about 132 feet away at an altitude of about 120 feet. Its maximum length from the vertical "tail" at the left to the right end of the horizontal line of light was only about 2.5 feet.

The small size of this other UFO was unexpected but not completely surprising. There are numerous reports of small UFOs going back over forty years. Of course, 2.5 feet is also "hoax size," but in this case it would make little sense to claim that he had supported a 2.5-foot model over the water at a distance of 132 feet and 120 feet up *and* a 25-foot-diameter model at a distance of 475 feet and 150 feet up. I concluded that if these were hoax photos, they had to be done with small, movable models to defeat the parallax-measuring capability of the camera.

About the same time that I received the May 1st photos, I also received a set of Nimslo camera test photos from Tom Deuley. Now I could complete the analysis of the stereo photos of February 26th. It required many hours of patient work with a traveling microscope to make the necessary measurements, but I finally succeeded in calibrating the camera so that it could be used to measure distances. I found that the UFO that Ed photographed with the Nimslo camera could have been anywhere between 40 and 70 feet away and therefore between 2.5 and 4 feet long.

When I completed my calculations, I was immediately struck by the coincidence between the 2.5-foot minimum size calculated from the Nimslo camera data and the 2.5-foot length I had calculated for the smaller of the two May 1st UFOs.

There was also a coincidence involving the estimated minimum distance to the February 26th UFO. Ed had said that the UFO had passed on the other side of a treetop. At my request, he and Donald Ware had measured the distance to that tree and its height. I then calculated that the top was 38 feet from the camera. Thus the minimum distance to the object could have been as short as, but not much less than, the 40 feet that the Nimslo camera photos indicated.

Ed's claim that the UFO passed by on the other side of a tree is also consistent with the Nimslo camera images. These images consist of small dots and clusters of lights. In some of the images various lights or clusters are missing, as if something (the treetop) partially blocked the view of the UFO.

The short distance I calculated contradicted Ed's claim made at the time that the UFO was a long distance away. (Frances had the impression that it was not very far away, however, and therefore not large.) Of course, if this were a hoax, Ed would have known that the model was close. The fact that he claimed it was very far away and therefore very large meant that, if it were a hoax, he did not know of the distance-measuring capabilities of the Nimslo camera. This is consistent with his lack of knowledge of photography.

The more I thought about it, the more impressed I was with the coincidence in the calculated size of the smaller UFO. I tried to figure out just what would be required to hoax both the Nimslo and the May 1st photos. I began to realize the extreme level of photographic sophistication required. It was true that the Nimslo photos, which show no background, could, in principle, be photos of a 2.5-foot model at 40 feet. It could have been a model with a unique shape, cleverly lit so that its pattern of lights could be changed slightly for each photo. On the other hand, the May 1st photo, which clearly shows the same type of UFO but with a somewhat different pattern of lights, could not be a photo of the same size model. It could not be the same size because if it were, Ed would have had to figure out how to support it at a high altitude over water and more than 130 feet away (but not more than 200 feet away in order to be consistent with the UFO size range allowed by the Nimslo camera photos). While this is, of course, possible to do with sufficient equipment, technical ability and probably an accomplice or two, I considered it to be impossible for Ed under the circumstances.

A more reasonable hoax would use a small, movable model to defeat the parallax-measuring ability of the SRS camera using the method previously described. However, after some thought I realized how difficult this would be. To make the May 1st photo consistent with the Nimslo photos, Ed would first have to calculate the size of the small model that he would place at some short distance from the SRS camera to assure consistency with the 2.5-to-4-foot size range. He would then have to calculate exactly how far to move the small model between photos in order to synthesize a parallax equipment to 132 to 200 feet. If he missed on either calculation, he would produce pictures that would be inconsistent with the February 26th photos.

And then, as if this weren't enough, to fake the May 1st photos, he would also have to have the other type of UFO model within the field of view and he would have to figure out how to make it, also, appear to be large and far away.

When I realized how difficult it would be to hoax the May 1st and Nimslo photos in a consistent manner, I began to realize that this was, indeed, the last straw. I had to be honest with myself: I had not found any proof that Ed's sightings were a hoax. Therefore my tentative conclusion was that Ed and his family were telling the truth: *The sightings really happened.* I did not tell anyone of my tentative conclusion, however, because I still thought it a possibility that some investigator might discover convincing proof of a hoax.

June 1988: The MUFON Symposium

At the MUFON symposium on June 26th I presented my paper. I covered Ed's sightings in detail and also presented a reasonably complete history of the other sightings and related events from November 11th to May 1st. I did not report my conclusion. Instead I said that I could find no convincing proof of a hoax. I also pointed out that there were many details of Ed's sightings and photos, not to mention the sightings by others in the area, which made a hoax extremely difficult to imagine.

My paper was presented in an atmosphere of controversy. Questions from the audience kept the Gulf Breeze session of the conference going past midnight. I had the difficult task of answering the questions without alienating any of the UFO investigating groups, one of which had publicly claimed that the sightings were probably a hoax.

July 1988

After the conference was over, investigations into various aspects of the sightings continued. Several people helped me with conventional and computer-aided photo analysis. The goal was to determine whether or not any photo could be definitely determined to be a hoax. Such a result could only occur if something like a suspending cord, a mechanical support, an odd reflection, or some other artifact of photographic trickery could be discovered in the photos. No convincing evidence of such an artifact has been found.

August 1988

I began a serious analysis of the December 28th videotape. A videotape, like a movie, can only be faked with extreme difficulty. The reason is that not only must the UFO *look* real, it must also behave in a manner that one might expect for a self-propelled vehicle. I have seen some movies of objects, claimed to be UFOs, which do not move like self-propelled vehicles. They swing back and forth and wobble as they move about. The reason for the swinging and wobbling, as opposed to simple rectilinear motion, is that they are suspended by a string or rope. (Sometimes the suspension is visible.) This swinging or wobbling would occur with any object forced to move back and forth if it were hanging by a suspension. I wanted to check very carefully for any evidence that the UFO in Ed's videotape was not self-propelled.

Ed's video was made in the dark. In the foreground is a bush that was dimly lit by porch lights that were behind Ed as he looked eastward toward the large field. He said he had ''hidden'' behind the bush so that he wouldn't be seen by the UFO. There are dim images of a windscreen board at the south end of his pool and there are images of streetlights and security lights around the school buildings on the other side of the field. With these images as reference points it is possible to determine where the camera was pointing during most of the videotape.

The UFO was visible for a total of about ninety-four seconds. During the first forty-seven seconds it moved generally from the right to the left, with several pauses and direction reversals. During the last forty-seven seconds it moved generally back to the right, again with pauses and direction reversals. At the end of this time it simply disappeared in one frame (two TV raster scan fields, one-thirtieth of a second).

During the first few seconds of the tape, when the UFO image was the largest, it passed on the *far* side of the rightmost windscreen board. About forty-five seconds into the videotape it was at the far left and the image was the smallest. At this time it passed on the *far* side of a tree that was about fifty feet from the camera. Ed turned off the camera for about a minute after he lost sight of it when it went behind the tree.

The UFO is quite clear during the first section of the videotape, especially during the first twenty seconds or so. One can easily see that it is the same type of object Ed photographed in the "road shot." The top light is dim, and the bottom "ring" light, which appears as a short, thin horizontal line, is quite bright. The brightness of each light fluctuates, seemingly in a random manner at a rate comparable to the TV scan rate. The central portion (main body) of the UFO is easily seen during the first half of the video. The top light was not exactly over the center of the bottom light. Instead, it was to the left of center as if the UFO were tilted to the left slightly. This tilt remained constant as it moved back and forth. The main body gives the visual appearance of rapid rotation as the UFO travels along. However, this seems not to be a real effect, but rather an artifact of the TV scan combined with the electronic noise in the dim image.

The angular height of the UFO at its closest was about 0.018 radians, corresponding to about 1.8 feet if it were 100 feet away or about 7 feet if it were 400 feet away. At its farthest distance, at the far left of its travel, the angular size was about 0.011 radians. This means it was about 1.6 times farther away at the far left than at the far right.

During the second section of the videotape only the top light and the bottom ring were visible. The center part was completely invisible, which indicates that the glow from the central portion can be turned off. Again, as in the first half of the videotape, the top light was not directly over the center of the bottom ring light. However, this time it was to the right of center. This slight tilt did not waver as the UFO moved back and forth. The angular height of the UFO image at the beginning of the second section, when it was still at the far left, was about 0.015 radians. This is larger than it was at the end of the first section, which means it had moved closer while it was not visible. Just before it disappeared the angular height was again about 0.018 radians.

The videocamera recorded faint sounds such as the nearby leaves rustling and even the whistle of a distant train. However, there were no sounds associated with the presence of the object, as nearly as I and others could determine.

The motion of the object during and after the direction reversals is of particular interest because these would be the times when any pendulumlike swinging, characteristic of a small suspended model, would be most noticeable. I looked carefully but couldn't see any oscillations or tilting of the UFO as I played the video at full speed or slowed down. This made me suspect that there were no oscillations, but to be sure I made a graph of the horizontal position of the UFO as a function of time for a portion of the videotape. The graph covers about fourteen seconds of time (320 frames of the video at 30 frames/second) and includes a period of time when the object was stationary as well as periods of steady motion and motion reversal. I looked for any telltale oscillations in the graph, which I couldn't see just by viewing the video. I didn't find any. Instead the UFO accelerated and decelerated smoothly. There were a few times when it changed its state of motion rather abruptly, yet there were no small oscillations of motion. I had imagined that, if this were a hoax, the UFO might be a small model hanging below a pulley and (horizontal) rope arrangement such as is often used for clotheslines. The failure to detect any oscillations made this hypothesis unacceptable.

If the UFO were a model, one would expect it not only to swing left to right but also to rock or tilt back and forth. Since the top and bottom lights are visible, if this rocking occurred, it would be apparent because it would make the top light move by small amounts to the left and right relative to the bottom light. However, after many careful inspections of the film I have concluded that there is no rocking of the UFO. This is another reason to reject the suspended-model hypothesis.

Yet another reason is that the hypothetical rope-pulley suspension or any other means for transporting the UFO model would have to be able to maintain a sloping trajectory with no up-and-down oscillations over a distance of forty feet or more. A pulley-rope arrangement with a tight rope could not do that. Any jerky motions such as would be caused by a sudden direction reversal could cause the horizontal rope to oscillate up and down. Although the UFO did change its altitude a couple of times, it made no up-and-down oscillations.

I have studied two other methods that might be used to create a video hoax. One is to have a model on a track and the other is to have a model supported by a person walking back and forth. The first of these would require that a large structure be built to support the track. This would be a lot of work and would be easily noticed by Ed's neighbors. The second of these would be easily detected in periodic erratic motions of the UFO as it moved back and forth.

I consider the above arguments to be valid reasons for rejecting the idea that the videotape is a hoax based on the physical (photographic) data itself. A further, nonphysical but nevertheless important, reason is that any hoax scenario would have to assume that Ed had an accomplice. The video camera was not stationary; Ed moved it and panned with the UFO. Therefore, barring some extremely complicated remote-control mechanism, Ed would have had to have an accomplice to move the UFO. No such person has been discovered, however.

September 1988

I visited Gulf Breeze for a second time and spent two days with Ed and Frances. We reenacted one of their sightings and talked to some of the other people who had reported sightings. I also talked to Dr. Dan Overlade, a clinical psychologist who had been working with Ed to try to discover what happened during the period of missing time on May 1st. Before carrying out any hypnosis sessions, however, Dr. Overlade administered a standard set of psychological tests to Ed (Wechsler Adult Intelligence Scale Revised, the Minnesota Multiphasic Personality Inventory, the Thematic Apperception Test, the Draw-A-Person Test, and the Rorschach ["ink blot"] test). This was an attempt to determine whether or not he had any unusual characteristics or personality traits. It required about eight hours to administer these tests. The test results showed no evidence of psychopathology. In other words, Ed was found to be normal by accepted standards.

A few weeks later I had a long conversation with Harvey McLaughlin, who administered two polygraph ("lie detector") tests in February. I learned that Mr. McLaughlin had been skeptical of Ed's stories, yet he had found no evidence that Ed had a "sociopathic" personality, that is, he is not the type of person who, in a sense, doesn't know the truth from fiction and therefore can pass the electronic part of a polygraph examination. Such a person cannot easily fool a practiced examiner, however. Mr. McLaughlin also told me that he saw no physiological changes in Ed during the two two-hour examination periods, so, in his opinion Ed was not on drugs when he took the tests. In summing up, Mr. McLaughlin said that, in his opinion, Ed really believes what he is saying. Dr. Overlade had voiced the same opinion.

Summing Up

By the end of 1988 my investigation was mostly completed. I had studied all of the photographs, I had studied the complete history of Ed's sightings and the sightings of others in Gulf Breeze, I had analyzed the videotape and I had talked with all of the local investigators. I had corresponded with several of the critics of Ed's sightings and had responded to their criticisms. It was now time for a final opinion.

In reviewing the situation I considered many factors, the most important of which are summarized below:

1. Ed has produced numerous photos that would have taken a lot of time and considerable technical skills and equipment to produce; some of these photos, the March 17th, 20th, and May 1st SRS camera photos in particular, would even tax the capabilities of professional photographers. The videotape taken on December 28th would require a structure or mechanism of considerable sophistication to move a hypothetical UFO model in the manner shown on the tape. All of this pictorial evidence could, presumably, have been hoaxed by someone with lots of capability and time to spare, but I have found no evidence that Ed had either the capability or the time.

   Ed is not the only person in his family to report that he took photos in his backyard. If he were the only one, I would be extremely suspicious of a hoax. However, the other family members have also attested to having seen the UFO and to watching Ed photograph or film it. For example, they watched the UFO as he videotaped it on December 28th. Frances has even reported that she took two of the photos in the presence of her husband and daughter.

   There is no way that Ed could have successfully hoaxed his family. Therefore one must choose between the conclusion that the whole family is involved in the photographic hoax and the conclusion that the photos are real.

2. There were nonphotographic multiple-witness sightings. Frances was personally involved in several nonphotographic sightings. For example, she saw the creature outside the bedroom, she saw the UFO on December 27th when Patrick Hanks came to visit, and she was with him when they saw a UFO fly over on April 21st. Patrick also saw the UFO. Thus two people, one of whom

is not a family member, attest to seeing a UFO at times when Ed took *no* photos.

3. The story of the sightings as told by Ed and Frances is rich in details. The story and photos make a coherent whole, which would tax the capabilities of a Hollywood scriptwriter. The complexity makes a hoax less likely than if the story were simple and therefore easy to remember (memorize).

4. Ed is a rather wealthy man. He and his family have lived for a number of years in a manner befitting those who have more than the average income. He is a man who certainly appears to be perfectly happy with his daily life without UFOs. He is well respected in his community. I can't imagine why he would even think of creating a UFO hoax. But, assuming he did think of it, I can't imagine that he would take the chance of being caught at it and thereby losing his community standing. Moreover, one would expect that his wife, in particular, would be concerned that a hoax would have a detrimental impact on their lives and resist his efforts to perpetrate the hoax. She has, in fact, demonstrated that the sightings have concerned her greatly, but there is no indication that she blames her husband for the impact of the sightings. In fact, she supports Ed's claims.

    Was this all a simple attempt to "get rich quick" by selling a story about UFOs? Hardly. The fact that Ed turned down a large sum of money early on indicates his reluctance to promote the story.

    Ed has demonstrated a sincere concern for a loss in his standard of living as a result of going completely public. For that reason he requested that investigators and reporters keep his name confidential. It seems to me that he had more to lose than to gain by releasing his story.

5. One would expect a hoaxer to resist efforts to uncover the hoax. Yet Ed has cooperated with the investigators. He has provided me and the other investigators with information that could be damaging to his case if it were a hoax. He has changed cameras upon request and has provided me with numerous measurements that I needed to carry out analyses of the photographs. In many cases I have not revealed why I wanted certain information. Would a hoaxer take a chance that I might uncover some damaging evidence if he provided the information? I think not. Ed has allowed

his house to be searched. He has no basement, no photographic studio, or even any books on photography (so far as I could tell). He has allowed a personal-background search. Would a hoaxer be so cooperative?

6. The strange circular area in the field behind Ed's house near where he had numerous sightings is physical evidence that something unusual happened, yet Ed said that he never actually saw a UFO right over the ring. One would expect that, if he were a hoaxer, he would make use of this physical evidence, whether he caused it or not, to support his story.

   Ed's reluctance to use potential supporting evidence if he thought it was not actually related to a sighting is evidence of his desire to present an accurate description of what happened. This desire was displayed with regard to the circle in the field and again when he did not point out to the investigators some deep tire tracks on the shoulder of the road where the January 19th event took place (Route 191-B). He could have pointed to these very obvious tire tracks as evidence to support his claim that he drove away as fast as he could to escape from the oncoming aliens. Instead, he pointed to much less obvious, less convincing tire tracks twenty or so feet from the deep tracks. The subsequent analysis of the photo showed that he had been correct: the deep tracks were too far down the road to have been made by his truck.

7. At the suggestion of Budd Hopkins, Ed took a polygraph exam. He was actually given two tests about a week apart. The second test was a surprise for Ed. He passed both tests. The examiner said that, in his opinion, Ed believes what he is saying. He has also been tested by a Psychological Stress Evaluator. The PSE analyst found no evidence of stress as Ed recounted details of his sightings. These results might be explained if Ed were a pathological liar (a "sociopath"), who couldn't tell truth from fantasy or falsehood. However, no one has detected such tendencies in Ed, including a clinical psychologist who has spent many hours with Ed and who administered a series of personality tests. The conditions under which the lie detector tests were administered precluded the use of drugs to defeat the test.

8. If Ed, alone, reported sightings, I would be extremely suspicious of a hoax in spite of all of the previous arguments. If Ed and his family alone reported sightings, I would still be suspicious. How-

ever, Ed and his family were not alone in the community in reporting UFO sightings during the same time frame as his sightings. Some of the other sightings have been described in the preceding text and some are presented in more detail in Appendix 2. A conservative estimate, based on published sighting reports, is that well over a hundred people in Gulf Breeze and nearby areas saw UFOs between November 11th and the middle of April. Several of the other sightings took place on some of the *same days* as Ed's. Of particular interest are the reports of sightings on November 11th. There had been very few sightings reported in the area for years, and then on that one day there were seven or eight sightings besides Ed's (the exact date of one of the early November sightings is not known; it could have been November 11th). One of these was a daylight sighting (Jeff Thompson) and one mentioned an object with a bluish beam coming down (Mrs. Billie Zammit). One of these occurred only minutes before Ed's sighting (Charlie and Dori Somerby).

Other dates when Ed and others had sightings were December 2nd, February 26th, March 17th, and March 20th.

The newspaper received photos from two anonymous photographers as well as from Ed. The images in these photos show that the photographers did, in fact, photograph the same thing that Ed photographed.

Duane Cook did not see the UFO, but he was present as Ed underwent severe stresses and he did watch the photo develop on January 24th.

The existence of these numerous other people who have reported seeing UFOs in the area, many of whom have said they saw the identical objects pictured in the local news media, suggests that either something real has been flying around or else many people in the area are in collusion with Ed. If the latter were true, one would expect that somebody would have come forward by now to testify against Ed's sightings, especially in view of the local publicity about the possibility that Ed's photos were all part of a hoax. (The initial conclusion by some UFO investigators that the photos were hoaxes was publicized in the latter half of April 1988.) I find it unbelievable to assume that numerous people in the community, including some of the foremost citizens (e.g., the county coroner and his wife), are in a grand collusion with Ed.

Considering the large number of sightings by other people in Gulf Breeze it would be bizarre, indeed, to reject Ed's sightings as a hoax and accept any of the other well-witnessed sightings of the same sort of UFO as Ed photographed.

Conclusion

Having studied these sightings "every which way" for more than a year I have concluded that they are proof of the existence of UFOs. But what is proof for one person is not necessarily proof for another. What would convince you? You have to make up your own mind.

The investigation is not yet complete. Ed was abducted on December 17, 1987, and again on May 1, 1988. The investigation into what happened during these and previous abductions is ongoing.

UFO sightings have been reported since the late 1940s. In the intervening years the reports of hundreds of honest people have been ignored or even publicly disputed and disparaged because of a lack of thoroughly convincing proof that true UFOs were actually flying through our atmosphere. Now, however, that proof is here. Now is the time to begin reexamining the situation. Now is the time for us to finally learn what has been happening throughout the world over the last forty-odd years. And now is the time to prepare for what the future has in store for the whole human race.

APPENDIX 1

The Critics and False Evidence

Thespectacular nature of the Gulf Breeze sightings has been accepted by the general public with remarkably calm perception. The few who have chosen to disregard the importance of the sightings and turn their backs on even the possibility certainly have that right. There has been very little ridicule forthcoming from those who are of the opinion that "this just can't be real."

However, there are always a few who seem to be compelled to attack any and all who testify to having seen a UFO. The attack is even more violent if there are photographs that support the testimony of the witnesses. These highly motivated and relentless attacks come from critics who are better described as debunkers.

The Gulf Breeze sightings involved hundreds of witnesses, several with photos, and a battery of photographic evidence. Therefore Gulf Breeze was an inescapable target for the debunkers. Without naming any of these emotional antagonists, I must at least point out some of their efforts.

The most common ploy is a news release, usually addressed to the local television stations and newspapers. The idea is to explain away the sightings as quickly as possible and avoid any prolonged attention to them by the local media. The debunker writes a very simple explanation on a powerful-sounding letterhead in which he claims that he is an expert and that what people saw was really only an "airplane behind a cloud" or "a meteor" or "a helicopter," etc., etc. To those other than the witnesses, it will sound quite reasonable and a lot easier to believe than UFOs, so . . . end of case, the debunkers win.

312

However, in Gulf Breeze, the debunkers had to deal with the hundreds of witnesses and dozens of photographs that look nothing like an airplane, helicopter, or meteor. Deprived of that explanation, they had to find an alternative. In such cases, the next-best choice is often either hoax or an incredible secret military aircraft. In this case, the debunkers settled on hoax.

To support the hoax theory, the debunkers usually try to cast doubt on the photographs. If that doesn't work, then they create as much distraction as possible by attacking the photographer. It wouldn't matter who the photographer was. If he was the chief of police . . . no problem. Maybe he was divorced. Simply start a rumor that he beat his wife and that was the cause of the breakup. What if the witness was a priest? That's even easier . . . start a rumor of impropriety. Debunking a UFO case isn't difficult because suddenly the witness who took the photographs has to defend himself against rumors and ridicule. The debunkers don't concern themselves with proof.

My Gulf Breeze UFO photos were supported by dozens of other witnesses, photographs from five different cameras, and my reputation as a well-known businessman with solid ties to the community and a deep concern for its young people. My house was a frequent location for youth activities. Pool parties, treasure hunt parties, Halloween parties—dozens of area teens found their way to my house on any given weekend.

How could this be ridiculed? Easy, for a debunker. Start a rumor that the parties were actually "ritual seances" with the attendant negative implications. Presto, my character has been attacked and the debunker has succeeded in distracting attention from the UFO.

Fortunately, the truth is hard to deny, and this, as well as other bizarre efforts, was exposed. For example, one debunker found out that my family and I had gone to New York in November of 1988 for a vacation. He had a photographer fake a Gulf Breeze–type UFO hovering over the Chrysler Building and sent out copies with a statement alleging that I had taken the photo. The professional photographer who had made the photos for the debunker came forward when he found out about the trickery, and exposed the so-called scientist as the real hoaxer for spreading fake evidence.

For the record, and in the event that some fake evidence is still circulating, the following is a brief review of some of the efforts of a few motivated debunkers. Their attempts to debunk sometimes involved dozens of pages, some with detailed mathematics, but they didn't offer any evidence to refute the authenticity of the photographs.

Photos 1 through 5

- The photograph direction has been verified to be northwest. A debunker changed the photo direction to southwest. (Debunkers always assume that their audience will not know the details, so they can change them to suit a hoax theory.)
- The UFO is shown in the videotape to illuminate itself, and later in the same tape, to cloak its midsection. A debunker ignored this self-illumination and boldly said, "It is obviously not glowing." (The debunker expected us to believe that he knew how UFOs are designed and operate. He further demonstrated his knowledge of UFO design with his argument that the "window" spacing is arbitrary.)
- The National Weather Service verified that the clouds in these photos were at approximately 18,000 feet and moving at ninety knots, which supports the four minutes of elapsed time between the photos. A debunker faked the weather reports to read thirty-knot winds so he could increase the elapsed time to thirty minutes. (He needed more time between the photos to support his hoax theory.)
- In photo 5, the clouds cannot be seen and seem to have moved away in the ninety-knot wind. As the debunker ignored the ninety-knot wind-speed weather report, he could claim the clouds should be seen in his fake thirty-knot wind.
- The weather reports also verify that the wind was blowing the clouds from left to right. A debunker printed a multipage report to the contrary, saying that he would resign from his position if he was wrong. The next day he was forced to admit he was wrong and retract his statement, but he did not resign.
- The first sighting (photos 1 through 5) has been reenacted to demonstrate how I held the camera and obtained similar framing. Contrary to the photo evidence, a debunker pretended that a tripod had been used.
- Two computer analyses of photo 5 ruled out any evidence of a support for the craft, as alleged by a debunker.

Photo 6

- The electric transformer on the light pole is dull gray. A debunker claimed it was aluminum and that, therefore, it should be reflective.

- The photo shows that I moved the camera to follow the UFO's direction; therefore, the background is slightly out of focus. A debunker said he did not believe that. (He did not, however, offer any proof, only opinion.)

Photo 7

- The computer analysis of this photo, using the original photograph, confirmed that the UFO was beyond the tree and the tree overlapped the UFO. A debunker ignored this analysis.

Photo 14

- The UFO rocked back and forth as it hovered. A debunker argued that we should not see the bottom edge of the UFO. He ignored the witness testimony to the rocking of the craft, which explains why this happened.

Photo 16

- Photos 16 and 17 were taken more than fifty feet apart. A debunker changed the location of number 17 to the same as 16. A team of reporters verified the true location, and later tossed out the pages of mathematics that the debunker used to try to impress them and said, "This guy can't be a real scientist. Even we can see that his figures don't measure up."

Photo 17

- I reported that the UFO had appeared "overhead" (but not 90 degrees overhead). A debunker picked out the description "overhead" and then used a page of mathematics to show that the UFO had not been 90 degrees overhead. (Unwittingly, he supported my testimony, because I never said the UFO had been 90 degrees overhead.)
- The photo shows the glow of the UFO bottom to be an uninterrupted circle. A debunker claimed the glowing circle to be a round fluorescent light. (He ignored the fact that a fluorescent light has a dark power plug that interrupts the circle.)

Photo 18

- The trees in this photo were measured at 175 feet away. A debunker filled another page with mathematics, moving the trees to 440 feet away to fit his theory better.
- This photo and most of the others have white spots and emulsion streaks that have been verified by Polaroid engineers as film defects caused by the rollers in the camera. A debunker called these defects "water drops" or "supports" or anything else that would help his theory.

Photo 19

- As recorded in the early reports, the UFO was rocking back and forth. The debunker ignored the testimony and again questioned the tilt of the UFO over the road.
- There was no rain at this time, as verified by the National Weather Service. The debunker "created" rain so he could claim that there should be reflections off the roadside trees.
- During the photo 19 incident, I did nothing that could be described by the word *calmly* and I didn't use that word in my report. A debunker changed my testimony to include *calmly*.

Photo 21

- I reported the UFO to be "over the truck toward the trees 150 feet away." A debunker dropped the "toward the trees 150 feet away" and used several pages of mathematics to show that the UFO had not been "over the truck" (90 degrees above). Again, he unwittingly supported my testimony.
- The two other witnesses testified to being 600 feet away and reported seeing an orange glowing light through some trees between them and the UFO. A debunker changed their testimony by moving their location to within 100 feet and said they'd seen nothing.
- Earlier the debunker boldly said the UFO and its "arbitrary windows" were never seen again after photos 1 through 9. Later he changed his mind and said photo 21 was similar.

- The photo evidence shows the UFO to be self-illuminating. Again a debunker pretended to know the correct design properties of a UFO with regard to illumination and symmetry.

Photos 22 and 23

- The camera used was the same Polaroid 108 verified to have a manual adjustment focus. A debunker changed the camera and said it was a fixed-focus type. (It's easy to debunk a photo if you change witness testimony and the camera type.)
- Again, a debunker asserted his design knowledge of UFOs and insisted they could not self-illuminate.
- When we are outside, our spitz dog is always at our feet, particularly my wife's, unless the dog is fending off an intruder. In photo 22 the dog is shown in an agitated state, alternating her attention between my wife and the UFO. A debunker said the dog was "totally indifferent."
- A daytime reenactment of photos 22 and 23 showed that the top of the wooden windscreen did not reflect in the pool. A debunker ignored the reenactment and wanted the UFO to reflect in the pool even though the angle made such a reflection impossible.

Photos 25 through 34

- I had been given the special four-lens camera and asked to use it if I had an opportunity to photograph the UFO. Sixteen days later, four days more than the time between previous sightings, I took these photos while out with my wife. A debunker commented that it took "a long time (almost three weeks)" before I had the opportunity.
- As I looked through the four-lens camera viewfinder, the lights from the UFO seemed very far away and the UFO seemed to me to be very big. The photo analysis showed it to be small and close. This small "probe" showed up again in photos 38L and 38R. A debunker argued that I had lied when I said the UFO looked big to me, and ignored the fact that my wife had reported that what she saw with her naked eye, while wearing contact lenses, appeared to be small and close.

NOTE: I find it interesting that the debunkers have avoided the video-tape and the stereo photographs when they could just as easily distort the testimony and evidence about them as well.

Nonphotographic Debunking Efforts

At first, my wife and I deliberately omitted reference to the blue beam and telepathy, and intentionally changed minor points to withhold our identities, reporting the first sighting as if a friend, "Mr. X," had taken the photos. The debunkers find this unreasonable and say the blue beam and telepathy were added later, after other witnesses had reported them.

I am well known in my community as Ed Walters (my birth name). However, in respect to my deceased stepfather, the only father I can remember, I sometimes add his name (Hanson) to mine. I may one day have my name legally changed to include Hanson. The debunkers have twisted this, trying to make something sinister out of it.

I am an average family man. The debunkers describe me as "not prominent or outstanding in any perceptible way."

There were several other photographers of UFOs, all of whom have photos of lesser quality. The debunkers ignore these photos and the hundred-plus witnesses.

I have never photographed the UFO in the presence of an investigator. A debunker said that I had, but he did not tell us who this investigator was.

I speak basic "countryside" or "street" Spanish, which I picked up during the approximately four and a half years I lived in Costa Rica. One debunker is fluent in Spanish and doesn't like my improper use of the language.

One debunker added a basement to my house. He needed to make space for a darkroom. In Florida, houses near the coast generally do not have basements, and certainly mine did not.

When I passed two lie detector tests, the debunkers said, "It is well known that a sociopathic personality can pass lie detector tests." When I passed eight hours of psychological tests that proved my sanity, they said nothing. When I underwent eight hours of hypnotic regression that verified my UFO testimony, they said nothing.

This recap of the debunking efforts points out that these highly motivated, and sometimes emotional, people offer no evidence. They only change the witness testimony, then alter or omit the real details.

I believe that these few people are indeed very determined. I believe that they will stop at very little to discredit the photographs, my family, and all the other witnesses in the Gulf Breeze sightings.

Their personal attacks go a long way in portraying the desperation of their desire to suppress the Gulf Breeze sightings. They have tried to label me a con man, liar, occult master, etc., but my community knows me and rejected these charges.

Now that this book has detailed all the sighting accounts, the debunkers will no longer find it so easy to twist the testimony. The documented account is here for all to see.

The overwhelming events that rocked my family and our small town will not be hidden away by a few debunkers. Questions will be asked and the answers will one day be discovered.

Who are they and what do they want?

APPENDIX 2

Additional Sightings and Reports

Additional Sighting Report by Ed and Frances—Thursday, April 21, 1988, 10:30 P.M.

After taking the kids to a movie, we returned home and Frances and I decided to take an evening walk. As we approached the corner of Dracena and Silverthorn, just down from our house, an object came overhead quickly and stopped to the east of us.

I'm sure the object was the same as that of February 26 in Shoreline Park (the one photographed with the MUFON camera). We didn't have a camera with us this time.

It was either large and far away or close and very small. The more Frances insists that it was close, the more I am influenced to agree. If she is right, then where it stopped and hovered for about four seconds would be at the end of the street. It then left, moving very fast to the northeast toward the school.

No hum. No sound.

I consider the following sighting important because of its location, near where I took the road shot on January 12, and because the sighter also saw the blue beam. This report is from the MUFON files. It details the sighting that took place on Thursday, April 28, 1988, at 10:00 P.M.

Word of Truman Holcomb's UFO sighting came to Mark Curtis of WEAR-TV through the wife of an employee. Mark told Donald Ware and Bob Reid on May 4, 1988, while they were in his office investigating other sightings. These two investigators interviewed Truman Holcomb in his home that evening.

At about 10:00 P.M. on April 28, 1988, Mr. Holcomb was driving east on Highway 98 near 191-B. He saw a circular object with a very bright orange light on the bottom. It was staying just ahead of his van and a little above the trees to his right as he drove for about forty-five seconds at 45 miles per hour. The object then hovered about 100 feet east of Ocean

320

Breeze Lane, where Mr. Holcomb lives. As he turned south on Ocean Breeze Lane, he could see a blue beam coming from the lower side of the object and shining north across Highway 98. He stopped and watched it for another ten or fifteen seconds. He was about 150 feet from the object, which was about 100 feet above the ground. It appeared half the size of the city water tank. His window was open, but he heard no noise. There was a short blue streak perpendicular to the beam near the object. He got excited, and as he accelerated to get his wife half a block away, the lights blinked out.

His wife said he was very excited when he got home and that this is quite unusual. She went outside but did not see it. Mr. Holcomb said that about ten to fifteen minutes later three small airplanes appeared and circled for about ten minutes. He also said a neighbor's dog barked for some time after the sighting and that several dogs across the highway where the blue beam was shining continued to bark until about 2:00 A.M. the next morning. Also, about 11:00 P.M. he got a glimpse of what he thinks was the same object over the bay north of Highway 98.

Other cars were on Highway 98 at the time of the sighting. Efforts are being made to interview an independent witness. It is interesting to note that this sighting was less than half a mile from where Ed photographed a UFO hovering over 191-B on January 12, 1988. Mr. and Mrs. Holcomb said that at about dusk on January 12th their TV and the TVs of their neighbors displayed considerable interference. The TV was not being watched at the time of Mr. Holcomb's sighting.

Mr. Holcomb is retired from the USAF and is now commander of Chapter 141 of the Disabled American Veterans. He was an aircraft technician. His hearing is good, and his vision is corrected to 20-20. This is considered a significant unknown because of the blue beam and the proximity to other sightings in the area.

There were so many sightings that often they didn't get reported or printed until days or even weeks after the fact. These next reports still may not represent all the known sightings, they are just the rest of those that were printed in the *Sentinel*. MUFON may have others in their files.

Because there were so many sightings, it didn't seem possible or practical to include all of them in the main text of the book. They are, therefore, included here in chronological order of the sighting regardless of when they were first reported. In a few instances a second sighting by the same witness will be included on the date of the first sighting.

October 1987

Back in October 1987, Pam Strickland and her son, Yancey Spencer IV, were driving west on Highway 98 toward Gulf Breeze. As they neared Breeze Plaza, they spotted an oval-shaped craft in the distance where the sun was setting. The UFO hovered for a moment, then seemed to "turn on an axis" and disappeared from sight. They were both startled by what they saw, but since there had not been any reports of sightings at the time, they dismissed the incident.

Second Week in December 1987

Eleven-year-old Christina Holscher is a fifth-grade student at Oriole Beach Elementary. She has seen a UFO twice since December. The first sighting was two weeks before Christmas. She was with two other girls; all reported seeing a round craft engulfed in a bright white light that moved smoothly and silently, then disappeared behind trees.

Christina wrote her version of the second, more recent sighting:

On a dark night three weeks ago, I walked home from my friend's house. She lives on another street. I use a trail to get to and from her house. That night when I got out of the trail, I got a surprise. There was a streetlight where it shouldn't have been. [Christina saw the light at the end of a long straight road.] I thought it was nothing. Then, just as I was going to turn around to walk to my house, the sun-golden "streetlight" moved! Shocked, I turned around again. Now the wheels in my head began to click. What was that thing? I decided it must be a UFO. I was not afraid, though. I simply followed it until it silently cruised behind the trees and houses and I saw the strong, unblinking, sunny golden light no more. Then a bomb of fear exploded in me. I ran down the street as fast as I could until I got to my house. I look into the night sky more than ever now. But I try not to be afraid of what I don't know. There is something here, I believe. But I don't think it wants to see us in our world.

February 6, 1988

Linda Wilson woke up early, at about 5:00 A.M. on the morning of Saturday, February 6, expecting to find the snow that had been predicted the night before. She went to her back door to look outside and noticed a very bright, very large oval-shaped light above the streetlight outside her house.

The first thought that came to mind was the moon, "but I knew it shouldn't be that low in the sky," Linda reported. "I noticed the streetlight at the top of our telephone pole, this light was maybe another hundred feet high."

Linda describes the light as being a "bright white, fluorescent-looking light." She described a "wavy look, exactly like looking through the heat waves coming off the hood of a hot car engine."

The light did not move and Linda heard no noise as she stood on her deck watching for two or three minutes. In her groggy state, she tried to rationalize what she was seeing.

"I just couldn't believe that I was actually seeing what I had been hearing about," Linda said. "I thought there had to be some explanation."

She went back to bed without seeing any movement and didn't really think about what she had seen until she woke up later in the morning.

After checking the lunar position in the newspaper, she realized there was no possibility that she had seen the moon.

February 8, 1988

A twelve-year-old Midway girl was visiting an aunt in Gulf Breeze when she noticed a copy of the *Sentinel* with a picture of a UFO. She told her aunt, "I've seen this thing at my house." She claims that the craft hovered above her Midway home making a slight humming sound.

March 4, 1988—about 9:15 P.M.

After watching the Channel 3 TV news special *The Sightings,* concerning the Gulf Breeze UFO phenomenon, a *Sentinel* reader and his date decided to ride to the beach to see if they could find the controversial object. They drove down Soundside Drive to the water and waited. After seeing nothing, they left and drove north on Soundside. As they stopped at the Stop sign on Highway 98, they abruptly found the object of their search.

"It was the same object I had just seen on the news special—the one in Ed's photos," the viewer stated. "It was very low, about twenty feet above the trees. It moved over 98 through a vacant lot by the Junior Food Store, then hovered for a moment and rotated. It had very bright, white lights, but no sound.

"As we sat there with our mouths hanging open, it moved again, coming directly toward us. I grabbed my camera and started shooting. My date began pleading with me to back up and get out. She was clearly frightened. The only thing I could think of was to get the picture.

"Then, as it crossed 98, it turned and went toward town, finally disappearing."

Unfortunately, the viewer said, his camera was loaded with 200-speed film, and none of the shots turned out.

The viewer claims to have seen the object about four times since that night, "but that was the last time I saw it up real close."

About 10:30 P.M. on Thursday, April 21, 1988, his camera now armed with 1,000-speed film, he was driving home to Gulf Breeze from a baseball game in Pensacola. As he approached the National Seashore, he saw an object just over the trees on the south side of Highway 98. It was moving east, the same direction he was driving. Traveling at a very high rate of speed, it quickly passed him, eventually crossing 98 and disappearing on down the highway ahead of him.

"But," he said, "it was a different object. This one was round and flat, with yellow-orange-colored lights. It was definitely not like the ones I'd seen before."

He was able to snap some shots, but "I don't know if I got anything. It was moving very fast."

March 11, 1988

The first witness Friday was apparently eleven-year-old David Sominski of Sand Piper Village, who related the following story:

"It was about 6:30 P.M. and I was out in right field at Shoreline Park during baseball practice. I was kinda bored, so I was looking around and I saw it over in the direction of the high school. I saw a bright light at the bottom, a small light at the top, and a row of little lights around the middle.

"At first it was flat [level]. Then it tipped up on an angle and started spinning around. Then it tipped the other way and started spinning around again and started to move to one side.

"Then I heard somebody hit the ball and I looked to see if it was coming to me, and when I looked back, it was gone."

About the same time, thirteen-year-old Jayson Carter was out in his yard at home in Sandpiper Village. This is what Jayson had to say:

"I walk outside a lot with my camera since I've been looking for the

UFO. I saw a bright light moving very fast from west to east, so I took four pictures as it went over. It may have had more than just the one bottom light, but I'm not sure as I was busy taking pictures. I knew it wasn't an airplane or a helicopter because it didn't make any noise.''

Friday evening when David got home from practice, he saw Jayson in the yard and said, ''You're not going to believe this, but I think I saw the UFO.''

After hearing David's story, Jayson shared his own experience and showed David the UFO pictures in the *Sentinel* to see if that was what he saw. David said it was, so Jayson arranged for them to come in and tell their stories.

March 14, 1988

The following is the complete report from the *Sentinel* of the family whose son heard a telepathic message that was condensed in the body of the book:

> ''We picked it up as it was coming at an angle to Gulf Breeze from the southwest like it was coming in from the beach. It was about 8:00 P.M. It proceeded on an easterly course, I would say running right over the beach and the sound, right over Gulf Breeze. And it ran like that until it got into the National Seashore and at some point, I couldn't say where, it crossed over 98 [Highway 98] and got on to the north side. We were coming on down 98 and I picked it up again as we turned into Villa Venyce, I could see it probably over Whisper Bay. When I turned in to Villa Venyce, it was 8:09, and at that point it moved on a westerly course and it ran back to where it was exactly due north of us. We backed up and came out of Villa Venyce, went across 98 and turned at Ford's. At that point it was right directly in front of us. It started moving away and I couldn't tell if it was moving back toward Gulf Breeze or out over the bay, but it appeared to be moving out over the bay. We turned behind Ford's and tried to get a closer look, but it disappeared.''
>
> How close were you or could you see any details?
>
> ''Well, I really couldn't see any outline. When I picked it up in Gulf Breeze, it was probably 500 feet above Western Sizzlin' and we were on 98, so it was fifteen hundred to two thousand feet away from us, hard to judge at night. At that point I thought it was Lifeflight coming into the hospital. That's what it looked like to

me, it had a bright light, which I thought was on the rear with a greenish-blue smaller blinking light above it. Forward it had another bright light. At one time I saw three bright lights and then another time the third light in front disappeared and I saw a bright orange circular light or glow. But that didn't last too long. I don't know if it was because of the angle it was moving from us, I couldn't tell. When we got down to Villa Venyce, all I saw was three bright lights, the greenish one had disappeared. My wife saw a red light on it at one time, but I didn't see it. But I did see the orange circular glow. I thought, that can't be a helicopter, a helicopter doesn't have that kind of lights, and it moved away from the hospital. Then I got to thinking if, well, if that is some kind of propulsion system, it would seem strange that would be on the front of it as I perceive the front of it, because it was moving in that direction. I would think that that would be on the rear of it pushing it.''

You say it was about the size of a 747?

"It was big, yes, it was pretty darn big, much bigger than a helicopter. After I got to looking at it real good, I was determined in my mind it couldn't be a helicopter. It was too large."

So, if you've been reading the paper, it was much bigger than the craft that we've been printing the picture of for so long?

"I was thinking after we got home. I remember the twelve-foot-diameter circle that was behind the school. It was much bigger than that. I would say it was somewhere in the neighborhood of a DC-9, DC-8.

"I'm skeptical. When I first picked it up, you always try to rationalize it, I thought it was Lifeflight, but I saw it was much larger than a helicopter. It was too low to be a plane, then the bright orange ring appeared and blew any plane theory.

"There was an airplane that was looking right at it; when we got to Villa Venyce, I picked up an airplane to the northeast of the UFO at about one thousand feet above it and to the east. It was circling right above it. It was a small plane. It was small in comparison to the UFO and to the distance. But you could see the lights on it and you could recognize it as a plane.

"We saw some other cars moving very slowly on the highway and I said they were looking too. We saw one stopped.

"I would be very interested to see if anyone calls tomorrow to say if they saw it."

Quotes from mother and son:

The son, who was sitting in the backseat of the car while watching the object, screamed that he heard an adult male voice in his head. He screamed to his parents, "It's talking!" But the parents couldn't hear anything. The son said that it said, "Stop," not loudly, just quickly as if it were a command.

"It was like the voice wasn't talking to me, but to someone else," explained the son.

The mother said the son, who usually enjoys gory television movies, is not easily scared. But later at home, after seeing the object and hearing the voice, he "didn't feel right, like something was going to happen." He was really frightened. He also felt nauseous, vomited a few times, and suffered lack of breath. "He just did not feel right the rest of the night."

The mother advised, "If anyone wants to see it, they have to look for it, which we were."

March 14, 1988

Ann Hurd, a *Sentinel* employee, was driving home from work about 8:00 P.M. on March 14th, and made the following report:

I left the *Sentinel* office and was driving east. About maybe one mile out on 98 I noticed a bright set of lights shining through the trees in the National Seashore Reservation on the bay side of the highway. It looked like four bright lights and they seemed to be staying in one place. I thought, "If that's a plane circling to land at the airport, he sure is low." I kept watching through the trees as I was driving, and when I came around the curve, I noticed that it appeared that the lights had not moved.

I decided to get on home and if this had been a sighting, someone would be calling the office in the morning to say that they had seen the same thing.

Going past Santa Rosa Park Road, I noticed two cars stopped down there and I thought, "I bet they are trying to see it too." I had already seen a lady in a car off the road at the National Seashore soundside entrance. It was obvious that she had pulled off far enough to face back north. She had her window down and was looking out north. I went on past Santa Rosa Park. I checked my watch to verify the time in case anyone called the office Tuesday morning; it was 8:08 P.M.

In addition to calls, the *Sentinel* received a letter to the editor after the stories about the sightings on the 14th were in the paper. Although this letter didn't appear in print until the March 24th edition of the paper, it's included here:

I, too, saw the glowing bright orange object on March 14th at about 8:45 P.M. I was coming across the beach bridge at about that time and noticed an object over toward the ball parks. It was not moving. At first I thought it was a streetlight, but it was much brighter. I turned into the Bahama Bay Club parking lot to cut over to the road that leads to the new rec center and ball parks. By the time I rounded the corner it vanished!

I was waiting to see if anyone else reported the sighting. Sure enough, it came out in your March 17th paper. I knew then that what I had seen was what everyone else had been reporting.

I want to remain unknown at this time but am willing to come forward if I should ever see this object again. I will tell you that I am a schoolteacher and have had two cousins about six years ago see something that scared them half to death. Another one of my cousins was camping out with about six other teenagers along the Alabama River. They saw something hover over their campsite. These boys were so frightened that they left immediately.

I have shown your articles to the mother of one of my cousins, who thinks now that her daughter really did see a UFO. They kept her story a secret from the public hoping she would forget that night.

March 16, 1988

The sightings in this week's report occurred on Wednesday evening, March 16, beginning with testimony from two groups of people who saw the craft hovering "over" Gulf Breeze just north of the Bob Sikes Bridge.

The first witness, Nancy Reese, came into the *Sentinel* with the following report:

10:00 P.M., Nancy wrote that she and her friend first saw it from her balcony, took the camera and went to look for it.

About two blocks before the tollgate they saw it over Food World and pulled out to take a picture. They stopped again at the top of the Sikes Bridge to take another picture and described it as humongous with bright yellow lights separated by dark spaces. When they came down off the bridge, they couldn't see it anymore, so they drove through the Naval Live Oaks Reservation to look for it, then went back home.

11:00 P.M. After returning home, Nancy went to the balcony to look and again the bright yellow lights appeared as before, traveling east just above the treetops getting brighter and dimmer, then suddenly very bright just before it disappeared.

"Stephi, Lisa, and I all witnessed this scenario tonight," wrote Nancy.

When she was telling her story at the *Sentinel,* Nancy said that a deputy and a marine patrol officer saw it too, so we called to get their story.

The marine patrol officer, Nancy Andrews, was with Deputy Mike Delay when they saw unusual lights across the sound over Food World. Nancy described the configuration as very large and in the shape of a sausage. She said it looked like it was over Highway 98 but it could have been higher and farther north. Nancy, who's spent a lot of time at night on the waters around here, said it was not like any light she's ever seen before.

They all watched the mysterious craft until suddenly it took off to the east down the peninsula out of sight, "like it was shot out of a gun," said Nancy.

March 16, 1988

A Soundside resident, who like so many others saw what she believed to be Gulf Breeze's own UFO last Wednesday evening (March 16), says weird things have been happening out over the body of water her house sits on ever since her family moved into the subdivision in the early 1970s.

With a large family of kids, she is apprehensive about revealing her real name. But she is sure the object she saw hovering out over Little Sabine for at least forty-five minutes around dusk last Wednesday was real.

And since she can also cite several other unexplainable phenomena over the Santa Rosa Sound in the past ten years, she is not particularly surprised by what she and two of her children saw Wednesday.

Here is her story:

"We live right on the water in Soundside, and we've been seeing strange lights out over the sound for ten or twelve years. For fun, my sisters and I went out looking for the UFO with a jug of wine a week earlier. We didn't see anything, but I don't want to use my name because I'm afraid people will read it and say, 'This lady is crazy.' "

The Soundside resident said the object two of her children first saw hovering over Sabine on the island thirty minutes before dark last Wednesday looked like the Goodyear blimp.

"It had a flashing light, but it wasn't going anywhere," she said. "I can see Big Sabine from my house, and it looked like it was right over Big Sabine. It didn't go anywhere for forty-five minutes or so, probably longer.

"My son saw it first, and he went crazy. But it was nothing spectacular. There was just one flashing white light. It looked like the Goodyear blimp or a big cigar. I would almost be relieved if somebody told me the Goodyear blimp was in the area, even though I don't really think that's what it was.

"I couldn't see any details except for one blipping light. It wasn't red or green. It was a light like you would see on an airplane, but the object wasn't going anywhere."

The Soundside resident said her husband saw another strange light on the horizon toward Tiger Point from her home when he was taking out the garbage about an hour after dusk that same night.

"He saw what he thought was a star, but while he was watching it, the light dropped straight down," she said.

Wednesday's sighting was not a first for the Soundside resident. She said her son, who is now twenty-one, and his friend were followed by a UFO in their neighborhood about ten years ago.

On another evening, at least five years ago, she was awakened by a brilliant light shining into her bedroom balcony.

"I'm a very sound sleeper. Believe me, nothing wakes me up," she said. "But this light was so brilliant that it woke me up. I wanted to go out and investigate. But my husband told me not to. It was just a brilliant light hovering over the balcony. I don't know how long it was there. But it was long enough for us to discuss it. I was scared. But I was curious, too. I went as far as the screen door, but my husband told me not to go out to the balcony. It was just a very brilliant light, brilliant enough to wake me from a sound sleep.

"I don't remember exactly when this happened," she added. "I only know it was a reality that it did happen."

On another occasion, the Soundside resident and many of her neighbors were treated to a light show out over the sound.

"The lights were moving up and down and sideways," she said.

"What was even more particular was how the intensity kept changing from brilliant to dim. There were probably three lights. Everybody that lives on the water came down to the beach to watch. We thought they might be airplanes, but nobody had ever seen airplanes that could move horizontally and vertically like that.

"This has been getting a lot of attention since the first *Sentinel* article was published. But I'm here to tell you they've been around for a while."

Our witness said Soundside Drive has never been so crowded. "People are bringing shrimp and strawberries for UFO picnics almost nightly.

"One guy who has been a regular told my husband he was parked with his girlfriend in Whisper Bay when a brilliant light came through his front window and curled his dashboard. I said, 'Right.' But my husband saw the dashboard. This was right after the mystery man was beamed.

"I don't think they are hostile and I don't think it's a government project. Yes, I do believe we're being visited."

March 16, 1988

A third person reported a sighting that occurred on Wednesday, March 16, at 8:30 P.M., in the area of Villa Venyce and Blue Heron Cove. It was close, she reported, on the north side of her house, and very bright with a blue cast. She stated it was small and had windows. She watched it for approximately one and a half hours.

The viewer stated that it appeared again on Thursday, March 17. It began descending, then two airplanes approached it and it disappeared. When the airplanes were gone, the UFO reappeared.

On Sunday, March 20, around 8:30 to 9:00 P.M., the viewer again saw a colorful object that looked like a blue and red star above the tall trees at Soundside.

"It was huge, with blue and red lights—not blinking—and we could see windows in a circle. It was going down and went behind some trees over the sound. We pulled off Highway 98 to get a closer look as it went behind a house."

March 17, 1988

Another viewer states that she was at home in Navarre on Thursday evening, March 17, at 8:50 P.M., when she noticed a very large bright light moving from southwest to northeast. It was over the sound about five miles west of the bridge.

"It got close enough for me to see a light on the bottom, which was the brightest, lights on the top, and a spherical shape. The lights grew very bright and then dimmed. It was not a helicopter, nor an airplane."

The viewer watched as it stopped and hovered, then began a back-and-forth movement, north to south, then south to north, and north to south again, finally descending slowly near the shore.

"We climbed higher to keep it in sight, then it took on a red hue and went below tree level."

The mother and her daughters climbed up on the roof and watched a couple of minutes more, until they could no longer see it. The sighting lasted approximately fifteen to twenty minutes.

"Then we all got in the car to go looking for it, thinking we could see it through the trees. We drove about ten miles and, finding nothing, came back."

March 18, 1988

Dana Gibson, a hairdresser at Baybridge Hair Design, spotted a UFO on her way home last Friday night (March 18). She reports, "I was driving east on Highway 98 between 7:30 and 7:45 P.M. As I neared the Tom Thumb by Villa Venyce, I looked toward the bay. I saw what I thought was a plane. Then I realized it couldn't be a plane. There was a cluster of white lights . . . but they weren't really white. There were no blinking red or green lights. It was moving faster than a plane and it was not as high as a plane. It crossed over the highway, then hovered for a couple of seconds over the trees. Then it moved back over the highway and shot straight down toward the east."

By this time Dana had pulled into the Santa Rosa Bank parking lot to watch the object. Within a few seconds all of the lights on the object blinked out—and finally the entire craft went dark and disappeared from sight.

March 21, 1988

Testimony from a local mother and her twelve-year-old daughter, March 21, about 3:00 P.M., traveling across the Bay Bridge from Pensacola:

I always scan the skies, day or night, when I'm in or near Gulf Breeze. That day I and my twelve-year-old daughter saw an object hovering to the right of the water tower, but before the point of

Gulf Breeze. It just stayed there and the atmosphere around it wavered, but I couldn't figure out why.

From the time we spotted it until almost the end of the bridge [into Gulf Breeze] we could see it. We were excited because it might be the UFO.

We were not scared, because it was daytime and the UFO was far away. From what I could figure, it was over the sound before Pensacola Beach—because it was seen right above the line of trees of Gulf Breeze, but it didn't seem close enough or clear enough to be over Gulf Breeze.

But I don't think it was over Pensacola Beach or the Gulf, because the horizon would have hidden it from where we were on the bridge.

I thought it might be one of those big helicopters from the naval base, except that it hovered in one place the whole time.

The object seemed big and oblong and dark. We looked at people in other cars, and it seemed no one else noticed the UFO.

I regret I didn't have a camera, especially since it was daylight, and I wish I could have driven to check it out.

March 23, 1988

Wednesday, from 7:00 P.M. until 10:30 P.M. on Pensacola Beach overlooking the sound.

The viewer saw a total of three objects: two concentrated in Gulf Breeze east of the hospital, and the third over by the Tiger Point area.

"It had to have been the craft, because they were too erratic," said the viewer.

The objects were bright, clear lights, which hovered above the trees a few minutes, then dropped down and disappeared, then appeared again moments later.

"Then at one time, the lights would appear four or five times brighter, then drop down and disappear."

"I never saw them go up," said the sighter. "I just saw them go down, then reappear." The viewer also mentioned a large amount of air traffic in the area that night.

"But you could tell a distinct difference between the airplane and helicopter lights, and these weren't airplane or helicopter lights," said the viewer.

March 30, 1988

(Although this sighting occurred on Wednesday, March 30, 8:00 P.M., outside Grand Canal, it was not reported until late April.)

"It was the same kind of thing, in the picture we saw in the April 21st paper," said twelve-year-old Misti Brown, who, along with her friend Jennifer Hall, watched a strange object in the sky for about thirty minutes. The girls viewed the spiral object through binoculars.

"It was about the size of the dining room table," said Misti, "and it was spinning around with red, yellow, blue and green lights on it."

Both girls went inside a home for a few minutes, and when they returned outside, the object was gone.

"The next night, we checked in the same place, and it wasn't there," said Misti.

March 30, 1988

Sighting from two local Gulf Breeze females between the ages of twenty and twenty-three. March 30th at 10:30 P.M. turning onto Fairpoint from Highway 98:

A friend and I were returning home after spending the afternoon driving around "looking for the UFO" we had read so much about in the *Sentinel*. We had given up our search after only seeing "odd moving lights over the sound." We had to see some type of shape—like in the pictures before we really believed. Well, the object we saw was not like the *Sentinel* pictures, but it did spark our curiosity.

While turning onto Fairpoint, we saw a bright light coming from behind the Exxon building. As we looked over, a large, almost diamond-shaped object raised up and rolled over, then headed over the Big B building until it was out of sight.

The object was outlined with small white "light bulbs" and had red lights on its tail. My friend had her window down and we didn't hear any sound.

We talked for a while on what we had seen. A low plane? Maybe—but? We decided to see if anyone reported a similar object before we told our story.

On April 7th about 9:00 P.M., driving east on Highway 98, I saw the object again. I had just driven past the *Sentinel* when I saw the object moving toward Gulf Breeze downtown over the trees on the left side of the road. The object had the same shape, no sound, and an almost clear bottom that I could almost look into. For a moment I almost stopped the car, but being in the left lane and surrounded by traffic, I didn't.

March 31, 1988

A previous UFO witness and her husband and child reported a second sighting on March 31. At about 8:45 P.M. the family noticed a large craft hovering in the sky above their Villa Venyce home.

They described the craft as being elongated and having no sound. And although it was dark outside, they were able to see the craft "plain as anything."

There was a white light beside the craft that seemed to be either a small plane or a small ship. The light on the smaller craft went out for a few minutes, then reappeared later in the same spot.

The UFO moved in a "gliding motion" in a northeasterly direction until it disappeared from sight. The witnesses felt it probably passed over Whisper Bay.

April 4, 1988

Tiger Point resident Margaret Cunningham was on her way home from a meeting last Monday (April 4) when she saw what she believes was a UFO. "I was driving down Hillside Drive when I noticed something hovering over the golf course," Margaret told the *Sentinel*. "It had very bright white lights at either end and pulsating red lights coming from what looked like portholes."

Margaret had binoculars in her car and immediately grabbed them to take a closer look. It was dark—approximately 8:45 P.M. She was unable to see the shape of the object but guessed that it was about the size of a helicopter. She heard no sound coming from the craft.

"I watched it for about five or six minutes as it hovered in one place. Then it slowly moved below the trees and out of my sight."

April 7, 1988

Thursday, April 7, about 8:30 P.M. on Highway 98 by Western Sizzlin':

Grandma and Amy had been watching an object that had "real bright lights and it looked like a car with four big spotlights on it."

"When you look up into a light fixture," said Amy. "That's what I saw."

Amy, who saw the object the longest, described it as "an airplane with a big circle in the middle with blue lights shooting out and the lights attached."

The object flew over the car by Western Sizzlin', and farther down the road the two saw a second object.

"The small one went down behind the trees and came up again," said Grandma. "I was confused that an airplane could fly that low with such bright lights."

The objects were traveling "up and down and sideways," said Amy, as she moved her arms. As they drove farther down the highway, an airplane flew over Whisper Bay.

"I could tell the difference," said Grandma. "I heard the noise."

April 7, 1988

Thursday, April 7 over the sound:

"I saw mostly swirling red lights; I couldn't tell what shape it was," said the male Gulf Breeze viewer.

The object was seen four hundred to six hundred feet away from the back of the sighter's home, and about one thousand feet over the water.

"It just came right down the sound real fast," said the witness, "but it didn't make any noise."

April 7, 1988

On Thursday, April 7th, at approximately 9:30 P.M., a Gulf Breeze stockbroker was coming across the Bay Bridge from Pensacola when he spotted a small craft flying over the bay from the east.

"I was just coming to the base of the bridge . . . I pulled over into the left turning lane and got out of the car to watch." He described the craft as being triangular-shaped, small, maybe fifteen feet long. "If there were aliens inside, they would have to be pretty small."

As the craft neared the bridge, it slowed and hovered for a few seconds. The man was able to see the shape of the UFO, which was outlined in white lights with red and green lights in the center. "It looked kind of like a Christmas tree. Near the center, there were two indentations."

The witness watched as the craft turned and "glided" back over the bay toward Pensacola. "It made a tiny, low, aerodynamic sound as it moved away."

"I don't know what it was, but I'm sure it was not an airplane or any kind of craft that I know of," the witness told the *Sentinel*.

April 14, 1988

A Whisper Bay resident reported seeing "something strange" on Thursday, April 14th. "I know it was 9:02 P.M. because I called my sister on the CB radio as I was seeing it and she looked at her clock.

"I was coming down Highway 98 from Gulf Breeze coming home. As I neared the Naval Live Oaks area, I noticed some strange blinking lights in the air. There were red lights and white lights. They were about as high as an airplane, but it made a weird turn. The UFO moved out over the highway, then made a U-turn and went off into the opposite direction. I was trying to drive and watch at the same time, so I'm not too sure where it went."

Duane Cook has been interested and involved in the Gulf Breeze events almost from the beginning, at first as the editor of the *Sentinel* newspaper, later also as a friend. He has written firsthand accounts of two different nights. The first, January 24, 1988 was the night he videotaped me being tormented by the UFO. The second, March 17, 1988, was the night the first photos were taken of the UFO with the SRS camera. Here are those accounts:

January 24, 1988

It was late Sunday afternoon, January 24th. Ann was setting type, Dari was up front on the phone, Fran [Thompson] was in the darkroom, and I was in my office writing checks.

One of the other lines rang, but I didn't notice as Ann answered it in a couple of rings. My concentration was broken when Ann said, "Duane, it's Ed."

"Hi, Ed, what's happening?" is my usual opening remark, although I don't expect anything is actually happening. Usually when he calls, it's to tell me what happened the night before. Well, this time was different. Ed was at first hesitant, then he started to talk and talk fast.

"It's here! I know it's here . . . I can hear the buzz," Ed said, referring to the buzzing sound he had heard prior to each of several sightings he's made since his first UFO experience on November 11th.

"I can't get anybody on the radio," he said, "I don't know what to do."

The radio Ed was talking about was the walkie-talkie set-up between him and the MUFON investigators who had been "staking out" the area behind the high school since the December 23rd sighting when Ed got three craft in one photo.

"You want me to come over there, or do you want to come over here?" I asked, my own adrenaline pumping.

"I think I'm gonna get in my truck and come over there," Ed said calmly. "You be waiting out front."

As I hung up the phone and jumped from my desk, I shouted to Fran, "Where's my camera?"

Sensing the situation, Ann said, "Oh no, you don't mean it! . . . Can I go too?"

When I told Dari what was happening, she had mixed emotions about it. She didn't want to miss anything but she was afraid too many people would cause the UFO to pass up the opportunity to make contact.

When Ed drove up, I joined him in the front seat of his pickup and we headed east on Highway 98 through the Naval Live Oaks Reservation.

Ed was real nervous about the whole thing. He was afraid for himself because he didn't know what they wanted from him. He had had enough experience with them to know that they were powerful. He was also afraid for me. He didn't know how the UFO would respond to his bringing me along to photograph whatever happened.

Ed had come prepared with his Polaroid and his video camera, so I put down my 35mm and started recording the ride on videotape.

As he drove, we kept looking up and around for any sight of the UFO. He felt sure they were there as the buzz lingered, sometimes louder, sometimes softer.

"They spoke to me!!" Ed screamed. "They said, 'In sleep you know.' . . . I heard it in my mind.

"My right eye is moving!!" he screamed. "Look at my eye. Is it okay?"

I studied his eye through the lens of the video-cam and assured him his eye looked fine.

He wasn't too reassured, though, and was feeling stabs of pain in various parts of his body, too sharp and too random to be anything natural. He was sure they were hurting him on purpose, but why? That's what he had to find out.

"We've gotta get off this highway. . . . We've got to get some place where it's not so busy. . . . They'll never show themselves with this many people around," Ed said.

"How about Soundside Drive," I suggested.

"No way!!" said Ed. He had already had one confrontation with the UFO when he was alone on Soundside Drive earlier in the month and wasn't prepared to relive that experience. That was just a little too remote. He was looking for a big space, but where there were some houses around.

"There are some pretty undeveloped roads off to the right beyond Tiger Point," I suggested.

After we turned off into Tiger Point East, Ed became more nervous about my safety.

"I think you're in trouble . . . maybe I ought to take you back," he worried out loud.

I told him I wanted to stay and record whatever happened and that there wasn't any history of people being hurt or killed by UFOs, but if he wanted, I would get out of the truck and watch from a distance.

We turned east and stopped in the road beside a large cleared area on the right. By now it was dark and I didn't hold out a lot of hope that the videotape was going to work, but I left it on for the sound track and in case the UFO showed up.

Ed took his Polaroid and got out and walked about forty feet up the road calling out to the UFO to do something—either beam him up and get it over with or take their buzz and get out of his life.

Suddenly Ed screamed with pain. He said his left hand felt like it was in a vise. I told him to drop the camera and see if the pain went away since he had already confided in me how he had been told during an earlier confrontation that "photographs are prohibited."

It started to rain again and I knew it was too dark for the video camera so I got back in the truck.

He kneeled over in pain while constantly searching the sky for the craft to show up. He knew they were close since the buzz was a virtual roar in his head.

Then, slowly, it all seemed to subside. Ed stood up and walked back to the truck. He hollered toward the sky that if they wanted him, they missed their chance because he wasn't going to give them another opportunity like this again.

Then, just as he went to get in, he looked up and shouted, "There it is!" aimed his camera, and snapped the picture.

I scrambled to get out of my side so I could see it too, but the two seconds it took me were too long. It was already gone!

"Did you see it! Did you see it?" Ed cried to me hopefully.

I apologized for being so slow. I was, of course, sorry I had missed it, for both of our sakes.

Then it dawned on me that if he got it in the photograph, and I watched him take the photo out of the camera, and if I watched as he separated the negative from the positive, that would be as good as having seen it myself!

Meanwhile Ed was back out in the field beside the truck, shaking his fist at them and chastising them for being so elusive, camera still in hand.

I called to him, "Let's see what you've got in that picture. Bring the camera over here."

He came over to my door, pulled the photo from the camera, and handed it to me. I waited for the longest sixty seconds I can remember and carefully peeled the film apart to reveal the now familiar round object with a brightly lit ring on the bottom and small "portholes" around its midsection.

This photo was different from the others Ed had taken in that the craft started up just as the picture was snapped, giving the streaks of light on the film. You can imagine how fast it took off when the light streaks show it went from standstill to completely out of view in the span of time the shutter was open!

With this evidence in hand we decided it was time to go home. As we started to move, it occurred to us to mark the spot, as the MUFON investigators would want to put the exact location in their report. Turns out we were right in front of the Players Club. We wondered aloud what they would have to say about a UFO sighting in their front yard.

On the way back we theorized about why the UFO remains so elusive. Surely they are not afraid of us, even if there are some among us who would shoot first and ask questions later. They certainly appear to have the technology to avoid any encounter or aggressive action.

Oh, well, at least we got a picture and I witnessed the picture being made. For my purposes at the *Sentinel* that's better than seeing it and not getting the picture.

March 17, 1988

This week's UFO update begins with a personal account of my second near-sighting last Thursday and concludes with the testimony of a Wednesday evening sighting of what we are now calling "the mother ship" by two local residents, one of whom is a Marine Patrol Officer.

The story began Thursday afternoon at the *Sentinel* office. Ed had stopped in to visit and talk with witnesses to Wednesday night's sighting. Before he left, Ed shared with Dari and me privately that he was "hearing" the UFO. We, of course, became excited at the prospect of being present when it showed itself again. So that evening we called Ed to see if he was going to Shoreline Park to try out the new "stereo" camera arrangement he had built for the purpose. (Dr. Bruce Maccabee had asked Ed to mount two Polaroid cameras two feet apart so that they were parallel, thus giving a stereoscopic effect when fired simultaneously.)

Ed was at first reluctant but said if he could talk his wife into it, they would go down about eight o'clock.

When we arrived at about 8:30, they were already there. Ed told us he had called Peter and Phyllis Neumann, and Brenda and Buddy Pollak, in case they wanted to come watch also.

When Peter arrived, Ed asked him to open two new packs of film and witness as they were loaded into the cameras.

A few moments later Buddy arrived and joined the vigil.

After a while a couple of men who had been watching from out on the pier gave in to their curiosity and came over to see what we were doing. Buddy intercepted them, visited a while, and came back and said it was his old friend Carlos Hill. Carlos had been to Shoreline Park a lot lately with his video camera in hopes of catching a shot of the UFO.

Meanwhile, it was getting close to 10:00 P.M. and Ed confided to the group that he hadn't "heard" the buzz for about an hour, at which time I suggested that maybe he needed to be alone, considering the UFO's tendency to be shy around groups of people.

While the Neumanns went home, Dari and I just went as far as the new recreation center parking lot, then returned to Shoreline Park South with our lights out so that we wouldn't be seen returning. We saw that Buddy had returned also and was at the east end of the park with Carlos and Reggie White.

Seconds after we stopped, we saw the flash of Ed's cameras and thought he was just making another test shot. A moment later Ed emerged from the brush with a photo in each hand. When he saw us, he motioned for us to come see them in the headlights of his truck—two parallel photos of the same UFO he's been shooting since November 11th. Buddy, Carlos, and Reggie also saw the flash through the trees and Buddy and Carlos came over to see the photos.

They didn't see the craft, but examination of the photos showed that it was too low and behind the tree line when Ed saw it and shot the pictures. His wife agreed and said she wouldn't have seen it either if she hadn't seen which way he was aimed because it winked out seconds after the flash.

About this time Brenda Pollak drove up and joined the group having just returned from a Junior League meeting in Pensacola. We were telling her what she had just missed when she stopped us to relate what she had seen.

"I was at about the midpoint of the Bay Bridge when I saw an orange light over the area by the post office. It was unusually bright and low. Sometimes it was obscured by the trees. Instead of steady, it was pulsating dimmer and brighter, not fast like an airplane light, but occasional and without rhythm. When I got off the bridge, it disappeared in the trees.

"I turned on Shoreline to go home, then saw it again to the north as I passed the library. I pulled off at the recreation center to make sure it was moving, and indeed it was moving from northeast to southwest. I watched it for three or four seconds till it flashed out.

"I know it's a light I've never seen before," said Brenda. "It was orange like our new streetlights but much brighter, and it was moving."

With the time and proximity in mind, it is clear that what Brenda saw was probably the same object that Ed photographed at approximately the same time only a couple of blocks to the southwest.

Soil and Grass Sample Analysis

Results from the circular "landing site" behind the high school. Analysis by Max E. Griggs and the University of Florida.

Enclosed are nematode assay results from soil samples I took at the Gulf Breeze site. As you see, nematodes of approximately the same number were found inside the circle of dead grass (sample #1) and outside. This information, combined with the fact that the circle of dead grass was geometrically perfect, negates the possibility of the dead grass being due to lightning strike. The fact that no scorching or eruption of plant tissue was present further supports this idea.

Observation of plant tissue inside the dead area and adjacent areas of the healthy grass did not reveal any evidence of plant disease. No fungal, bacterial, or viral agent appeared to be responsible for the dead grass. Even if a plant pathogen had been actively causing disease in the grass, it would certainly have been unheard of to kill in a geometrically perfect circle with discrete boundaries of only two to three inches between dead grass and healthy grass. Considering also the fact that no other area of grass was dead within the immediate area, I think that plant disease can be disqualified as the cause of the dead grass.

Observation of plant tissue inside and outside the dead-grass area revealed no evidence of insect feeding to any portion of the plants. Here again such agents do not restrict themselves to such perfect symmetry and to only a single isolated instance. Insect damage that could have caused the grass to die to the extent we found it would have been easy to identify by inspection in the field.

As I told you on the telephone, I used squash seeds as a test plant to see if a herbicide residual were present. Squash belong to a group of plants that tend to be very sensitive to herbicides. Three out of three seeds planted in soil taken from the dead-grass site germinated and grew normally. This does not eliminate the possibility of a chemical agent being responsible for the dead grass, but it does lend support to this idea.

The physical condition inside and outside the dead grass circle was essentially the same. Texture, composition, and usable rooting depth the same. A nutrient deficiency of such severity to kill grass will not limit itself so discretely, nor will it be so sudden and homogeneous in its impact. It is safe to disregard plant-nutrient problems as the cause of this phenomenon.

As you can see from the text of this letter, I have attempted to disqualify physical, chemical, and biological causes that might normally kill bermuda grass. In short, I have not been able to identify the cause of the grass dying, but evidence supports either the influence of short-lived toxic chemical or exposure of the grass to an energy source capable of killing it. Either of these would have required mechanical precision to do what was observed on the field.

LABORATORY, INC.

11 EAST OLIVE ROAD   PENSACOLA, FLORIDA 32514
PHONE (904) 474-1001

```
Client:  EDWARD WALTERS              Lab I.D.#:       88-1746
22032    612 SILVERTHORN DR.         Order Number:    P12734
                                     Order Date:      05/17/88
         GULF BREEZE   FL  32561-0000  Sampled By:    E. WALTERS
                                     Sample Date:     05/17/88
                                     Sample Time:     N/S
Project Number: 88-1746
Project Name:   EDWARD WALTERS
Sample Site:    GULF BREEZE
Sample Type:    WATER
                                     N/S = Not Submitted
```

Lab ID	Sample ID	Parameter	Units	Results	Detection Limit
88-1746-1	GULF BREEZE	CALCIUM	PPM	226	0.1
88-1746-1	GULF BREEZE	CHLORIDE	PPM	7800	100
88-1746-1	GULF BREEZE	CONDUCTIVITY	UMH/CM	19850	0.1
88-1746-1	GULF BREEZE	MAGNESIUM	PPM	538	0.1
88-1746-1	GULF BREEZE	SODIUM	PPM	4130	200

APPENDIX 3

Position Statements

Position Statement on the Gulf Breeze, Florida, Case from Walter H. Andrus, Jr., International Director, Mutual UFO Network (MUFON)

As the International Director of the Mutual UFO Network, Inc. (MUFON), I have made three trips to Gulf Breeze to personally investigate this very significant UFO case and to meet with the prime witnesses, Ed and Frances. I have worked directly with Donald M. Ware, MUFON State Director for Florida; Charles Flannigan, Lead Investigator and State Section Director; Budd Hopkins, Dr. Bruce S. Maccabee, Thomas P. Deuley, and several other MUFON investigators directly involved.

The Gulf Breeze Case ranks as one of the most important UFO cases in the past forty years, since it contains all of the attributes categorized as close encounters of the first, second, third, and fourth kinds. This evidence is further documented by forty-one photographs made by the primary witness with a Polaroid camera, a video camera, a Nimslo 3-D camera, and a self-referencing stereo camera using two Polaroid 600 Sun LMS cameras. His wife, Frances, not only made two photographs, she was a witness to a majority of the others taken by her husband.

This is the first time in UFO history where scientific investigation and research could be conducted while a case was in progress with the full cooperation of the family.

The investigative team had access to the photographs from November 11 to December 23, 1987, soon after they were made. On January 7, 1988, the witness agreed to a full disclosure of all the photographs and events to date. Thereafter he cooperated with the investigators as the series of events unfolded, including photos with the Nimslo 3-D camera and a self-referencing stereo camera and concluding on May 1, 1988.

UFO photographs, per se, do not constitute valid evidence of a UFO experience. The credibility and character of the photographer and witness

345

is even more important than the photographs when evaluating them as documented evidence. I personally felt that it was imperative to the investigation that I obtain firsthand facts by meeting and interviewing the two prime witnesses in Gulf Breeze. After meeting Ed and Frances on three occasions, conducting over a dozen telephone conversations, and receiving numerous pieces of correspondence, I found Ed to be an enthusiastic, dramatic, sincere, and successful businessman in the Gulf Breeze community and very involved in civic activities. Both Ed and Frances are deeply devoted to the well-being of their two children and committed to chaperoning band trips and respectable parties for the high-school-age young people in their home and swimming pool.

Frances, in contrast to her husband, seems very reserved when she is meeting people for the first time. However, once she becomes acquainted, her friendly, gracious, and sincere personality emerges. The sincerity of both Frances and Ed was made even more evident when they volunteered to meet and answer questions pertaining to the case at the annual MUFON board of directors meeting in Lincoln, Nebraska, on June 26, 1988. After being literally bombarded with questions, their response removed any doubt that a hoax had been perpetrated upon the UFO community and the public.

The enormous question that plagues Ed is: "Why me? Why was I selected to take these photographs and have my family subjected to such a disruptive and traumatic experience for five and one-half months?" The competent team of investigators is endeavoring to answer this same question as they continue probing into the mystery, wherein Ed has volunteered to submit to regressive hypnosis sessions for a possible explanation.

If one were to briefly speculate on the solution to the enigma occuring in Gulf Breeze, it might take the following scenario: On or before November 11, 1987, the intelligence behind the UFOs implanted a tiny communication device within Ed's head whereby they could communicate by voice or a humming sound to alert him to the proximity of their craft. Based upon the brief exposure time of these objects, Ed was conceivably programmed to take the photographs for public distribution as part of the entities' ultimate plan to make themselves gradually known to the public and world governments. On May 1, 1988, when Ed was rendered unconscious by a white beam of light, after taking one set of stereo photographs, the implant was probably surgically removed, ending his UFO experience.

A successful businessman and civic citizen was probably selected for this ultimate disclosure so that the events and evidence would be thoroughly investigated and hopefully accepted by the scientific community as factual and not easily ignored as an obvious hoax. Ed was apparently chosen and programmed to fulfill a role in the ultimate disclosure by the intelligences controlling the UFOs. Continued scientific investigation and research into the phenomenon known as unidentified flying objects may indeed confirm this speculation.

Position Statement on the 1987–1988 UFO Sightings of Gulf Breeze, Florida from Donald M. Ware, Florida State Director, Mutual UFO Network (MUFON)

As MUFON State Director living only forty-four miles from Gulf Breeze, I have helped coordinate the activities of seven local investigators and three internationally known investigators of the many UFO reports in this area. There have been at least sixty-eight reports of objects that, after various amounts of investigation, we have not been able to identify as either naturally produced or made by man. These include 135 witnesses of which 4 reported alien beings, 6 reported blue beams, and 9 reported periods of missing time suggesting abductions. Over sixty UFO photographs have been taken.

I am convinced that these sightings are proof of alien visitation. The level of technology demonstrated indicates they can come and go at will and can reside in a variety of places: the bottoms of our oceans, inside major high-altitude ice fields, in earth orbit, on the moon, on Mars, etc. . . .

One might ask why one couple in Gulf Breeze has been allowed eighteen photographic sessions. The most obvious reason to me is the aliens want people to see the photographs. I hope this causes more people to give serious thought to the idea that we, as an intelligent species, are not alone in the universe.

The events that happened to me and my family during those five and a half months were both incredible and threatening. One of the threats was that of ridicule.

Many witnesses, both from Gulf Breeze and elsewhere, have wrestled with the same question about telling what they have seen and what some have photographed.

If you have had a sighting, been involved in an incident of "missing time," or taken photographs of a UFO and wish to share the event with me, I guarantee to withhold your identity, and I encourage you to write and send your photographs to me at:

> EDWARD WALTERS
> P.O. Box 715
> Gulf Breeze, FL   32562-0715